W9-AQN-870

"This book will do more to prevent premature cardiovascular disease than any modern textbook of medicine or health book written for the general public. . . . Every professional, every executive, and every literate layman should place this book on his 'must read' list."

"As a classic TYPE A trying to become a TYPE B, I urge that everyone read this book—especially if you're in a hurry. These ideas have helped keep me alive. I found out about them some years ago. Not only do these ideas help me live longer—they make my life so much more enjoyable."

Type A BEHAVIOR
AND YOUR HEART

Meyer Friedman, M.D.,
and Ray H. Rosenman, M.D.

FAWCETT CREST • NEW YORK

We dedicate this book to Mrs. Philip H. Little of San Francisco, a lady whom we have not yet met, but who in January 1962 wrote the following letter to us:

Gentlemen:

You will find enclosed a check for 100 dollars toward your research. For a Christmas gift to myself, I could think of nothing more necessary and deserving than a contribution to further cardiovascular research—a contribution in memory of my beloved husband, Philip H. Little, who was not granted a second chance for survival in September of 1960.

I regret I cannot afford a contribution many times this amount to help save others from his untimely fate—I am just an office worker and this is my pay for overtime work during the Christmas season.

Most sincerely,

Helen F. Little

Since that time, each year after Christmas Mrs. Little has sent us an additional contribution.

Contents

WHY WE HAVE
WRITTEN THIS BOOK

After more than thirty years studying coronary heart disease in the consultation room, at the hospital bedside, and in the laboratory, we are convinced that if the crippling and deaths caused by this disease are to be prevented, the average American must himself become involved in the process of protecting himself. The doctor alone cannot possibly do the job.

But though the layman has been deluged with information about what to eat, about exercise, about the dangers of smoking, he has unfortunately been denied the most important information of all: the facts about what we believe to be the major cause of premature coronary heart disease. This is the specific behavior pattern that we have designated Type A. *In the absence of Type A Behavior Pattern, coronary heart disease almost never occurs before seventy years of age, regardless of the fatty foods eaten, the cigarettes smoked, or the lack of exercise. But when this behavior pattern is present, coronary heart disease can easily erupt in one's thirties or forties.* We are convinced that the spread of Type A behavior explains why death by heart disease, once confined mainly to the elderly, is increasingly common among younger people.

This is the first book to identify and describe Type A behavior, and to show how it can be drastically altered—even abolished—by individual effort. If the book is widely read and the counsel contained in it faithfully followed, we believe that in the next few decades thousands of lives can be saved from the premature blight of coronary heart disease. And that is why we have written this book.

M.F. & R.H.R.

San Francisco
August 1973

Type A BEHAVIOR
AND YOUR HEART

Chapter 1

HEART DISEASE
AND YOU

"Some time ago, I quit worrying about what to do, or not to do, to keep from having a heart attack. I was so confused by all the conflicting theories that I began developing the symptoms." So wrote Los Angeles *Times* columnist Jack Smith recently.

Mr. Smith's irritation is justified, and he is probably speaking for many Americans. "Don't smoke," "don't eat animal fats," "eat whatever you please," "don't drink soft water," "drink any kind of bacteria-free water you want," "watch your weight," "obesity bears no relation to heart disease," "jog," "don't jog," "avoid cholesterol," "avoid sugar and starches," "avoid whiskey," "avoid sexual intercourse"—all these statements have been made at one time or another by physicians and researchers. Is it any wonder that some people figure none of us knows precisely what he is talking about?

Consider the problem this way. Coronary artery and heart disease is obviously the result of a variety of factors working together. Thus far, researchers have managed to locate and identify certain of these factors, meanwhile admitting a degree of doubt as to the precise function of each in the overall pattern. Ideally, taken as a whole, these factors should explain 100 percent of all heart disease cases. But they obviously do not. At least half the people who get heart attacks can be linked to *none* of the known and suspected causative factors—smoking, diet, exercise habits, other contributing diseases, and so forth. We estimate that perhaps a third (at best) of heart attacks can be avoided by medical attention to *all* of these factors, which is a pretty sorry record.

Plainly, another factor is at work here, and this is the one we have discovered and dubbed Type A Behavior Pattern. It is a particular complex of personality traits, including excessive competitive drive, aggressiveness, impatience, and a harrying sense of time urgency. Individuals displaying this pattern seem to be engaged in a chronic, ceaseless, and often fruitless struggle—with themselves, with others, with circumstances, with time, sometimes with life itself. They also frequently exhibit a free-floating but well-rationalized form of hostility, and almost always a deep-seated insecurity.

We will be investigating the Type A pattern more deeply later in this book. Suffice it to say that though it of course exists in different degrees in different individuals, it is in fact extremely common among urban Americans of virtually every class and occupation. For example, in one test group of twenty-five hundred Federal employees in the San Francisco area, using techniques to be described later, we were able to identify between 50 and 60 percent as authentic Type A's —with about 10 percent exhibiting the characteristics in a highly developed form. As we will show, their chances of getting coronary artery disease and a heart attack before reaching the age of seventy are far greater than that of the rest of the populace.

If you have already suffered a "coronary," you are painfully aware that heart disease can be a matter of intense personal concern. But perhaps you are fairly young, vigorous, and totally free of any heart symptoms. Is there any reason why you should worry?

The stark fact is that it will be almost impossible for you to reach forty years of age without realizing that coronary artery and heart disease is no respecter of youth. By then you will have suffered the anguish of watching it cripple or kill at least one of your relatives or close friends. How can we be so certain of this unhappy prophecy? Because current statistics make any happier prophecy overoptimistic.

Yet these statistics do not tell us much about your *own* chances of being felled. They only indicate how many of a very large group of subjects may be expected to suffer heart attacks in a given period; they do not describe or identify them. If you happen to indulge in certain habits or to suffer from certain specific diseases (which you have neglected to treat), the national statistics would give you a very false sense of security. They might show that you have a 90 percent chance of escaping a heart attack before you reach sixty, whereas actually, because of your particular habits or diseases, you may be almost certain to succumb before reaching fifty. On the other hand if you are free of those habits or diseases, chances are you will reach not only sixty but seventy-five without a heart attack. This will be true in spite of the gloomy national statistics showing that only half of all Americans remain free of heart disease to age seventy-five.

It is not, of course, the figures emanating from various Washington-based computers that will determine whether or when you may have a heart attack. It is *you*. So we do not propose to frighten you by harping on the incidence of coronaries. If—to feel secure —you must know the statistics, you can call your local branch of the American Heart Association. *Our* purpose is to show you ways to *avoid* heart attacks. But we would be failing in our duty if we did not make plain that no social group or class has a monopoly on heart disease. It is a catastrophe that strikes many kinds of Americans.

For example, it is certainly not a threat to corporation executives alone. Plumbers, butchers, candlestick makers—if indeed they still exist—and you yourself are just as prone to a coronary as are bankers, attorneys, and even doctors. The fact is that doctors suffer from heart disease just about as frequently as do truck drivers and garbage collectors. The prevalence of this ailment in America today, then, is independent of race, class, position, or economic means. We will emphasize its ubiquity again in later chapters because it is downright dangerous for a blue-collar (or even collarless) worker to think he is immune. But while it is not limited to the rich, the powerful, or the elderly, it has in the past preyed particularly on American men.

The latter situation is rapidly changing. In the last several decades, coronary heart disease has increasingly attacked *white* American women. In the 1920s a woman under sixty years of age suffering from coronary heart disease was almost as rare as one suffering from gout. Now no physician is greatly surprised when a white woman under fifty years of age has serious heart disease.

Therefore, if in this book we appear to concentrate our attention on the male sex, we do so only for the purpose of brevity. Suffice it to say at this point that if the dietary, smoking, and exercise habits and *behavior pattern* of any group of white American women are precisely identical with those of a group of American men, the *future* incidence of coronary heart disease will also be essentially identical. This will go for blacks as well.

So whatever your age, sex, or occupation, take heed. Preventing your coronary heart disease is your business, and what we have to say in later chapters will help you do it. First, however, we thought it would be of interest to provide some background information about the anatomy and function of the heart and its own blood supply, as well as about cholesterol and its role in heart disease. This information is useful to a clear understanding of the problem. But if you wish to skip this section, or better yet return to it later, please feel free to do so. *The real heart of the book—what Type A behavior is, how it works, and what to do about it—begins on page 69.*

Chapter 2

THE NORMAL HEART
AND CORONARY ARTERIES

Let us begin with the right half of your heart. It consists of a holding chamber (the right auricle) and a
pumping chamber (the right ventricle) (see Figure 1).
It receives the blood returning to the heart from all
other parts of your body. This returning blood, which
flows in vessels called veins, is low in oxygen content.
That is because every part of your body has extracted
some of this life-supporting gas from the blood flowing
through it. Because of its poor oxygen content this
blood appears more blue than cherry red.

The right half of your heart then takes up this oxy-
gen-poor, blue-colored venous blood and pumps all
of it directly into your lungs via a vessel called the *pulmonary artery* (see Figure 1). The blood, while in
your lungs, absorbs quite a bit of the oxygen contained in the air you are constantly breathing in. As
the blood receives this oxygen, it becomes cherry red
in color and again becomes arterial blood, which flows
directly back to the left half of your heart via the pulmonary veins. (Incidentally, these are the only veins in
your body that carry arterial blood.) The left auricle,

19

receiving this newly oxygenated blood, then pumps it in a rhythmical, gentle way into the "powerhouse" of your body, the left ventricle (see Figure 1). This tough, remarkably durable pump ejects the blood with considerable vigor into your aorta, the largest artery of your body, whence it passes to all the arteries serving your body.

This pumping cycle is governed and monitored by all sorts of nerve, hormonal, and chemical regulators. Each day your heart must go through 100,000 of these cycles (or beats), receiving and promptly pumping out again a total of 1,400 gallons of blood. This means that your heart, during the average lifetime of seventy-five years, has to pump well over 35 million gallons of blood in no less than 2.5 billion beats. For this truly astounding and necessarily unceasing work assignment, the muscles of your heart that do this pumping require a likewise *unceasing* supply of nourishment and—above all—of oxygen. The other muscles of your body can frequently continue to survive, even do work, at least for a while, without much oxygen, but not your heart muscle. Deprived of oxygen, it almost instantly dies. To prevent this, nature has seen to it that the first fraction of arterial blood pumped out at each beat by your left ventricle is returned directly to the muscles of your heart itself. The right and left coronary arteries (see Figure 1), the first branches springing from the aorta, bring back this bright red blood to nourish the pumping muscles of the right and left halves of your heart.

The coronary arteries (which surround the heart like a crown—*corona* in Latin—and thus get their name) are quite different from all the other arteries in your body. For one thing, most other arteries in your body are deeply buried and protected by overlying muscles and other types of supporting tissues. But your coronary arteries for most of their course lie on

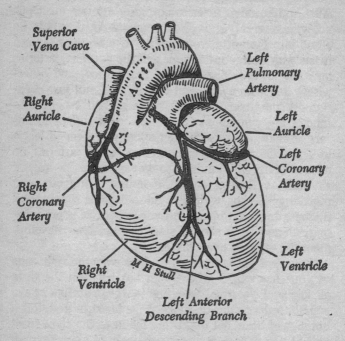

Figure 1. The right and left coronary arteries are shown. Note how the right coronary artery, after arising from the aorta, winds its way (indicated here by shading) to the posterior area of the heart, which it chiefly nourishes. The left coronary artery, however, arising from the aorta, gives off a major branch (the left anterior descending branch), which nourishes a major part of the anterior walls of the heart. After giving off this anterior branch, the left coronary artery also travels to the rear of the heart to furnish this area with some additional blood.

the surface of your heart, and receive very little buttressing, cushioning, or protection from other tissues. Also, unlike other arteries coronary arteries must put up with a great deal of movement. As it expels its blood into the aorta, your heart shortens, shrinks, and twists with each contraction, and the coronary arteries must do so, too. They are twisted, turned, and otherwise jolted with every beat of the heart, not just occasionally but over 100,000 times a day. No flexible tube of any synthetic we know of could withstand this sort of beating for more than a few years, much less a lifetime. Of course, the human coronary arteries do not remain totally immune to damage from this sort of rhythmic violence. Within months of our birth, in more than half of us they begin to develop tiny cracks, fissures, and even ulcers in their linings. It is probably these defects that set the stage for the later development of coronary heart disease.

The right coronary artery passes over the right side of your heart in a groove that lies between the right auricle and ventricle (see Figure 1). In its backward course to the posterior walls of the heart, it gives off a number of branches that bring blood to the right front half of your heart. Reaching the rear of your heart, it joins up with the terminal branches of the opposite left coronary artery to form a trunk that supplies the posterior or rear walls of both your right and left ventricles.

The left coronary artery divides into two major branches very shortly after it springs from the aorta. One of these branches runs down the front of your heart in a shallow groove lying between the right and left ventricles. We call this branch the *left anterior descending artery*. It is a terribly important branch because it serves as one of the chief sources of blood for the main pumping unit of your heart, the left ventricle. The second branch of the left coronary artery winds toward the rear of the heart, again in a shallow groove lying between the left auricle and ventricle. Reaching the rear of the heart, its terminal branches, as already described, usually team up with similar branches coming from the right coronary artery to form the trunk vessel mentioned above.

Although your heart does have these two major arteries supplying it, neither can easily or rapidly substitute for the other. For example, if your right coronary artery were suddenly obstructed or tied off, your left coronary artery could not immediately take over and bring blood to those portions of your heart previously supplied by the right coronary vessel. Nature for some inexplicable (but probably very wise) reason has thought it best that very few large interconnecting or "bypass" channels should link the right and left coronary circulations. It has permitted, however, some tiny connections to exist between the peripheral or terminal ramifications of these two major coronary arterial systems. Moreover, given enough time and demand, these relatively minute connections can grow larger, and carry more blood from one coronary arterial circulation to another. Hundreds of thousands of Americans whose left or right coronary artery has been severely narrowed or even totally occluded continue to survive and even flourish, probably because of the development and growth of these initially minute connections into moderate-sized vessels.

Although the coronary arteries serve solely to bring blood to your heart, just as metal pipes serve to bring water to your house, they differ from such pipes in that they are living tissues, and have a complex structure. For centuries, however, physicians and medical scientists conceived of arteries as inert and inanimate pipes. During the last century, we have come to recognize that an artery is an organ in its own right. It has a smooth lining, which we call the *intima* (see Figure 2).

The intima is composed of myriads of flat, smooth cells (endothelial cells), which serve as a selective sort of sieve through which certain elements of the blood passing over them can penetrate and nourish the inner parts of the artery wall. For example, endothelial cells easily allow the passage of oxygen and certain salts and sugars from the blood, but resolutely forbid the escape of red blood cells, and under normal circumstances allow only the very slow seepage of cholesterol-bearing proteins.

At birth the intima, or inner coat, of the coronary artery consists of a single layer of endothelial cells. This cell lining is far too fragile to withstand all by itself the pounding surge of blood flowing at such high pressure over it, so it is supported by the strong muscular component of the middle layer of the artery wall. This portion of the coronary artery is called the *media* (see Figure 2). But even this muscular coat could not indefinitely withstand the pulsating pressure of the blood flowing through the center channel (called the *lumen*), were it not for the millions of tiny elastic or rubberlike fibers intimately woven into it. These fibers permit the artery to expand without too great a danger of rupture.

The coronary artery has a third outer coat, too, the adventitia, a sort of tough, fibrous, glovelike tissue (see Figure 2) that sheathes and bolsters the muscular coat. It is in this outer coat that the tiny vessels bringing blood to nourish the artery wall itself are found. As we cannot insist too strongly, the artery lives and needs its own oxygen and other blood nutrients just as much as our brain needs these substances.

This, then, in very brief, is the structure of the coronary arteries, whose only job is to see to it that the muscles of the heart and its "rhythm-inducing" centers receive a continuous supply of blood. And quite a lot of blood this may be at times—as much as a

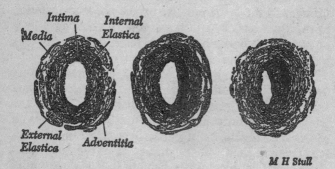

M H Stull

Figure 2. The microscopic cross-section of a normal coronary artery (*left*), of a coronary artery exhibiting early disease (*center*), and of a coronary artery harboring a well-developed atherosclerotic plaque (*right*). The three coats (intima, media, and adventitia) of the normal artery are indicated. Note that the normal intima, or lining coat, consists of only a single layer of cells. In the center drawing, the multiplication of a number of lining cells partially occlude the right half of the lumen in the first stage of disease. In the right drawing, a plaque of scar tissue has replaced the original excess lining cells. Cholesterol (dark black mass) has accumulated at the base of this structure. Note that the lumen is severely narrowed.

pint or more per minute! Indeed your heart, with every beat or contraction, receives back immediately via its coronary arteries about 5 percent of the blood it had just ejected into the aorta.

The coronary veins, of course, return the blood (now deprived of much of its oxygen, hence venous), brought to the heart muscles by the coronary arteries, to the right auricle. But the coronary veins have little or nothing to do with coronary heart disease. So, let's forget about them.

There is one other aspect of heart anatomy that does deserve attention. It is the very specialized tissue that we call the heart's *conduction system*. This tissue, which for the most part is half muscle, half nerve, is responsible for the heart's orderly contraction or beating. Prior to each actual contraction of the heart muscle, a brief electrical wave, beginning in a sort of miniature dynamo situated in the right auricle (the sinoauricular node), sweeps down, over, and within the entire heart along its own electrical pathways to ensure that the contractions of every single muscle fiber of your heart will follow or join in unison with every other fiber. This millivolt current is what the electrocardiograph picks up, amplifies, and then "scratches" out on specially processed paper to give us that very important and sometimes (but not always) revealing message we call the *electrocardiogram*.

It is absolutely imperative for the proper function of the contracting muscles of the heart that this electrical stimulus or excitatory wave be the directing and *unifying* force for contraction. Nevertheless, since every muscle fiber of the heart also generates its own current, sometimes an individual current will attempt to take over or "revolt" against the "master" current. If this muscle fiber does succeed in beating independently of the master current, it may also succeed in stimulating other muscle fibers to revolt and also beat independently. As a result of such muscular anarchy, the heart begins to shiver and writhe like a bag of crawling red worms, no longer capable of pumping.

When it is confined to the auricles, this sort of anarchy is called *auricular fibrillation*. If so confined, it is not too dangerous, because the auricles chiefly serve as "holding chambers" for blood, which can enter its associated ventricle by the pressure exerted upon it. But if it takes over the ventricles, the resulting ventricular fibrillation, if not corrected within a hundred seconds or so, becomes fatal. Effective pumping of blood from the heart immediately ceases; the brain receives no fresh blood and it *almost instantaneously* ceases to function.

In a sense, then, we possess a heart whose muscle components, many eons ago in the evolutionary process, reluctantly subdued their own capability of exciting themselves and agreed to tarry a bit until they received an excitatory stimulus from a central headquarters. But this evolutionary submission has not been and is not a totally irreversible one, as every cardiologist sorrowfully knows. If it were, the more than 100,000 Americans who die suddenly each year of ventricular fibrillation would still be living!

Chapter 3

WHAT IS CORONARY ARTERY DISEASE?

Coronary artery disease, as we shall employ the term in this book, is a still symptomless disorder characterized and identified by the thickening and deterioration of the blood-supply conduits to the heart (see Figure 2).

It is likely that over 100 million Americans already have some degree of coronary artery disease, in the sense that one or more small segments of either their right or left coronary arteries already have some degree of thickening. Such thickening probably began during the first few years of their lives. There are many theories about how and why these thickenings begin so early in life, but nobody is sure about what causes them to take place. We ourselves believe that they arise because the coronary arteries, in their incessant twisting, turning, and telescoping upon themselves, often receive many tiny wounds or tears in their lining during the first few months or years of life. Following the receipt of these wounds, the arteries try to heal or bridge them over with newly formed cells. Such collections of new cells probably serve as "patches," and are the arterial thickenings we first observe so early in life.

If our view is correct, then coronary artery disease actually begins when the artery attempts to heal itself of a traumatically induced wound or tear, but does not succeed in doing so. It is exceedingly unlikely that we shall ever be able to prevent these initial tiny arterial wounds, because they appear to represent part of the payment every human being must make for leaving his mother's womb. Therefore, if there is to be effective control of coronary heart disease, we must concentrate our efforts on ensuring that the healing of these wounds takes place without distortion.

The cells making up these relatively minute thickenings consist of a mixture of newly grown endothelial cells of the intima and muscle cells of the middle coat of the coronary artery's wall. Also, very frequently, there is an accumulation or deposit of cholesterol and fats in and around these overgrown cells. Initially these thickenings are minute, and may even be invisible to the naked eye. Frequently, too, the collections of cells stop growing, and the entire complex may disappear and be replaced by a tiny scar. This, of course, is the happiest of all possible outcomes. But as one complex disappears or is replaced by scar tissue, undoubtedly other segments of the affected artery sustain new damage. Thus a succession of new wounds and their repairs probably goes on continuously throughout infancy, childhood, adolescence, and even adulthood.

Unfortunately, instead of disappearing, too often these overgrowths of cells accumulate an excess amount of fat/cholesterol. This excess accumulation in turn promotes a further overgrowth of cells. The cell "tumors" continue to expand and encroach increasingly upon the main channel, or lumen, of the vessel, through which the vital blood supply for the heart passes. Such expansion and encroachment may continue throughout childhood and adolescence, until at some stage there is no possibility of the disappearance or the simple replacement by a thin scar of these grease-laden (that is, fat/cholesterol-impregnated), distorted arterial cells. This point of no return appears to occur when these masses of arterial cells are infiltrated by another type of cells, which lead to the formation of relatively huge and distorted scars, or what we call *arterial plaques*.

An arterial plaque, or a scarlike mass in the artery wall, will never disappear, and the best one can expect of such a wound or lesion is that it will remain quiescent or indolent. And this, an arterial plaque, thank goodness, very frequently does! It eventually becomes covered with a very tough scarlike "cap," which insulates the blood flowing through the lumen from the living overgrown arterial cells lying beneath. Gradually, too, all the excess fat/cholesterol is concentrated or sequestered at the base of the plaque, very near the still-intact original muscle coat of the artery.

Well over 50 percent of American men over the age of twenty-one years harbor one or more of these plaques. We therefore must admit that this same proportion, according to our definition, already harbor coronary artery disease. But most of the plaques are still small and do not seriously obstruct the lumen of the artery. Accordingly, there is very little diminution in the coronary blood supply to the heart. Even if one or more of these plaques have grown large enough to obstruct over half of the lumen of the vessel harboring it, the heart still receives sufficient blood for its needs. These facts make clear that coronary artery disease can and frequently does exist for many decades, indeed for the total biblical outlook of seventy years, without making its presence known.

A coronary artery plaque is of course a living, although rather monstrous, variety of tissue. It, too, needs blood for the support of the cells it contains. Such blood is provided by new, very tiny vessels, which have grown into the plaque from blood vessels originally located in the outer coat of the artery. But these newly formed vessels are rather makeshift and inadequate, so that very often a plaque really doesn't receive enough blood for the adequate sustenance of its cells. The excess fat/cholesterol present in these plaques also sometimes markedly interferes with the nutrition of their cells. Because of these two inimical factors, the inner cellular portions of many plaques die (or, in medical terminology, become *necrotic*). When such necrosis takes place, the area these cells formerly occupied is replaced by rough and unyielding bonelike material termed *coronary bone,* or by a pool of grease-laden debris, sometimes both.

Now an intact plaque, filled with living arterial and scar cells, is rarely life threatening, no matter how large it is. But when portions of a plaque deteriorate and these formerly living parts are replaced by either pools of necrotic debris or bone, or both, then the stage is set for possible future tragedies. Perhaps half a century ago plaques remained relatively intact past the fifth or sixth decade. But now it is not at all rare to find degenerated plaques in men and women who are in only their twenties. And perhaps 20 to 30 percent of American men under fifty years of age today harbor one or more coronary artery plaques that carry areas of necrotic liquefaction, newly formed bones, or both in their total structure.

But even a necrotic plaque still may not exhibit any evidence whatsoever of its presence. Not even an electrocardiogram taken after the severest sort of physical activity will necessarily reveal the presence of those potentially dangerous plaques. This is so because the electrocardiogram records nothing but the excitatory electrical stimulus coursing along the fibers of the heart. As long as all the muscle components through which these fibers run remain uninjured and receive sufficient oxygen, they will continue to conduct a normal electrical impulse. And the fibers will remain seemingly intact and healthy as long as they receive as little as 10 to 15 percent of their normal blood supply. Thus unless a plaque cuts down the blood flow through a coronary vessel 85 to 95 percent, its presence will not show up on an electrocardiogram. To be noticed, it must block 90 percent or more of lumen of the artery through which the blood is flowing.

If a deteriorating plaque thus usually pursues an "underground" course in man, it does not necessarily remain indolent. The areas of necrotic debris gradually enlarge, as do the areas of calcification (or "bone"). Either process only too often begins to approach and gradually eat away the firm, scarlike cap of the plaque. This cap, as we have already stated, isolates the blood traversing the lumen of the artery from the clot-producing potential of either the pools of debris or the "bones" of the sick artery. Undoubtedly, breaks in the cap much thinner than the thinnest strand of hair do occur from time to time. Blood-clotting elements of the blood flowing past this break then rush to the "leak in the dam" to seal it off. Perhaps such tiny breaks occur scores of times over a period of years.

But the blood-clotting elements laid down as an emergency sealant eventually turn themselves into plaque material, thus enlarging the original plaque and causing it to obstruct more and more of the lumen through which the heart's own blood must pass.

Unlike most other diseases, therefore, coronary artery disease pursues an underground course in man for many decades. Sir William Osler, probably the greatest physician our hemisphere has ever produced, has described this course hauntingly in the book he wrote on heart disease in 1897,* and we believe he deserves to be quoted.

Angeio-sclerosis, [i.e., atherosclerosis or coronary artery disease], creeping on slowly but surely, "with no pace perceived," is the Nemesis through which Nature exacts retributive justice for the transgression of her laws. . . . Nowhere do we see such an element of tragic sadness as in many of these cases. A man who has early risen and late taken rest, who has eaten the bread of carefulness, striving for success in commercial, professional, or political life, after twenty-five or thirty years of incessant toil reaches the point where he can say, perhaps with just satisfaction, "Soul, thou hast much goods laid up for many years: take thine ease," all unconscious that the fell sergeant has already issued the warrant. How true to life is Hawthorne in *The House of the Seven Gables*! To Judge Pyncheon, who had experienced a mere dimness of sight and a throbbing at the heart—nothing more—and in whose grasp was the meed for which he had "fought and toiled and climbed and crept"; to him, as he sat in the old oaken chair of his grandfathers, thinking of the crowning success of his life, so near at hand, the avenger came through his arteries.

As it was in Judge Pyncheon's era, and later in that of Osler's, so in our own times. The final surfacing of this so frequently poorly perceived disease only too often makes itself felt as an abrupt and sometimes irretrievable tragedy. We have inserted, however, "almost" before the word "irretrievable" in the last sentence because we know that in hundreds of thousands of cases the tragedy need not necessarily be an irretrievable one. Osler, for all his clinical acumen and ability to employ lovely descriptive prose, could not insert "almost" in this same sentence because he did not have at his disposal, when he wrote the above, the body of facts, the drugs, and the surgical techniques we now have at ours.

* William Osler, *Lectures on Angina Pectoris and Allied States* (New York: D. Appleton & Co., 1897).

Chapter 4

WHAT IS CORONARY HEART DISEASE?

Luckily, for the majority of persons coronary *artery* disease never becomes coronary *heart* disease. But in about 3 percent of American adults, coronary artery disease does worsen some time after the third decade to such an extent that the coronary arteries cannot carry enough blood to supply the muscles of the heart with sufficient oxygen and nourishment for them to perform *all* their functions under *all* demands made on them. When coronary artery narrowing has progressed to this point, then coronary *artery* disease may be considered to have evolved into coronary *heart* disease.

As we have pointed out, the mechanism of this development involves plaques lying upon and growing in the walls of the coronary arteries. When they begin to decay and rupture, the blood flowing through the lumen of an artery is permitted to come into direct contact with the shaggy, clot-generating elements lurking in the decaying areas of the plaques. At this point clots occur, and only too frequently totally close off the lumens of vessels already moderately or severely narrowed by the plaques.

Now, plaques rarely decay until they have grown relatively huge and are already *partially* obstructing the flow of blood. Thus, a person may possess coronary arteries studded with dozens of relatively tiny plaques, but because they remain small, these plaques usually stay intact. Hence, they do not generate clots. On the other hand, another person may possess coronary arteries having only a few plaques, but if one or more of these is growing so wildly as to exceed the blood supply available for *their* sustenance, they are likely to decay and rupture. The consequence may be a clot. Both of these individuals suffer from coronary *artery* disease, but only the latter may develop coronary *heart* disease.

Two plaques of equal size and containing the same amount of decay may still differ in their propensity to rupture and also in their propensity to generate clots. If one plaque harbors its areas of decay very deep in its structure, quite a distance away from the blood flowing through the lumen of the coronary artery, it may never rupture severely enough for the circulating blood to reach it and clot. Again, even if plaque may rupture in such a way as to allow the blood to touch decayed areas, a dangerous clot still may not form, due to conditions present in the blood itself.

You might well ask at this point why scientists are not concentrating more of their attention upon preventing the rupture of plaques and staving off the clotting phenomenon. We can only answer that not until the last few years have we learned that it is the rupture of plaques that changes essentially benign coronary *artery* disease into potentially cataclysmic coronary *heart* disease.

More and more attention will undoubtedly be focused in the future upon this serious pathological development. Meanwhile, since we are already reasonably positive that one of the causes of plaque ruptures must be the size of the plaques, we will continue to try to restrict their emergence and continued growth. More attention is being paid to the prevention of blood clotting, too. For over two decades, several anti-clotting drugs have been administered to patients with coronary heart disease. Unfortunately, however, these drugs apparently do not prevent the *type* of clot that occurs in coronary arteries.

Only too often, very serious coronary artery disease (in the sense that it may evolve into coronary heart disease almost instantaneously) may be present without either the patient or his physician being aware of it. No matter how thorough his last physical examination was, no matter how many different tests were done on his blood, urine, and feces, no matter how many X rays were taken, no matter how many ordinary electrocardiograms were obtained, a person could have coronary artery disease ready to erupt, in the space of a few fleeting seconds or minutes or hours, into coronary heart disease.

There are only two tests, both of them relatively new, that can offer a person assurance that he does not harbor serious coronary artery disease. The first, called *coronary arteriography,* a special X-ray procedure in which the coronary arteries are injected with a radio-opaque dye and then visualized, may be slightly dangerous. It is accordingly not often performed unless the patient is already suspected of suffering from coronary heart disease and surgical relief is being considered. The other, an electrocardiogram taken while the subject is undergoing a moderately severe, standardized type of exertion, is a relatively safe procedure, provided a doctor or his trained assistant with the proper equipment is in constant attendance. Now that it has been widely recognized that an electrocardiogram taken under resting conditions is not of much value (if it is normal), monitored electrocardiography under conditions of controlled exercise is being used more and more. It will be interesting to see what measures various prepaid medical care complexes will take in this regard in the next few years because this is a procedure that cannot safely be left to any system of automation in the absence of a real trained attendant. Also, if a subject is ever asked to exercise while an electrocardiogram is being taken, he should not do so unless not only a doctor is there but also a machine called a defibrillator is at hand and ready to use. But more about this later.

We have expanded a bit above about this matter of severe coronary artery disease because many people have been shocked when a seemingly healthy friend suddenly collapsed and died of a "heart attack." Their shock and surprise were even more profound if this same friend was pronounced "as sound as a dollar and as fit as a fiddle" by his physician after a *routine* checkup a few weeks or even a few hours before his demise. For anyone thirty years of age or older, a *routine* checkup might be very valuable for determining his blood pressure or the state of his lungs and stomach, and so on, but it is almost farcical as a means of detecting the presence of serious coronary artery disease.

But far more often than not, we are the first to detect the presence of coronary heart disease in ourselves. Sooner or later, the previously silent coronary artery disease makes itself known by inducing various complexes of symptoms and signs. At this point, coronary *artery* disease has passed over into coronary *heart* disease. The symptoms and signs are as follows:

ANGINA PECTORIS

Literally translated, angina pectoris means "pain of the chest." Various illnesses can, of course, cause chest pain. But in the two centuries since William Heberden first described and named this particular kind of chest pain, cardiologists have gradually come to limit their use of the term to that type of pain which arises at the moment when the heart muscle suffers from lack of oxygen because of an inadequate blood supply. This state is technically called *ischemia,* and it is now believed to be caused by a sudden change in a long-standing condition of coronary artery disease, a change so severe that the blood flow through one or more of the main coronary arteries has become very seriously compromised.

The pain of angina pectoris most often erupts when the victim demands more of his heart muscles than they can accomplish without running short of oxygen. At complete rest, the heart muscles can usually do a fairly decent job of pumping without becoming starved for oxygen, even though the coronary arteries may be partly blocked. But if the patient eats a very heavy meal, runs or even walks up a hill (particularly if it is windy), or becomes emotionally upset, then his heart is asked to beat faster and stronger. It manages to do so, but its own increased demand for oxygen cannot be met. The muscle itself thus becomes oxygen starved—or ischemic—and angina pectoris results.

Most medical textbooks locate the typical angina pain in the center of the chest, describing its squeezing, pressing, or crushing character and its frequent extension into the left shoulder and down the left arm. But often the pain may be perceived first in the pit of the stomach; in the neck or jaws; in either shoulder, elbow, or wrist; or in just a few fingers of either hand.

Wherever the pain appears, however, if it is true angina it rarely lasts more than a few minutes. Of course, if the person persists in the physical activity or remains in the same emotional state that brought on the attack, the pain may continue.

Although many laymen consider an episode of angina pectoris a form of heart attack, cardiologists usually do not, because no *permanent* or *significant* damage is done to the heart during or following the attack. To the cardiologist, angina pectoris is just a form of "body language" whereby the heart indicates to its possessor that it temporarily lacks oxygen. Accordingly, few patients are hospitalized because of an occasional attack of angina pectoris. This does not mean, of course, that it is nothing to worry about—far from it! It is, on the contrary, a sign of an abiding and dangerous condition. Just as there is no such thing as a "slight touch of pregnancy," there is no such thing as a "slight case of angina." See a doctor.

MYOCARDIAL INFARCTION

This event is one of the most common and also one of the most serious complications of severe coronary artery disease. It is also a complication that can take place quickly and unexpectedly. This is the catastrophe that is most often called a heart attack by the layman. Various synonyms have been and are still commonly used to describe it: "coronary," "acute coronary occlusion," and "acute coronary thrombosis." Indeed, cardiologists themselves, when talking with their colleagues, are most apt to employ the term *coronary* when they refer to a case of myocardial infarction. They would not, however, ever use this term in the writing of the history and progress of such a patient, either for a hospital record or for the medical literature.

A myocardial infarction is any area of heart muscle (almost always, however, located somewhere in the left ventricle) which has died (or become necrotic). It has died because it failed to receive a sufficient amount of oxygen or other nourishing substances *over too long a period of time*. In most of these cases (but certainly not all), a large, fresh clot or thrombus had formed over a crack or fissure in a deteriorating plaque of a coronary artery. The thrombus thus formed permanently obstructed the entire lumen of a coronary artery. In so doing, it cut off the already diminished blood supply to some portion of the left ventricle. This portion of living muscle tissue then died. The area involved may be a very small (less than pea sized) and discrete segment of the left ventricle, or it may be relatively extensive (larger than an olive) and not necessarily sharply delineated. Depending upon the size and location of the infarct, a patient may die, or recover with severe, slight, or no discernible impairment in the pumping power of his heart.

The occurrence as well as the location and general size of a myocardial infarct can usually be determined with rather stunning accuracy by the electrocardiograph. Of course, the severity and extent of the wound can also be surmised by other laboratory procedures, and sometimes may have to be if the infarction is a very small one, or if it occurs in a heart damaged earlier.

A myocardial infarction sometimes involves, in addition to heart muscle, a portion of the conduction system. In such cases, irregular and even dangerous bouts of irregular heart beating or conduction (what is known as *arrhythmia*) may occur.

If the patient survives his acute myocardial infarction (and 50 percent or more do so), the area of dead heart muscle is gradually replaced by scar tissue. But this scar tissue cannot contract or help to do its share in pumping blood from the left ventricle as did the heart muscle it replaced. It no more resembles the original heart muscle than does a scar on your face resemble the original intact skin it replaced. If the scar area is of very small size, its failure to do its share in pumping really doesn't matter; but if it is of good size, then its nonparticipation in the pumping process makes quite a bit of difference. The left ventricle's contractions may then be weakened. And depending upon how much it is weakened, the patient surviving an infarction may be permanently handicapped by easily induced shortness of breath or fatigue. For example, whereas he may have been able to play a grueling three sets of tennis singles prior to his infarction, afterwards he may not be able to play a single set. He may not even be able to walk to the tennis court!

But in most cases of infarction, the dead muscle area is not that great. Its replacement by scar tissue rarely immobilizes a patient permanently, particularly if it is his first heart attack.

Still, patients who have suffered an infarction tend to die at an earlier age than subjects of their same age who have not had one. There are probably several reasons for this. First, their coronary arteries had to be quite severely diseased before they suffered their infarction. And having the infarction hasn't changed the seriousness or the degree of their *basic* coronary artery disease. Second, most patients who have suffered a heart attack or infarction *continue to indulge in certain habits* avoided by most of their healthy friends. We seriously believe that if these habits are changed— and they can be—it is quite possible that the patient having a heart attack need not have a second one any sooner than many of his so-called "well" friends. As matters now stand, of a hundred patients having their first heart attack in 1974, fifty will have a second one before 1979 arrives. And this is really a ridiculous sort of tragedy, because it is so readily preventable.

The other type of danger faced by heart attack survivors involves the heart muscle fibers lying near the scar and indeed sometimes surrounded by tiny strands of scar. While not actually dying, as did the heart muscle fibers replaced by the scar, these fibers *almost* died. Lacking a sufficient flow of coronary blood, and perhaps also interfered with by strangling strands of scar tissue, they exist in a chronically malfunctioning state. Sometimes, when their blood flow is perilously diminished, they appear ready to die, and then at other times, with *just about* enough blood to *almost* satisfy their wants, they appear viable and able to endure as typical contracting muscle fibers. But in this conflict, which begins whenever the blood flow diminishes, these struggling fibers can no longer be depended upon to follow unquestioningly the master electrical rhythm set by the heart's central pacemaker. Instead, they may send out their own electrical wave, thus interfering with or destroying the lifelong, seventy times-a-minute tempo of the master stimulus. This may cause a simple extra or premature beat of the heart or a run of extra beats. But sometimes this new rebellion inspires general disorder, causing the heart to race completely out of control at a rate of one hundred fifty to two hundred or more times a minute (ventricular tachycardia); or even worse, tragically worse, it may send every muscle fiber in the heart into a chaotic frenzy (ventricular fibrillation). As a result of this state of arrhythmia, what had been a beautifully synchronized pumping heart turns instantly into a quivering mass of totally useless flesh.

Once this latter type of asynchrony is initiated, the heart cannot of itself ever revert to its normal beating. Death—until a few years ago—was inevitable. Now an electrical countershocking machine can abolish this electrical revolt of the heart. How unforgettably dramatic it is to witness this therapeutic intervention! The dials are twisted, the red lamp lights up, all the doctors momentarily step away from the dying patient, then one doctor applies the paddle electrodes directly to the bare chest. "Turn it on!" he yells. The powerful current pours in, and the whole body of the patient jerks. Usually, the revolt is quenched, and the original pacemaker of the heart again takes over. The patient opens his eyes and begins to breathe again!

But this electrical "revolt" may take place in the heart when its possessor is looking at television; riding a plane, car, or bus; sitting and working at a desk; or even jogging. With no countershocking machine available, chest massage sometimes has been used to keep the patient alive until he can either be moved to the machine or it to him. But this form of emergency treatment fails much more often than it succeeds. A far more effective measure—but infinitely less dramatic, of course—would be the medical prevention of the "revolt" itself, and we shall discuss such possible medical prevention in a later chapter.

But a note of caution! Irregularities in the rhythm of the heart can occur in patients with coronary heart disease who have never suffered a myocardial infarct. Then, too, at least a quarter of the patients who have suffered a myocardial infarct never knew it. These being the facts, it seems to us that if ever a person begins to observe *any* type of irregularity in the beating of his heart, he should consult his physician. And if the physician attempts to reassure him by telling him of the total inconsequence of such irregularities, it would be wise, we believe, to ask for a more practical type of reassurance: namely, that the irregularity be permanently corrected.

CONGESTIVE HEART FAILURE

Congestive heart failure is another form of coronary heart disease to which patients possessing severe coronary artery disease sometimes become susceptible. But once again, one or more of the three main coronary arteries must be totally occluded before this variety of coronary heart disease can occur. In congestive heart failure, the heart muscles gradually weaken and fail to contract vigorously enough to do a good job of cycling the total volume of circulating blood. If the muscle fibers of the left ventricle, weakened by a poor blood supply from the thickened coronary arteries and interfered with by areas of scarring from earlier infarcts, begin to pump poorly, the blood accumulates in the lungs. Meanwhile, the right ventricle (which is rarely attacked in coronary heart disease) continues to pump more blood into the lungs. The immediate result is shortness of breath, and if the process continues, actual flooding of the air spaces of the lungs with fluid seeping from the distended blood vessels. We call this last phenomenon *pulmonary edema*.

Sometimes, following this initial partial failure in the pumping ability of the left ventricle and the consequent damming up of blood in the lungs, the right ventricle also begins to weaken in its battle to eject blood into a lung already filled almost to bursting with stagnant blood under high pressure. When it weakens, then the venous blood coming to it from all parts of the body begins to accumulate in veins and distends them, and the liquid portion of this blood, because of the pressure exerted upon it, begins to leak out of the veins. The liver may enlarge, the ankles and legs swell, and fluid begins to accumulate in the abdomen. To correct this situation, drugs are given that restore the pumping capacity of the left ventricle, thus interrupt-

ing the vicious circle. Other drugs are also given to
encourage the kidneys to excrete the excess fluid.

There are many persons who have no symptoms of
coronary heart disease even under severely stressful
circumstances (physical or emotional), although one
of their three main coronary artery branches has been
completely occluded (a so-called "silent" coronary occlusion). By our definition, such persons still cannot
be said to have coronary *heart* disease, because of the
absence of symptoms and electrocardiographic abnormalities.

It is even possible that *two* of their three coronary
arteries may be totally occluded and still they experience no symptoms of heart disease. How can this happen? Because these arteries have developed new blood
vessels that bypass the obstructions. But such arteries
(we call them *collateral vessels*) must traverse a sinu-
ous and circuitous pathway. They rarely transport as
much blood as the original artery had. As a result,
those areas of the heart muscles receiving the diminished blood supply may be at a serious disadvantage,
despite the fact that they have never given any indication of their distress. The owner of this type of heart is
thus unaware of his nearness to danger.

It is precisely this condition, present but undis-
cerned, which afflicts those hundreds of thousands of
Americans who, hale and hearty at breakfast, nevertheless collapse later at their office, in the subway, at
the football game, at the concert, at the bowling alley,
or even that night during their sleep. What takes place
in such persons so that heretofore "silent" coronary
artery disease seemingly instantaneously erupts into
"symptomatic" coronary *heart* disease? Sometimes an
additional clot or thrombus has taken place, perhaps
in that portion of the artery above a previous occlusion, which had supplied blood via the new collateral

vessels. Just as frequently, however, no new arterial event can be discerned. We are forced to assume that, for reasons still incompletely understood by our colleagues or by us, a focal area of muscle in the hearts of these patients is deprived of sufficient blood *(if only for a few seconds or minutes)*. The muscle area either dies, causing an infarct; or it revolts against the dominant rhythm-making center of the heart, and in so doing gives way to the fatal chaos of ventricular fibrillation.

This chapter has probably not been a pleasant one to read, particularly for anyone who is now suffering from coronary heart disease. Yet we have chosen to tell the whole truth about the consequences of coronary artery disease. In later chapters, however, we will go on to tell the whole truth about the ways in which the tragedies caused by this disease can probably be averted or indefinitely forestalled.

Chapter 5

CHOLESTEROL: THE PRIME SUSPECT IN CORONARY ARTERY DISEASE

If the mass media has not eliminated cholesterol from your diet, it has nevertheless succeeded in making some of you feel just a bit guilty when, for example, you nibble at a hard-boiled egg or dash your coffee with full-strength cream. Millions of Americans besides yourself have been convinced during the past few decades that cholesterol-rich foods play a part in bringing on coronary artery disease and heart attacks.

It is only fair to say that hundreds of heart researchers today are honestly and wholeheartedly convinced that if nature had not invented and foisted cholesterol upon us, coronary heart disease would be almost nonexistent. In view of these convictions, it seems to us that it might be appropriate at this juncture to review for you some of the facts concerning this extraordinary substance.

THE NATURE AND NORMAL
FUNCTIONS OF CHOLESTEROL

Cholesterol is a highly complex alcoholic substance that at room temperature exists in rather greasy, yellowish-white crystals, relatively insoluble in water but quite easily dissolved in certain fats, ether, and simpler alcohols. Because of the large number of hydrogenated carbon atoms making up cholesterol, it superficially shares some of the physical characteristics of simple fats. Moreover, like fats, it is a relatively passive, inert compound that reacts poorly or not at all with most metallic chemical compounds. If properly coaxed, however, by various enzyme systems in the animal body, all sorts of chemical alterations of cholesterol can be effected. One of the simplest changes cholesterol may undergo in the body is its transformation into what we call a *cholesterol ester*—a modification brought about when cholesterol loses its terminal alcohol group and takes up a fatty acid.

Cholesterol was first extracted from human gallstones in the eighteenth century. For many decades after its initial extraction and partial purification, cholesterol continued to be obtained from gallstones and also from a far more macabre source, charnel "wax" —the oleaginous material emanating from decaying human bodies. It was only in the last half of the nineteenth century that researchers began to realize that cholesterol was a bit more important than the stuff of which most gallstones were composed or one of the stuffs into which most human bodies decomposed. Certain pathologists began to worry about the fact that this material could also be found in the arteries of living man.

But it was early in our present century that the real importance of cholesterol was discerned. Scientists discovered that cholesterol could be found in every cell of the animal body, and that it was synthesized not only in the liver but in virtually every tissue and organ. It was found to serve as a necessary component of the microscopic wall encompassing and protecting each cell, providing a framework of support for the animal body just as cellulose does for a plant. It was clear, in short, that the body could not maintain even a vestige of cellular integrity if this substance were removed.

We now know that nature employs cholesterol as its most effective insulator. It is primarily cholesterol that serves to keep separate the individual electrochemical reactions taking place in each of your active brain and nerve cells. If such cholesterol were removed, your thought, mobility, indeed your life itself would cease almost instantaneously, because all the electrochemical processes, no longer shielded from each other, would instantaneously "short-circuit."

Besides serving as an indispensable component of cellular structure and as an insulator, cholesterol has also been found to be the precursor of your sex and adrenal gland hormones and also all your bile acids. Again, if the body were deprived of the cholesterol needed for these purposes, life would end quite abruptly.

So, regardless of how this substance has been maligned by the organs of mass media, you would do well to remember that almost every cell in your body has been busily synthesizing and then utilizing it for one or more of the specific purposes described above. As a matter of fact, many of these processes started in your body long before you were born. Some of them began at that instant when your father's sperm met and conjoined with your mother's ovum.

But busy and also as capable as so many of your organs and tissues are in making their own cholesterol, they always seem quite pleased to accept cholesterol coming to them via the bloodstream. In turn, your blood seems as pleased to receive the cholesterol present in your food as that which the liver manufactures and gives to it. We don't know yet *why* your body's organs and tissues are so eager to receive cholesterol from sources outside themselves, but at least we are beginning to learn *how* they receive it.

THE SOURCES AND FUNCTIONS
OF CHOLESTEROL IN THE BLOOD

Cholesterol arrives in your blood from many sources. A continuous, small stream of molecules of this substance enters the blood from all tissues of your body as some of your cells die and release their cholesterol content. But the two chief providers of blood cholesterol are your liver and intestine. These two organs function ceaselessly every minute of your life. Before either of them releases cholesterol for its journey in your bloodstream, however, they must "package" it. Pure cholesterol, being very poorly soluble in water, just wouldn't dissolve in the watery medium of your blood.

The liver packages cholesterol by joining it to various proteins that it manufactures and that are quite soluble in water. To these combinations of cholesterol and protein, the liver also adds varying amounts of pure fat and a fatlike substance called *phospholipid*. Together, these complexes of cholesterol, protein, fat, and phospholipid are called *lipoproteins*.

Ordinarily, your liver packages cholesterol in three different kinds of lipoproteins. We designate these *alpha, beta,* and *pre-beta* lipoproteins. They differ from each other chiefly in the amounts of protein, fat, and cholesterol each contains. The alpha lipoproteins possess a minimum of fat and not too much cholesterol compared to their protein content. As a consequence, they are the most soluble, hence the most easily transported of the three lipoproteins. They are also relatively small molecules. The beta lipoproteins, in contrast, contain a far larger fraction of cholesterol and fat compared to their protein component. They therefore are less soluble and form larger-sized molecules. The pre-beta lipoprotein molecules contain even less protein and cholesterol than the beta lipoproteins, but they are intensely rich in fat. As a consequence, these pre-beta lipoproteins are the largest, least soluble, and least stable of all the lipoproteins the liver ejects into the bloodstream. Recently, certain studies have suggested that pre-beta lipoproteins may also be formed directly in the blood from the cholesterol coming from the food you eat.

Since you probably are not a medical student, it isn't at all necessary that you remember all the structural and compositional details of these three lipoproteins. Certainly you can forget about the alpha lipoprotein molecules, for no investigator even suspects that they play a part in coronary artery disease. But you might remember that the beta lipoprotein and the cholesterol it contains is very heavily suspected by hundreds of scientists of primary complicity in the "crime" of coronary artery disease. And just now the pre-beta lipoprotein is also being viewed with ever-deepening distrust.

Unlike your liver, your intestine prefers to package the cholesterol it receives from the food passing through it in a very different fashion. After it absorbs the cholesterol, it dissolves it in a minute but microscopically visible globule of pure fat, adds some phospholipid to this combination, and then sprinkles a very light covering of protein—a protein that is extraordinarily similar to the alpha lipoprotein—over the spherical surface of the total globule. This "ball" of cholesterol dissolved in fat is called a *chylomicron*. Myriads of these chylomicrons begin entering your blood within minutes after you have eaten a fat- and cholesterol-containing meal. Moreover, they will continue to enter your blood for many hours after this single meal.

Where do they go? What happens to them? Well, they are carried in your blood as solid, fat little cholesterol balls, bumping along looking for any arterial or capillary leak or crevice to escape from or settle in, but usually getting swept inexorably along in the forward rush of blood. Peculiarly, the liver at first almost totally ignores these fat, cholesterol-rich pellets and allows them to pass through its multiple channels relatively unscathed. However, cells lying in the fatty tissues of your body "attack" these chylomicrons and extract large fractions of their fat (but not their cholesterol) content. The chylomicrons, seriously ravaged and deprived of their fat, then circulate as cholesterol-rich remnants, which, when they reach the liver now, are not allowed to escape a second time. The liver seizes them and extracts from them all their cholesterol and what little remains of their fat and phospholipid content. They are, in short, totally destroyed and absorbed.

From this account you can see that the life of any single tiny chylomicron may not be more than a few minutes. But millions of these cholesterol-fat globules constantly enter and circulate in your blood for many hours after the ingestion of any meal containing fat. If you eat three meals a day containing fat and cholesterol, it is most probable that your blood during most of your waking hours will teem with millions of these particles. Moreover, the more cholesterol your meal contains, the more is contained by each of these millions of chylomicrons.

But why worry, when the liver is so adept at flooding the blood with its own manufactured cholesterol bound to alpha, beta, and pre-beta lipoproteins? One reason: the cholesterol contained in chylomicrons is not securely bound to any soluble protein but just suspended or barely dissolved in fat. Furthermore, if some of these chylomicrons, and particularly if some of the chylomicron remnants (chylomicrons whose fat has been almost totally removed), escape from the lumen of an artery to enter its lining wall, then although the fat portion of the chylomicron or chylomicron remnant may manage to escape and return again to the blood, the cholesterol portion precipitates out and remains in this artery wall for an indefinite stay.

We believe such accidental escapes of chylomicrons or chylomicron remnants into arterial walls occur quite frequently. Furthermore, these escapes are particularly apt to occur at the site of any arterial injury, no matter how slight such an injury may be. As we've already stated, it is extremely probable, indeed inevitable, that you have had tiny injuries in your own coronary arteries since soon after you were born.

It must be clear to you that we sharply distinguish between the cholesterol that your body itself makes and that which comes from your food. It is not that we believe that the cholesterol molecules that your body makes are chemically different, but rather that body-made cholesterol is *firmly* packaged in a very soluble lipoprotein "carton," whereas food-derived cholesterol is *flimsily* packaged in a fat-stuffed pellet. Let alpha lipoprotein cholesterol (which is made by the liver) escape from the blood and enter the wall lining of an artery, it will quickly return to the blood. But if a cholesterol-rich chylomicron makes the same type of escape, the cholesterol more often than not will remain indefinitely in the arterial wall. This fact has been repeatedly demonstrated in the laboratory, and you might do well to remember it the next time you hear a layman or even a doctor claim that the cholesterol the body makes is identical to that in the food as far as its potential for causing arterial damage is concerned. This statement is not simply untrue, it is dangerously untrue. The potential danger posed by chylomicron cholesterol should be considered by anyone led by best-selling diet books to believe that eating animal fats freely is a harmless way to lose weight. Perhaps he will lose weight, but it may be at the cost of his arterial integrity, a rather heavy price to pay for "gourmet dieting."

We have already pointed out that your liver removes cholesterol from your blood and converts it into bile acids, even though, like your sex and adrenal glands, it is wonderfully adept in manufacturing its own cholesterol for this same purpose. Since your liver both introduces new and removes old cholesterol simultaneously, it seems reasonable to believe that this organ constantly scans and inspects the various lipoproteins entering its meshes to be certain of their structural fitness for their blood journeys. Lipoproteins that fail to pass this conjectured muster are removed and replaced by newly made ones. Such a mode of replacement might explain why your liver is simultaneously removing from and adding cholesterol to your bloodstream.

THE REGULATION OF BLOOD CHOLESTEROL CONTENT

Although the red blood cells contain a fixed, unvarying amount of cholesterol, most of the cholesterol in blood is carried in its cell-free aqueous component, the blood serum. We measure the cholesterol content of serum when we wish to follow the cholesterol dynamics of either laboratory animals or human beings.

We usually express this amount as the number of milligrams (mg.) of cholesterol in 100 milliliters (about 3 ounces) of serum. For example, if a person has 250 mg. of cholesterol in 100 ml. of his serum, we say that his serum cholesterol content is 259 mg./100 ml. or 250 mg. percent or just 250.

Why is the serum cholesterol level of an elephant only 67 mg./100 ml., while that of a woolly bear caterpillar is 240 mg./100 ml.? Or why is the serum cholesterol level of a dogfish only 25 mg./100 ml. and that of a Columbia River salmon 500 mg./100 ml.? And you could also ask why the blood cholesterol of the monstrous hippopotamus is only 38 mg./100 ml., whereas that of the lowly but vicious viper is 390 mg./100 ml.? To all these questions, our answer at present would have to be the same: We don't know!

In fact, we truly don't know what determines the *basic* serum cholesterol level in man himself. Indeed, there is little agreement among scientists on just what the normal level of human serum cholesterol ought to be. This fundamental debate may surprise you, in view of the number of articles describing how easily your serum cholesterol level can be altered by the ingestion of various foods or drugs or by changes in some of your habits. But though the statistics remain in flux, there is no doubt that the cholesterol level of many persons can be changed by new food habits and by a few drugs or by modification of certain *specific* habits. Any change so effected, however, rarely alters the cholesterol level more than 20 to 25 percent, and often much less.

We know some of the organs that are involved in serving as a "cholesterolstat" for your serum level of cholesterol. Unquestionably, the liver is very deeply involved in the job, contributing its newly formed lipoprotein cholesterol to the blood when the latter's cholesterol content falls too low, and conversely, removing cholesterol when its concentration in blood rises to too high a level.

The intestinal tract is also able to synthesize cholesterol independently of that which it absorbs and passes on to the blood from the food traversing through it. Moreover, like the liver, the intestine is also able to extract excess cholesterol from the blood and get rid of it along with other bodily wastes. At our present level of knowledge, we are inclined to consider the liver and the intestine as the prime and chief monitors for the regulation of the cholesterol level in your blood.

But what system or center tells these two organs when and when not to add cholesterol to or remove it from your blood? This question, as we've already mentioned, cannot yet be answered with certainty. However, we have good reason to suspect that the cholesterol activities of both of these organs are partially paced by certain hormones. It has long been known that if too much thyroid hormone circulates in your blood, cholesterol content falls, chiefly because your liver, under the influence of this excess thyroid hormone, extracts huge amounts of cholesterol from the blood to convert it quickly into bile acids. If too little thyroid hormone circulates in your blood, cholesterol content slowly rises, chiefly because your liver becomes sluggish in manufacturing bile acids, hence extracting less cholesterol from your blood.

More recently, we ourselves have found that two other hormones, namely pituitary growth hormone and glucagon (a hormone secreted by the pancreas), also play a very important role in regulating the cholesterol level of your blood serum. These two hormones, like thyroid hormone, probably exert their influence upon the cholesterol activities of your liver and intestine. Finally, it is highly probable that the cholesterol content of your serum can be altered whenever there is a marked change in the blood content of various other hormones besides those we have already described.

We suspect that the ultimate center for the control of your serum cholesterol level lies in one or more centers in your brain. It is probably from these nerve centers that a continuous stream of neural messages are sent, not only to your liver and intestine, but to any other of your organs or tissues concerned with cholesterol metabolism. Such messages probably set the regular pace or rhythm at which cholesterol is to be added to or extracted from your serum. And to supplement these neural messages, these various brain centers also govern directly, as well as indirectly, the secretion rate of the hormones mentioned above. These latter probably supplement the neural messages sent directly to the cholesterol-handling organs.

A nice concept, but is it valid? We believe it is, for several reasons. First, although we physicians constantly forget it, no organ of your body is an island. Left to itself, unsupported by other organs and receiving no "supreme" directions, no organ in your body would long survive. But besides a willingness to support each other, these organs require uncompromisingly meticulous direction and coordination of even their tiniest and most trivial functions. Such direction and coordination must emanate from some central locus or headquarters, which is doubtless the brain. If there is some other organ or tissue in the body besides the brain from which such central direction and coordination issues, no anatomist or physiologist has yet been able to find it.

There is another reason why we believe our concept concerning the brain control of cholesterol regulation is valid. Several years ago, we found that as soon as we electrically injured several areas lying in the emotional center of a rat's brain, the rat promptly exhibited a doubling, tripling, even a quintupling of his serum cholesterol level. And as we suspected, the livers of these brain-disturbed animals, receiving unusual neural messages, also handled cholesterol quite differently than did the livers of normal animals.

We believe you may assume that your *basic* serum cholesterol level is regulated by certain brain centers both by means of direct (that is, neural messages) and indirect (that is, by hormones) agents. But if you have ingested certain foods and indulged in certain habits, and continue to do so, your blood serum cholesterol might (and usually does) rise above your normal basal level. Just what should your basal serum cholesterol level be? As we've already mentioned, there is little agreement about this matter. We ourselves suspect that a *normal* basal serum cholesterol level for an adult man or woman (when *all* dietary, drinking, and behavioral habits are controlled, we have found no essential sex differences in serum cholesterol levels) should be somewhere between 150 and 175 mg./100 ml.

Admittedly, very few of us will possess a serum cholesterol this low. The average serum cholesterol of adult American men and women is somewhere between 225 and 250 mg./100 ml. Most epidemiologists (medical investigators who attempt to determine the frequencies and distributions of various diseases in the human community) believe that a serum cholesterol level that is 275 mg./100 ml. or greater is an abnormally high one. We believe that these researchers came to such a conclusion chiefly because the average cholesterol level of any large American community of persons is usually below this figure. Nature, however, really doesn't feel one bit constrained by man-made rulings. We still suspect that it regards any cholesterol value above 175 mg./100 ml. as abnormally high. What we are saying, really, is that because of our dietary and behavioral habits, the majority of American men and women possess a serum cholesterol value that is too high.

It is indeed precisely this hypercholesterolemic value (above 175 mg./100 ml.) which we in the laboratory strive to obtain in some of our animals in order that they may begin to incur arterial lesions. A rabbit, for example, does not easily develop arterial atherosclerotic plaques if its serum cholesterol level never rises above 150 to 175 mg./100 ml. We might add that neither does man easily begin to develop atherosclerotic plaques in his coronary arteries if his serum cholesterol *always* remains below 175 mg./100 ml.

Incidentally, as far as we know there are no abnormally low serum cholesterol values. In extreme malnutrition and sometimes in severe liver disease, the serum cholesterol level may drop well below 150 mg./100 ml., but the body never suffers any bad effects from such declines per se.

What may elevate your serum cholesterol? First, let us look at the food you eat. There is more or less agreement among scientists that if your total daily intake of food contains more than one-twentieth of a teaspoonful (approximately 200 mg.) of pure cholesterol, your basal serum cholesterol level may *possibly* rise. If your daily food intake contains more than one-eighth teaspoonful (approximately 500 mg.) of cholesterol, your serum cholesterol level will *probably* rise. And if you take in one-quarter teaspoonful of cholesterol in your food each day, your serum cholesterol level is almost certain to increase. How much depends upon a lot of factors, including the quantity and quality of fat you ingest and also possibly upon the amount of starch and sugars you eat. But excess dietary cholesterol (that is, 200 mg. or more per day) alone can elevate your serum cholesterol 10 to 20 percent.

If you ingest most of your fat in the form of beef, pork, or chicken fats (but not fish oils), your serum cholesterol might rise 5 to 10 percent (rarely more) above your basal level. If you happen to be a particular type of person, the ingestion of simple sugars (and probably starches, too) may also elevate your serum cholesterol 5 to 10 percent. (Further on, we will describe the sort of person who may exhibit cholesterol sensitivity to the ingestion of sugars and starches.)

Besides the ingestion of dietary cholesterol, animal fat and sometimes sugar/starches, one of the most potent of all cholesterol-elevating agents is a hereditary disorder in which there is a defect in the normal handling of cholesterol. We will describe this disorder later, when we discuss the causes of coronary artery disease. In addition, certain acute and subacute disorders of the liver (viral and alcoholic hepatitis) and the kidney may also elevate the serum cholesterol level. But perhaps the most common and certainly the most medically neglected cause of an abnormally high serum cholesterol in man is the particular complex of emotional stresses we have designated as Type A Behavior Pattern. We shall describe this pattern at length later; suffice it to observe here that it is probably the major process at work in the majority of Americans whose serum cholesterol is too high (above the epidemiologically determined limit of 275 mg./100 ml.). If your own serum cholesterol is too high, chances are good that you also have this behavior pattern and that it is playing a major role in sustaining your hypercholesterolemia. Unfortunately, this state of affairs is commonly unrecognized.

What processes will cause man's serum cholesterol level to fall? Certainly, if a person's serum cholesterol level is elevated because his diet is rich in cholesterol, animal fat, or—in particular cases—sugar/starch, a drastic reduction in the intake of cholesterol, a substitution of vegetable fats (that is, polyunsaturated fats) for animal fats (that is, saturated fats), and a reduction in the sugar/starch intake should reverse the hypercholesterolemic process. Likewise, if a person's cholesterol level has been elevated because of his Type A Behavior Pattern, modification of this pattern will also bring it down again.

Peculiarly, an anxiety state of severe degree—that is, one in which the subject is profoundly depressed and seeks the help of others rather than relying upon his own possible powers for coping with his situation —is extraordinarily likely to reduce the serum cholesterol to unusually low levels. This phenomenon has not been widely recognized.

Hyperthyroidism, a disorder in which too much thyroid hormone is being produced and circulated, almost always reduces the serum cholesterol level of its sufferers.

We have drugs, too, which many times are remarkably successful in lowering a previously elevated serum cholesterol level. The most commonly used ones at this writing are clofibrate (marketed as Atromid-S in the United States), dextrothyroxin (marketed as cholestyramine or Questran in the United States), which by combining with bile in the intestine interferes with the absorption of cholesterol. Relatively recently, a form of surgical therapy has been introduced for the lowering of a very high serum cholesterol in persons who have not responded to other measures for lowering serum cholesterol, but this is not a procedure without its own great dangers, and is indicated only in cases of unusual severity.

WHY IS CHOLESTEROL SUSPECTED OF COMPLICITY IN CORONARY ARTERY DISEASE?

There are very few heart investigators working in laboratories who are not convinced that cholesterol plays a major role in the causation of coronary artery disease. On the other hand, there are more than a few investigators (particularly in the United Kingdom) who doubt the essential importance of cholesterol in those later processes which succeed in converting coronary *artery* disease into coronary *heart* attacks. In short, most of us agree that cholesterol strikes the first "blow" in coronary artery disease, but we differ considerably about how important its subsequent "blows" are in the total evolution of the disorder.

We experimentalists who work in the laboratory are positive that cholesterol plays an important part in initiating coronary *artery* disease in man for a number of reasons. First, without adding cholesterol to the diets of our laboratory animals, we just can't induce arterial lesions in them that bear any resemblance whatsoever to those found in man. Even if we scratch, prick, tear, burn, or freeze arterial segments; or if we inject acids, alkalis, or any other noxious chemicals into arterial walls of animals not receiving cholesterol in their food, we cannot simulate the grease-laden, multicelled plaque we observe in the early diseased human coronary artery. All we produce in the end, in these injured arteries of our animals, is a well-defined, well-healed scar. But if we inflict any of these same injuries on the arteries of almost any animal (rabbit, pig, rat, baboon, monkey, guinea pig, cow, chicken, duck, turkey, and pigeon, among others) and then add a bit of cholesterol to its diet, we no longer get a well-healed, self-limiting scar, but a proliferating, grease-filled plaque, a virtual duplicate of a human arterial plaque.

Actually, of course, it is not at all necessary to injure the artery of an animal prior to feeding it cholesterol in order to induce human-like plaques. Just the inclusion of cholesterol in its diet will do the job within a few months. Apparently, sufficient spontaneous injuries take place in the coronary arteries of the experimental animal (just as we assume take place in human coronary arteries) to prepare the ground for the deposit of excess cholesterol from the blood of these animals. The excess cholesterol not only prevents the healing process that would have led to a small, innocuous scar, but as we already have stressed, it *stimulates* a wild new growth of arterial cells. These new cells in turn attract more cholesterol, thereby producing, for all practical purposes, a tumor. In other words, pure cholesterol lying in wounded tissue transforms the otherwise scar repair process into a form of "cancer." This strange property of cholesterol is probably its most noxious characteristic.

But please note that it is necessary to *feed* cholesterol to these laboratory animals to create arterial plaques. We have the means to elevate the serum cholesterol level of animals tremendously by causing them to manufacture too much of their own cholesterol; yet under such circumstances they develop few or no arterial lesions. We believe that the explanation for this is that in the latter circumstances the excess cholesterol in the animals' blood is mostly in soluble lipoprotein forms. It therefore leaves the injured arterial areas almost as easily as it entered them. This is not the case with the cholesterol in the blood put there as part of a high-cholesterol diet. It enters the injured areas and stays there, initiating the cancerlike process. *If animal studies on coronary artery disease have told us any-*

thing it is this: The extent of an arterial atherosclerotic lesion is probably far more dependent upon how *cholesterol travels in blood than upon* how much.

And there happens to be other evidence available that strengthens our convictions about the atherogenic potential of *dietary* cholesterol. Certainly the detection of large amounts of cholesterol in any coronary artery plaque, whether this plaque is examined at its earliest appearance in the first few years or studied in its final, degenerative state in the adult or senescent years of a person's life, suggests the possibility, at least, that this substance may have borne some responsibility.

Then, too, from direct clinical studies, all physicians know that, in general, the higher the blood cholesterol of a person becomes, the more likely that person is to succumb to some type of coronary heart attack. Indeed, in those unfortunate children who suffer from a hereditary form of hypercholesterolemia and whose serum cholesterol may reach levels of even 800 to 1,000 mg./100 ml., heart attacks are the rule rather than the exception before the age of twenty-one years.

But once again a note of caution. There can be little question that in those subjects possessing serum cholesterol values of such huge magnitude, the excess cholesterol must be producing the coronary lesions or plaques that are inevitably observed. But there *is* some question whether we can similarly blame cholesterol alone for producing the coronary lesions that may be present in an adult whose serum cholesterol is normal or only moderately elevated (250 to 275 mg./100 ml.). Indeed, we may be quite wrong in so doing, because now we know that moderate elevations of the serum cholesterol frequently occur when certain other noxious agents are at play in the human body. The question is the old familiar one: how do we distinguish a symptom or sign from a cause?

Do we have any other data that makes us suspect that cholesterol bears the major responsibility in causing coronary artery disease? Some epidemiologists would say yes. They would point out that their studies have demonstrated (conclusively, at least to them) that coronary heart attacks are rife in populations and groups whose diet is rich in cholesterol and relatively rare in populations and groups whose diet is poor in cholesterol. While this would not be direct proof that dietary cholesterol is the cause of the coronary heart attacks, nevertheless it would serve as very good indirect evidence—if it weren't for one rather nettlesome detail: these same epidemiologists in publishing their data have completely overlooked the studies of some of their fellow epidemiologists. And for good reason, too, because these other studies described groups who had few or no coronary heart attacks despite their *heavy* intake of dietary cholesterol. These sorts of "omissions," of course, strike the rest of us as directly misleading. They also make it clear that epidemiological studies do not appear to be the finest way to find out and correct the causes of contemporary heart attacks in Western society.

Chapter 6

THE KEY CAUSE—
TYPE A BEHAVIOR
PATTERN

We believe that the major cause of coronary artery and heart disease is a complex of emotional reactions, which we have designated Type A Behavior Pattern. Such being our conviction, and also because less than a handful of medical investigators have concerned themselves with the possible relationship of your brain to your heart and its nourishing arteries, we mean to deal with the subject at thorough and, we trust, convincing length.

When, sometime between 1955 and 1958, we first began to approach the possibility that the brain and its functions might have some relevance to coronary artery and heart disease, we each had been seeing scores of coronary patients in our private consultation rooms for well over a decade. We greeted them, asked them how they felt, took their blood pressure, listened to their hearts, and then had a nurse take their electrocardiograms and obtain a blood sample for cholesterol analysis. Depending upon the results of these examinations, we might or might not have altered the dosage of their various drugs. Of course, each patient was routinely exhorted (1) to continue to eat his low animal fat/high unsaturated fat/low cholesterol diet, (2) to continue his exercise program, and (3) to avoid excess cigarette smoking. They in turn always asked what their blood pressure reading was, how high their last serum cholesterol measurement had been and whether their present electrocardiogram showed any "improvement." Having received such information (sometimes good, sometimes bad), they said good-bye, stopped at the secretary's desk to make their next appointment, and then departed.

Sometimes, however, we would ponder over the coronary status of some of these patients and wonder whether we really were helping them in any meaningful way. If we concluded—as we often did—that our therapeutic measures were actually far more impressive than helpful to a patient, we immediately rationalized that, after all, we had done the best that we could and no other physician could have done much more.

But we could have done far more in those earlier years. We could have surveyed each patient *in his entirety, as an individual.* We could have studied his face, his gestures, listened intently to the quality of his voice and to the content of his informal speech. We could have asked questions about his aims, dreams, principles, fears, and anxieties. Why didn't we do these things? you might ask. Possibly because we thought we were too busy to do so, or perhaps because we couldn't see how his answers to such questions could have any relevance to his coronary problem. You see, we hadn't realized then that each of our coronary patients was actually sending us signals, trying to tell us—albeit unconsciously—of the rather odd behavior pattern he possessed.

Indeed, it is quite probable that if one of our coronary patients had said to either of us in 1952, "Doctor, I rather suspect that the true cause of my coronary heart disease is the emotional stress that has been harassing me for many years," either of us would have nodded affirmatively, and quite politely waited until he had finished talking. Then we might have told him that his serum cholesterol level "had improved somewhat," but his reference to emotional stress would probably not have elicited any comment. Like all our peers, we were not intellectually prepared twenty years ago to accept emotional stress as a relevant component of coronary heart disease. In our defense (admittedly a miserably weak one), may we refer to the fact that most of our scientific endeavors at that time were focused on cholesterol and also that we were not psychiatrically oriented physicians?

But now, in retrospect, we are a bit abashed when we recall one particular incident that took place about then. We had called in an upholsterer to fix the seats of the chairs in our reception room. After inspecting our chairs, he asked what sort of a practice we had. We said we were cardiologists and asked why he had wanted to know. "Well," he replied, "I was just wondering, because it's so peculiar that only the front edge of your chair seats are worn out." Had we been sufficiently alert, we might have thought about that chance remark and what it indicated about the behavior pattern of our coronary patients.

We first began to consider the personality of these patients seriously when we had to search the medical literature prior to writing a review article on the role of dietary cholesterol in coronary heart disease. Too many finely executed studies suggested that neither the cholesterol nor the fat content of various diets could always explain the coronary heart disease developing in persons ingesting such diets. Other factors just had to be playing a part!

This impression grew to a certainty after we investigated the dietary habits of both a representative group of volunteers from the San Francisco Junior League and their husbands. We had expected (because American white women develop coronary heart disease much less frequently than their husbands) that our study would show that these women ate much less cholesterol and animal fat than their husbands. But the dietary intakes were exactly the same. What, then, was protecting the women? Their female sex hormones, that's what, most of our medical colleagues had been clamoring for a number of years. Yet if our colleagues had investigated and mulled over the total enigma in their minds, they would not have jumped to such a silly conclusion. They would have recalled that not only is the female laboratory animal as susceptible to experimentally induced coronary disease as her male counterpart, but also—and far more relevantly —white women of various countries other than the United States are as prone to coronary heart disease as their husbands. Also, in several separate studies done in different areas of the United States, the *black* woman was found to be slightly *more* susceptible than her black husband to coronary heart disease. If, then, the American white female owed her relative immunity to coronary heart disease to her female sex hormones, these hormones must be chemically and biologically different from those of most other women on our planet. We considered (and still consider) such a thesis to be ridiculous.

If we were in a mental stew following this dietary study, the then-president of the San Francisco Junior League wasn't confused at all. "I told you right from the first," she said, "that you would find that we are eating exactly as our husbands do. If you really want to know what is giving our husbands heart attacks, I'll tell you."

"And what is that?" we asked, possibly a bit patronizingly (as doctors can't help behaving at times when confronted with laymen who are certain that they know the immediate answers to age-old medical puzzles).

"It's stress, the stress they receive in their work, that's what's doing it," she quickly responded.

And that's when our concept of Type A Behavior Pattern and its probable relationship to coronary heart disease was born.

Obviously we had a bit of work cut out for ourselves. We first decided to send out a questionnaire to one hundred fifty businessmen immersed in the industrial and commercial milieu of San Francisco, asking them to check what particular phenomenon or complex of habits (we listed approximately ten for them to choose from) they believed had preceded a "heart attack" in a friend of theirs. We were only mildly surprised to find that more than 70 percent of these men believed that indulgence in "excessive competitive drive and meeting deadlines" was the outstanding characteristic exhibited by their coronary-stricken friends. Less than 5 percent of these responding businessmen thought that their friend's heart attack had been precipitated by a possible excessive ingestion of fatty foods, by smoking too many cigarettes, or by failure to exercise. Because we knew quite well that no medical editor would publish just these data, we similarly surveyed one hundred internists who treated coronary patients. The majority of them also thought that the phenomenon most frequently found to have preceded the heart attack in the patients they had treated was the indulgence of these patients in "excessive competitive drive and meeting deadlines."

Given these answers, we couldn't help feeling a little bewildered. Although the patient-to-be and his physician-to-be were both agreed about the probable cause of a "heart attack," this cause was not being even remotely considered by the medical pundits of that time. We could explain away the responses of the businessmen as being due to their medical naïveté, but we could not similarly account for the unorthodox answers of our medical respondents. At that time it was difficult to open any medical journal without finding yet another study indicating that the cause of a "heart attack" was almost without question due to dietary indiscretion, too much cigarette smoking, or too little physical exercise.

At this distance, we are rather proud to see that the majority of doctors charged with the responsibility of treating heart patients even then preferred to make up their own minds about the probable causes of coronary heart disease, regardless of what the "experts" were publishing. As for us, we knew quite well that there now could be no turning back. We were committed to find out, once and for all, whether man's personality and behavior did play a part in coronary artery and heart disease.

One of our earliest difficulties was to determine precisely which emotional traits had relevance. This determination has not been easy, and now, well over a decade since we first began this analysis, we are still adding features to the total complex of characteristics we have designated Type A Behavior Pattern. But from the beginning we did know that whatever else this pattern might encompass *in its entirety*, whenever any person felt within himself a chronic sense of time urgency and also exhibited *excessive* competitive drive, he invariably possessed the Type A Behavior Pattern. Knowing this, we were capable of performing various biochemical and epidemiological studies while we were still ferreting out the possible other traits making up the total pattern.

We discovered that time urgency and competitive

overdrive were components of the behavior pattern by reconsidering our own private coronary patients. Almost invariably, if these patients were under sixty-five years of age, they exhibited an habitual sense of time urgency and *excessive* competitive drive. Often, perhaps because of their excessive competitive drive, these same individuals showed an easily aroused hostility, which was likely to flare up under very diverse conditions. Involuntarily, our patients had been trying to tell us about these traits for a long, long time, but we had been too busy or too preoccupied with other matters to receive, much less comprehend, these "signals."

At the outset, we reasoned that if Type A Behavior Pattern did predispose its sufferers to coronary artery and heart disease, then subjects still ostensibly free of this disease but possessing Type A Behavior Pattern might nevertheless be expected to show some of the biochemical abnormalities common to most, but certainly not all, patients sick with coronary disease. We accordingly either chose or had chosen for us seemingly healthy men who were well known to have both a very intense sense of time urgency and a very strongly developed competitive drive or free-floating hostility. We have now been studying selected groups of these men for over twelve years. What have been the results of these studies?

First, there is no question about the fact that the serum cholesterol level may vary directly with the intensity of the Type A Behavior Pattern. For example, we followed the serum cholesterol level of a group of accountants from January to June. When the April 15 tax deadline approached, and the sense of time urgency of these accountants rose sharply, so did the level of their serum cholesterol. Conversely, in May and early June, when their sense of time urgency almost disappeared, their serum cholesterol fell. This change in serum cholesterol, then, could only have been due to their emotional stress—because neither their food, smoking, or exercise habits had changed during the period of our surveillance.

Here then was the first completely documented and *controlled* demonstration that the brain and its functions could alter the blood or serum cholesterol level. We vividly remember the occasion when we announced the results of this particular study at the annual national convention of the American Heart Association. Following our exposition, there was an absolute silence—no questions, no comments, no criticisms, just silence! Have these results been confirmed by others? Yes, repeatedly. Are we able to experimentally influence the brain of animals as well, so that their serum cholesterol will rise? Yes, we finally succeeded in doing this, too.

Having discovered that Type A Behavior Pattern can influence the serum cholesterol level, we then investigated its possible effects upon various other blood substances. Summarizing these results, we found that subjects *severely* afflicted with this type of behavior pattern exhibited every blood fat and hormone abnormality that the majority of coronary patients also showed. In other words, the same blood abnormalities that so many of our colleagues believe precede and possibly bring on coronary heart disease were already present in our Type A subjects. To us, the logic is irresistible: the behavior pattern itself gives rise to the abnormalities.

Of course, some physicians have asked us how we can be sure that the blood abnormalities do not precede and bring on the behavior pattern. When we are asked this question, we respond: "Dr. Jones, do you really believe that a high serum cholesterol or fat level might give a man a chronic sense of time urgency? And do you really believe that mild diabetes can make a man excessively competitive? If you do, then you must believe that mere mass may move spirit, and that really would be a phenomenon infinitely more interesting than coronary heart disease itself."

While these biochemical studies were being done, we also performed some epidemiological studies of our own. The first one was a study in which we had chosen and collected for us approximately eighty men from the general business and professional community of San Francisco who were believed by persons who knew them well to possess the Type A Behavior Pattern. For comparative or control purposes, we also had chosen for us approximately eighty men who possessed the converse behavior pattern, which we named Type B—men who felt no sense of time urgency, exhibited no excessive competitive drive or free-floating hostility. It wasn't very easy to find eighty men in San Francisco who were not under any time pressure and who did not experience any competitive strife or hostility in their workaday world. But fortunately, from the municipal clerks' and the embalmers' unions, we finally obtained them. The results again showed that the eighty Type A men had a higher serum cholesterol than the eighty Type B men.

What, however, was surprising to us then (it would not be to us now) was that 28 percent of these seemingly well Type A men (age thirty-five to sixty years) *already* had coronary heart disease. Indeed, they had *seven times* as much coronary heart disease as the Type B men, but their diets and exercise habits were almost identical.

We were not surprised when we observed that the average serum cholesterol level of our Type B men was approximately 210 mg./100 ml., despite the fact that their dietary intake was typically American in being heavy in cholesterol and animal fats. Why weren't we surprised? Because our earlier studies with our volunteer accountants had already shown us that a man's serum cholesterol may be determined just as much by what he feels as by what he feeds himself. That is why our Type B man, eating fully as high on the hog as his Type A counterpart, nevertheless exhibits a serum cholesterol level not a bit higher than some "primitive" races whose diet is quite low in cholesterol and animal fat.

Having finished these studies on groups of men exhibiting Types A and B behavior patterns, we then studied Type A and B groups of American white women. Again we found that the Type A women exhibited a much higher serum cholesterol level than the Type B women (interestingly enough, the average blood cholesterol level of our Type A women was even higher than that of our Type A men). The prevalence of coronary heart disease was also far more frequent in the Type A women than in the Type B women. Our Type A women, in fact, suffered as much coronary heart disease as their male counterparts.

If our own data were correct, "then why," you might ask, "do most American white women nevertheless appear to possess so much protection against coronary heart disease?" Because there are *comparatively* few Type A American white females as completely immersed as males in the contemporary economic and professional milieu that nourishes the development of Type A Behavior Pattern. Most American women, at least in the immediate past, have remained in their homes, and although they have had many chores to do, relatively few were constrained to work under conditions whose essence consisted of deadlines and competition and hostility. The mother of growing children, of course, does suffer many anxieties, and she at times does have too many tasks to perform, but the effects are clearly less pernicious.

Of course, many women now are entering the business community and are competing, and are also finding themselves short in time reserves. Will they begin to suffer a greater incidence of coronary heart disease? Recent statistics suggest that this is already happening. In this connection it might be of interest to note that ever since General MacArthur "liberated" the Japanese female from her previous domestic isolation, her incidence of coronary heart disease has quadrupled. This startling increase—which is now receiving close attention by Japanese epidemiologists—in just twenty-six years certainly cannot be explained by any significant change in dietary, smoking, or exercise habits. Finally, it must be remembered that the American white woman, although she does have less coronary heart disease than the American male, nevertheless already suffers from this disease more frequently than the males of many non-Western countries.

These earlier studies of ours did not, however, convince too many of our colleagues a decade ago. Some did consider our data rather "interesting," perhaps "provocative," but our conclusions at best were deemed "controversial" (and on the whole, in medical circles, the word "controversial" is distinctly pejorative). It was suggested to us that if we really were correct in our beliefs, then we should be able to study a group of men without a single discernible trace of coronary heart disease and then "predict" which men would succumb to coronary heart disease in the future.

We accepted this challenge, and in 1960-1961 we invited healthy men to join such a study. Thanks to the encouragement given us by the Bank of America, Standard Oil of California, Kaiser Industries, the Bechtel Corporation, Safeway Stores, United Air Lines, and the Lockheed Aircraft Corporation, we enlisted over thirty-five hundred men. They were classified according to their behavior pattern, and examined in numerous other ways at that time.

Now over ten years have passed, and well over two hundred fifty of these initially healthy men have suffered coronary heart disease. Did the dietary data we obtained at the beginning help us to predict who was most apt to succumb later to coronary heart disease? Not at all! Did the amount of physical exercise they took help us to discern those who later fell prey to heart disease? Not at all!

The most pronounced danger signal back in 1960-1961 was, above all, the presence of Type A Behavior Pattern. If a subject exhibited this pattern in 1960 (and was over thirty-five and under sixty years of age), he was almost three times more likely than a Type B man to get coronary heart disease in the subsequent decade. Indeed, not one man (with a normal blood pressure and without diabetes) exhibiting Type B behavior, a truly normal serum cholesterol (that is, one below 225 mg./100 ml.) and fat level (that is, one below 125 mg./100 ml.) has yet succumbed to this disease. Such individuals, no matter how much cholesterol and fat their diet contained, no matter how many cigarettes they smoked (most of these men, however, smoked few cigarettes), no matter what they weighed, no matter if one or both their parents had suffered coronary heart disease and no matter whether they were under or over weight, still appeared to be immune to the early advent of coronary heart disease in their lives. To these men, obviously most of the risk factors tabulated by the various committees of the American Heart Association did not appear to pertain.

Of course, those men who were found in 1960-1961 to be suffering from or exhibiting signs of one or more of the *certain* causes of coronary artery disease, to be described in Chapter 10 (high blood pressure, diabetes, and hereditary hypercholesterolemia), or who were smoking in excess of fifteen cigarettes a day, also proved more susceptible to the later advent of heart disease than persons without these diseases or habits. But their susceptibility was no greater, and usually less, than those men who exhibited Type A Behavior Pattern alone. Of course, many of the Type A men also smoked excessively (most Type B men do not), and some of them did suffer from high blood pressure (most Type B men do not).

These "predictive" results, of course, made us terribly suspicious that the Type A Behavior Pattern not only preceded the emergence of coronary heart disease, but might be in great part responsible for such emergence. But long ago the great bacteriologist Robert Koch insisted that the tubercle bacillus could not be accepted as the cause of tuberculosis simply because this particular bacterium was always found in the sputum or other excretions of the tuberculous person. It was also necessary to demonstrate that tuberculosis always occurred in an experimental animal when such an animal was injected with the tubercle bacillus. This rigid insistence of Koch upon the laboratory reproduction of an illness or condition by the suspected agent before the latter could be called the agent causing the disorder under study was the kernel of his famous postulates, postulates that by and large have kept medicine more than once from committing the grievous error of indicating a factor, agent, or condition as a cause, when in truth it was but an associated or accompanying phenomenon.

Before Koch, for example, swamps or even the night air were considered as the probable causes of malaria. Even today, in many parts of Italy, educated Italians who should know better still resist the idea of sleeping in a room with an open window. The pertinence to heart disease is this: Of all the suspected and propagandized so-called risk factors, only one has been demonstrated unequivocally to induce coronary artery disease in the experimental animal—the elevation of the serum cholesterol of the experimental animal by the feeding of sufficient cholesterol. In other words, all other so-called risk factors of coronary artery disease could simply be those which accompany or are even produced by the true cause or causes, which therefore remain hidden.

Thus, even though we detected the presence of Type A Behavior Pattern both in those who already had coronary heart disease and in those who subsequently came down with the disorder, and also detected in subjects with this behavior pattern all the biochemical abnormalities known to precede the onset of coronary heart disease, we still could not indict the behavior pattern as an indubitable cause of coronary artery or heart disease. Were Dr. Koch alive and were he to look at our results, he would still have insisted that we demonstrate in the laboratory animal that an experimentally induced emotional change could either produce coronary artery or heart disease or give rise to one more of the biochemical abnormalities that in turn might be expected to bring on the coronary disorder.

We succeeded several years ago in doing just this. Following deliberate damage to a rat's hypothalamus, the emotional center of the brain, the affected animal almost instantaneously exhibited the rat equivalent of the human Type A Behavior Pattern. No longer did this brain-altered rat scamper timidly and gently with his fellow cage mates. Rather, he stared fixedly at us without fear, and were we to open the cage ever so slightly, he would lunge to attack us almost immediately. Nor would he tolerate a single cage mate without jumping upon its back, ready to sink his teeth into the flesh of the other animal. If the cage mate were a shy, gentle control rat (exactly similar to the Type A rat prior to his brain surgery), the Type A rat eventually sensed absence of competition, dismounted him, and ignored him. But if the second rat were also another Type A rat, a vicious, no-holds-barred battle ensued, which if not interrupted would end only with the death of either or both of them.

Interesting as this change in behavior was to us, it really was the marked elevation in the serum cholesterol of such Type A rats that truly excited us. Because now even Dr. Koch, had he mentioned these studies, would have had to admit that we had demonstrated in a very clear fashion that an alteration in the function of an animal's brain leading to a changed emotional state could and did induce a very distinct rise in the animal's serum cholesterol—and an increased serum cholesterol level just happens to be the one unequivocal laboratory method of inducing chronic coronary artery disease.

It has been a long and at times rather arduous scientific trek. We cannot truthfully assert that our course over these past fifteen years has been as direct as a crow is reputed to fly, but we believe we at least are beginning to home in on the true target responsible for the epidemic-like increase in coronary artery and heart disease during our own lifetime. We base this optimism on four findings: (1) the ubiquity of Type A Behavior Pattern in those already ill with coronary heart disease, (2) the extreme vulnerability of Type A subjects to this disease, (3) the identification of the cluster of coronary biochemical abnormalities in Type A subjects, and perhaps most important of all, (4) our success in experimentally inducing a facsimile of Type A Behavior Pattern, followed by emergence of the most dreaded of all coronary biochemical derangements. It is now appropriate that we explain to you precisely what it is that we have termed Type A Behavior Pattern, and its probable causes.

WHAT IS TYPE A BEHAVIOR PATTERN?

Type A Behavior Pattern is an action-emotion complex that can be observed in any person who is *aggressively* involved in a *chronic, incessant* struggle to achieve more and more in less and less time, and if required to do so, against the opposing efforts of other things or other persons. It is not psychosis or a complex of worries or fears or phobias or obsessions, but a socially acceptable—indeed often praised—form of conflict. Persons possessing this pattern also are quite prone to exhibit a free-floating but extraordinarily well-rationalized hostility. As might be expected, there are degrees in the intensity of this behavior pattern. Moreover, because the pattern represents the reaction that takes place when particular personality traits of an afflicted individual are challenged or aroused by a specific environmental agent, the results of this reaction (that is, the behavior pattern itself) may not be felt or exhibited by him if he happens to be in or confronted by an environment that presents no challenge. For example, a usually hard-driving, competitive, aggressive editor of an urban newspaper, if hospitalized with a trivial illness, may not exhibit a single sign of Type A Behavior Pattern. In short, for Type A Behavior Pattern to explode into being, the *environmental challenge must always serve as the fuse for this explosion.*

The person with Type B Behavior Pattern is the exact opposite of the Type A subject. He, unlike the Type A person, is rarely harried by desires to obtain a wildly increasing number of things or participate in an endlessly growing series of events in an ever decreasing amount of time. His intelligence may be as good as or even better than that of the Type A subject. *Similarly, his ambition may be as great or even greater than that of his Type A counterpart.* He may also have a considerable amount of "drive," but its character is such that it seems to steady him, give confidence and security to him, rather than to goad, irritate, and infuriate, as with the Type A man.

In our experience, based on extensive practices in typing and then observing many hundreds of individuals, the general run of urban Americans tend to fall into one or the other of these two groups. The Type A's, we have found, predominate; they usually represent somewhat over half of all those in the open samples we have tested. These are somewhat fewer true Type B individuals, perhaps 40 percent of the whole. People in whom Type A and Type B characteristics are mixed account for about 10 percent. If our testing procedures can be further refined—and we are, of course, constantly trying to do this—we believe that the number in this middle group can be reduced. In other words, most Americans are in fact either Type A or Type B, though in varying degrees.

Again we should like to reiterate that, with exceedingly rare exception, the socioeconomic position of a man or woman does not determine whether he or she is a Type A or Type B subject. The presidents of many banks and corporations (perhaps even the majority) may be Type B individuals. Conversely, many janitors, shoe salesmen, truck drivers, architects, and even florists may be Type A subjects. We have not found any clear correlation between occupational position held and the incidence of Type A Behavior Pattern. Why is this so? Because (1) a sense of job or position responsibility is not synonymous with the Type A sense of time urgency; (2) excessive drive or competitive enthusiasm may only too frequently be expended upon economic trivia rather than affairs of importance; and (3) promotion and elevation, particularly in corporate and professional organizations, usually go to those who are wise rather than to those who are merely hasty, to those who are tactful rather than to those who are hostile, and to those who are creative rather than to those who are merely agile in competitive strife. (And if you who are reading this happen to be a wife of a Type A executive, attorney, physician, or florist, this last should not be forgotten, even if your husband insists that it isn't true.)

Before we begin to draw a detailed portrait of the Type A man, we should like to forestall one rather important source of misunderstanding. We are not psychologists. What follows is an honest description of symptoms and signs as *we have observed them*. We are convinced that they form, in themselves, a significant behavior pattern, and we *know*, by virtue of our own professional expertise, that this group of traits is closely linked to the pathology of coronary artery and heart disease. It is possible that our *psychological* analysis may be criticized as superficial, perhaps rightly so. But this by no means invalidates its *medical* significance. The Type A man is prone to heart disease; these characteristic behavioral habits identify the Type A man.

SENSE OF TIME URGENCY, OR THE MODERN DISEASE, "HURRY SICKNESS"

Overwhelmingly, the most significant trait of the Type A man is his habitual sense of time urgency or "hurry sickness." Why does the Type A man so often feel that he doesn't have enough time to do all the things that he either believes should be done or that he wishes to do, whereas the Type B man feels that he has quite enough time to do all that he believes ought to be done? The answer is quite a simple one. The Type A man incessantly strives to accomplish too much or to participate in too many events in the amount of time he allots for these purposes. Even if by some miracle time could be stretched adequately just once for his activities, the Type A man still would not be satisfied. He would then seek to stretch time a second or third or fourth time.

The fundamental sickness of the Type A subject consists of his peculiar failure to perceive, or perhaps worse, to accept the simple fact that a man's time can be exhausted by his activities. As a consequence, he never ceases trying to "stuff" more and more events in his constantly shrinking reserves of time. It is the Type A man's ceaseless striving, his everlasting *struggle* with time, that we believe so very frequently leads to his early demise from coronary heart disease.

In an attempt to save time the Type A man often creates deadlines for himself. He subconsciously believes that if he fixes a date for the execution of a particular task that is actually too soon, somehow or other he will succeed in triumphing over his inveterate enemy, time. Since he very often has created not one but as many as a dozen such deadlines, he is subjecting himself to a more or less continuous time pressure. This voluntary tyranny frequently forms the very essence of Type A Behavior Pattern. To fill a life with deadlines to the exclusion of life's lovelinesses is a peculiarly dreadful form of self-punishment.

If this ever-increasing harassment by a sense of time urgency is not checked, eventually the Type A subject begins to indulge in a phenomenon that can and only too often does subvert his creative and judgmental attributes. This phenomenon is stereotyped thinking and action. More and more, again to save time, the Type A subject tends to think and do things in exactly the same way. Consciously or not, the Type A man apparently feels that if he can bring the previously "coded" thought and action processes again to bear on a new task, he can accomplish it *faster*. He more and more substitutes "faster" for "better" or "different" in his way of thinking and doing. In other words, he indulges in stereotyped responses. He substitutes repetitive urgency for creative energy.

But his challenges may demand nonstereotyped responses. It is particularly this tendency that so often makes the Type A person vulnerable to what he in the past had contemptuously regarded as the snail-like, noncompetitive pace of the Type B subject. The *intelligent* Type B man is capable, at least at times, of freeing himself from the steel meshes of stereotypal thought and behavior. He *does* find the time to ponder leisurely, to weigh alternatives, to experiment, to indulge in the sort of dialectical reverie from which two, three, or even four seemingly totally disparate events, facts, or processes can be joined to produce strikingly new and brilliant offshoots.

Far more often than not, then, the Type A man, because he tries so desperately to accomplish more and more in less and less time, finally impairs his creative power and only too often the acuity of his judgment. Thus bereft, he desperately seeks to substitute speed of execution. If sometimes he still seems to display brilliance, it usually is due to those original and creative concepts which he may have formulated in his younger years—before he became *totally* enslaved to his Type A Behavior Pattern. But this earlier collected cache of concepts can serve him well only as long as the milieu and its demands remain relatively unchanged.

One of the real tragedies of Type A Behavior Pattern is its tendency to erode the adaptability of its sufferer to the totally new challenges of contemporary society. It has been distressing for us to observe the severely afflicted Type A subject when he is confronted with one of these utterly new challenges. Desperate, he tries to run faster in his old ways to overcome a problem whose solution cannot be achieved by stereotyped and hasty thinking, but only by creative, time-free contemplation and deliberation. The ranks of corporate middle management contain more than just a few thousand such condemned hangers-on. Type A Behavior Pattern may be felling their hearts. It is almost certainly making tatters of their spiritual fabric.

THE QUEST FOR NUMBERS

Man's fascination with the quantitative accumulation of material objects is a trait, like speech or awareness of future time, which is not shared by any other species. Admittedly, squirrels accumulate nuts and bees honey, but they do so for strictly utilitarian reasons—to forestall winter's famine. They do not do so simply for the "human" joy of adding to that of which they already have enough.

This almost innate delight in acquisition probably begins quite early in our childhood. All of us have witnessed, for example, the delight a small boy takes in his first electric train set, even though it only consists of a locomotive and several freight cars. Later, as he experiences more birthdays and Christmases and receives more toy locomotives, freight cars, and tracks, he begins to *count* (rather than enjoy) the number of units he has. A similar process takes place when he begins to collect marbles, postage stamps, or anything else.

Most of us mature sufficiently to realize that it is better to love, marry, and mate with one rather than with a constantly increasing number of attractive girls.

We tend to lay aside our childhood collections of trains, marbles, dolls, stamps, bottle tops, and so on as we buckle down to single, rather than to multiple, vocations. As parents, few of us strive to beget as many children as we can. We content ourselves with rearing several children well. Even in our vocations, at least half of us, while reasonably anxious to accumulate some of the goods of this world, still manage to preoccupy ourselves with matters that have nothing whatsoever to do with numbers. However, the severely afflicted Type A subject rarely matures in this regard.

Because of his obsession with numbers and because so many of the world's activities are expressed in currency units (that is, dollars, pounds, francs, and marks), the Type A subject more often than not appears to be absorbed in money. Before we thoroughly understood our own Type A patients and friends, we were inclined to believe that they were inordinately fond of making money for its own sake. This, however, is not true. The Type A businessman is not intrigued with money as such, nor is he miserly, nor is he necessarily eager to buy a better and bigger house or automobile than his friends (even if he frequently ends up doing just exactly that). Money for him merely represents the tokens or chips of the "numbers game" to which he has dedicated himself. "Last year my company grossed a profit before taxes of five million dollars," the Type A businessman proudly states. "Last year I performed one hundred fifty appendectomies," the Type A surgeon just as proudly announces. "Last year my laboratory published eighteen articles," the Type A scientist even more proudly announces. You will note that each is proud of his kind of "numbers."

The Type A individual simply uses money as a numeral of his prowess or achievements and then more often than not liberally disposes of a large fraction of it. You might compare a Type A man at work with an enthusiastic adolescent playing Monopoly. Both pay avid attention to their opportunities for acquiring the paper tokens necessary to win, but when the game is finished the Monopoly player counts them and then without a pang puts them away in the box. Likewise, the Type A man, after having striven for and obtained a certain *number* of dollars, doesn't care any more—and frequently even less—than the Type B about what use is made of the money. It is the *number* of dollars, not the dollars themselves, that appease—but unfortunately only partially—the insecurity of the Type A man.

THE INSECURITY OF STATUS

Perhaps no man, at first glance, seems less insecure than the typical Type A man. He bristles with confidence and appears to exude lavish amounts of self-assurance and self-conviction. How can we indict a man as being insecure who is always so eager to ask, "What is your problem and how can I help *you?*" a man who is so loath to say, "I have a problem and I need your help"? We do so because we have found, after many years of studying the Type A man, that he either lost or never had any intrinsic "yardstick" by which he can gauge his own fundamental worth to his own satisfaction.

Somewhere in his development process he began to measure the value of his total personality or character by the *number* of his *achievements*. Moreover, these achievements invariably must be those he believes capture the respect and admiration of his peers and superiors. He does not, however, care whether these achievements gain him the love or affection of his fellow man, although he does not particularly care to be disliked.

Having chosen this yardstick, he has committed himself irretrievably to a life course that can never bring him true equanimity. The *number,* not the quality, of his achievements must constantly increase to satiate an appetite that, unchecked by other restraints, ceaselessly increases. Second, he believes that the number of his achievements are always being judged by his peers and subordinates, and since the latter are constantly changing as he ascends in the socioeconomic scale, he feels that the number of his achievements must continue to rise.

A young Type A bank clerk, for example, will strive first to accomplish a number of tasks that will be admired by his fellow bank clerks and the assistant cashier, his immediate superior. At this stage in his development, their respect and admiration are necessary to him. Later in his development, when he becomes a senior vice-president of the bank, he then strives to obtain the respect and admiration of his fellow vice-presidents and the president and chairman of the bank's board of directors. How enormously unhappy he would be if he failed to obtain their esteem and had only the awed admiration of the bank clerks. In a pinch, this Type A senior vice-president would gladly trade off the esteem of even the thirty or more other vice-presidents for the sole approbation of the president; it is probably not an exaggeration to say that the respect of a single superior is more sustaining to the personality of a Type A man than that of a score of his peers. It may be in only this particular matter that even the Type A subject prefers *quality* to sheer *numbers.*

Perhaps we are all of this mold in that we all desire the approbation of our peers and superiors. But not all of us are so constantly and all-consumingly possessed with frenzy to gain this esteem. Then, too, many of us, unlike the Type A person, do want affection and do find considerable emotional satisfaction from the continuing admiration of those we may have left behind in our economic ascent. We must add also that the Type A man is not a snob, if only because the social amenities appear a complete waste of time to him unless they further what he considers to be his cause. Certainly, if a Type A lieutenant were invited to a party at which his commanding colonel's wife were present, he would be more inclined to attend her than the other ladies in the room, regardless of their possible charm. (We describe these traits, you must remember, not because we wish to condemn the Type A man; we only wish to portray him to you.)

From what we have written so far, it should be obvious that the Type A man isn't very concerned about simply sustaining himself. He feels that he always can obtain food, shelter, and clothing (and the modern welfare state, of course, buttresses his confidence in this regard). Nor is his insecurity exclusively focused solely upon his status at any given instant. Rather, it appears to be directly attuned to the *pace* at which his status *improves*. This brings us, then, to the key reason for the insecurity of the Type A man: he has staked his innermost security upon the *pace* of his status enhancement. This pace in turn depends upon a *maximal* number of achievements accomplished in a *minimal* amount of time, achievements recognized as significant by constantly changing groups of his peers and superiors.

His only possible surcease from this almost continuous self-harassment occurs at those fleeting moments when he believes that the number of his achievements are increasing at a satisfactory rate. These moments have to be rare. In his frenzy to accumulate achievements, he necessarily tends at the same time to subvert their quality. Noting unconsciously this fall-off in quality, he desperately attempts on a conscious level to make up for the deficit, by heaping up a still greater number of achievements.

The never-ending conflict in which the Type A subject is involved is a solitary one. It is, moreover, one frequently unrecognized by his associates or even his wife and children. So very few of us can muster sympathy, particularly in these antiestablishment days, for a successful banker, an attorney, or a physician whose sole difficulty, it seems to us, is only that he may appear to be somewhat short of time and sometimes rather irritable.

How can the president of a city's largest bank, whose spirit is being torn to shreds by his enormously compulsive drive to prove to the board of directors that he is making a better president than the one he succeeded or the president of a rival bank, expect sympathy or solace, even from his wife? Or how can the professor of medicine in a mediocre state medical school, who is publishing reams of medical trash in order to attract the attention of his peers at Harvard, expect understanding of his plight from the rather insouciant, but far better adjusted, members of his department?

Even if a Type A subject's friends were to recognize his potentially deadly struggle and tried to help him, he would probably reject their sympathy as of no value whatsoever. Again, only an increasing number of achievements and their recognition by his peers and superiors could serve as a temporary respite for his struggle. And one more thing. Even if a Type A man's peers and superiors were to laud his achievements, such praise would still not appease him unless he himself was certain that the number of such achievements truly warranted such encomium. The Type A man may have his faults, but hypocrisy and downright dishonesty are not among them. If a Type A man is found to be dishonest, you would be well advised to attribute this to ordinary human weakness, not to his behavior pattern.

AGGRESSION AND HOSTILITY

No man who is eager to achieve is totally lacking in aggressive spirit. Certainly we have met few if any Type A subjects who are deficient in this trait. On the contrary, most Type A subjects possess so much aggressive drive that it frequently evolves into a free-floating hostility. But excess aggression and certainly hostility are not always easily detected in Type A men, if only because they so often keep such feelings and impulses under deep cover. Indeed, very few of these men are even aware of their excess aggression, and almost none is aware of his hostility. Indeed, it is maybe only after fairly intimate acquaintance with a Type A man that his hostility becomes manifest.

Perhaps the prime index of the presence of aggression or hostility in almost all Type A men is the tendency always to compete with or to challenge other people, whether the activity consists of a sporting contest, a game of cards, or a simple discussion. If the aggression has evolved into frank hostility, more often than not one feels, even when talking casually to such men, that there is a note of rancor in their speech. They tend to bristle at points in a conversation where the ordinary person might either laugh self-deprecatingly or pass over the possibly contentious theme.

There are some persons whom we consider Type A, not because they are engaged in a struggle to achieve a maximal number of goals in a minimal amount of time (the usual complex making up this pattern), but because they are so hostile that they are almost continuously engaged in a struggle against other persons. Of course nature does not distinguish between a man struggling against time and one struggling against another man, but makes the organs of this struggling man discharge the same kinds of chemicals regardless of the exact causes of the struggle. No Type A man is more difficult to treat than one whose pattern stems directly and wholly from his free-floating hostility. But more about this in a later section.

Chapter 7

HOW TO TELL
A TYPE A
FROM A TYPE B

From the very time we began to think that a particular behavior complex bore responsibility for an increased risk of coronary artery and heart disease, we have been developing and refining methods of identifying individuals characterized by such patterns. Clearly the best method, and the one we use most to this day, is an interview conducted by trained personnel. At the moment, we have several interviewers especially skilled at spotting Type A behavior using a standardized questionnaire. The questions themselves, of course, are far less important than the *manner* of response to them. We find it necessary to emphasize this point repeatedly to those asking to have our list of twenty or so questions in order to run their own tests. Type A and Type B persons may give identical answers, but the *way* they give them is sufficient for our interviewers to differentiate the types almost all of the time.

In an attempt to make the classification process still less "subjective," we have tried using a voice analysis technique. Its basis is a two-paragraph diatribe, presumably the words used by a military commander exhorting his troops before a battle. This is the text:

This is the way that you and me, every God damned one of us are going to lick the hell out of whoever stands in our way. And I don't give a damn whether you like what I'm telling you or not. This is the way I say it's got to be done. First, we're going to smack them hard with mortar fire, understand? I want you to pour it on them! Let the bastards feel it get hot, really hot around them. Singe the hell out of them! Scorch the bastards, fry them, burn their guts out. Make ashes out of them.

After the mortars, I'll tell you when to advance. And when I give the signal, don't crawl, you run forward! Remember, it's your skin or theirs! All right, enough talk, now let's get the lead out of our pants and get going. Hey! One more thing, good luck!

A subject is invited to first read the monologue over to himself silently, until he is sure he can read it aloud without stumbling. Then he is asked to read it aloud, pretending that he is in his own home, alone. After this is done, and recorded, he is asked to imagine that he is the officer on the battlefield and to read it again.

A variety of tests are used to analyze the results. The most vivid by far are the electronically recorded voice-prints, which display in visual form the oscillations of each subject's voice during the readings. The Type B subject shows very little expression while reading to himself, and even during the more rapid hortatory reading inflects key words only moderately. The Type A subject, on the other hand, throws himself into the project with a certain violence. Even the trial reading displays wide oscillations caused by his typically harsh, explosive speech rhythms. His hortatory reading sends the needle flipping wildly.

This sharply aggressive manner of speech is one of the most common telltale signs of a Type A individual. Other signs are rather more subtle—for example, in many people a slight darkening of pigmentation around the eyes is a sign of certain pituitary secretions, an indication in turn of reaction to stress. But ordinarily the pattern is obvious without recourse to such points. Indeed, identification is easy when a person with a *fully developed* complex presents himself.

Yet even then, if the procedure is wrong, the investigator can be tricked. Several years ago we thought we had devised a clever objective test for screening Type A's. Subjects were asked to listen to a girl incoherently and maddeningly relating a story with no point whatsoever. As they listened, their breathing and body movements (such as wriggling or fist clenching) were carefully monitored by a polygraph machine. It seemed obvious that a Type A would show his impatience readily. But to our surprise a large-scale test failed. What we had forgotten was the Type A man's ability to simply quit listening if he was bored, and how easy it is for him to pretend to be listening when he is actually thinking about something else.

The following section is intended to help you determine for yourself whether you are a Type A or Type B personality. If you are honest in your self appraisal—and if you are actually aware of your own traits and habits—we believe that you will not have too much trouble accomplishing this. The details of the behavior pattern vary, of course, according to many factors—education, age, social position. But most of you will be able to spot yourselves. Incidentally, we have found that Type A persons are by and large more common, and that if you are not quite sure about yourself, chances are that you, too, are Type A—not fully developed, perhaps, but bad enough to think about changing. And after you have assessed yourself, ask a friend or your spouse whether your self-assessment was accurate. If you disagree, *they* are probably right.

YOU POSSESS TYPE A BEHAVIOR PATTERN:

1. If you have (a) a habit of explosively accentuating various key words in your ordinary speech even when there is no real need for such accentuation, and (b) a tendency to utter the last few words of your sentences far more rapidly than the opening words. The vocal explosiveness betrays the excess aggression or hostility you may be harboring. The hurrying of the ends of sentences mirrors your underlying impatience with spending even the time required for your own speech.

2. If you *always* move, walk, and eat rapidly.

3. If you feel (particularly if you openly exhibit to others) an impatience with the rate at which most events take place. You are suffering from this sort of impatience if you find it difficult to restrain yourself from hurrying the speech of others and resort to the device of saying very quickly over and over again, "Uh huh, uh huh," or, "Yes yes, yes yes," to someone who is talking, unconsciously urging him to "get on with" or hasten his rate of speaking. You are also suffering from impatience if you attempt to finish the sentences of persons speaking to you before they can.

   Other signs of this sort of impatience: if you become *unduly* irritated or even enraged when a car ahead of you in your lane runs at a pace you consider too slow; if you find it anguishing to wait in a line or to wait your turn to be seated at a restaurant; if you find it intolerable to watch others perform tasks you know you can do faster; if you become impatient with yourself as you are obliged to perform repetitious duties (making out bank deposit slips, writing checks, washing and cleaning dishes, and so on), which are necessary but take you away from doing things you really have an interest in doing; if you find yourself hurrying your own reading or always attempting to obtain condensations or summaries of truly interesting and worthwhile literature.

4. If you indulge in *polyphasic* thought or performance, frequently striving to think of or do two or more things

simultaneously. For example, if while trying to listen to another person's speech you persist in continuing to think about an irrelevant subject, you are indulging in polyphasic thought. Similarly, if while golfing or fishing you continue to ponder your business or professional problems, or if while using an electric razor you attempt also to eat your breakfast or drive your car, or if while driving your car you attempt to dictate letters for your secretary, you are indulging in polyphasic performance. This is one of the commonest traits in the Type A man. Nor is he always satisfied with doing just two things at one time. We have known subjects who not only shaved and ate simultaneously, but also managed to read a business or professional journal at the same time.

5. If you find it *always* difficult to refrain from talking about or bringing the theme of any conversation around to those subjects which especially interest and intrigue you, and when unable to accomplish this maneuver, you pretend to listen but really remain preoccupied with your own thoughts.

6. If you almost always feel vaguely guilty when you relax and do absolutely nothing for several hours to several days.

7. If you no longer observe the more important or interesting or lovely objects that you encounter in your milieu. For example, if you enter a strange office, store, or home, and after leaving any of these places you cannot recall what was in them, you no longer are observing well—or for that matter enjoying life very much.

8. If you do not have any time to spare to become the things worth *being* because you are so preoccupied with getting the things worth *having*.

9. If you attempt to schedule more and more in less and less time, and in doing so make fewer and fewer allowances for unforeseen contingencies. A concomitant of this is a *chronic sense of time urgency*, one of the core components of Type A Behavior Pattern.

10. If, on meeting another severely afflicted Type A person, instead of feeling compassion for his affliction you find yourself compelled to "challenge" him. This is a telltale trait because no one arouses the aggressive and/or hostile feelings of one Type A subject more quickly than another Type A subject.

11. If you resort to certain characteristic gestures or nervous

tics. For example, if in conversation you frequently clench your fist, or bang your hand upon a table or pound one fist into the palm of your other hand in order to emphasize a conversational point, you are exhibiting Type A gestures. Similarly, if the corners of your mouth spasmodically, in tic-like fashion, jerk backward slightly exposing your teeth, or if you habitually clench your jaw, or even grind your teeth, you are subject to muscular phenomena suggesting the presence of a continuous *struggle,* which is, of course, the kernel of the Type A Behavior Pattern.

12. If you believe that whatever success you have enjoyed has been due in good part to your ability to get things done faster than your fellow men and if you are afraid to stop doing everything faster and faster.

13. If you find yourself increasingly and ineluctably committed to translating and evaluating not only your own but also the activities of others in terms of "numbers."

The characteristics above mark the fully developed, hard-core Type A. Many people properly classified as Type A exhibit these characteristics in a lesser degree, however. If you are a moderately afflicted Type A subject, for example, you rarely feel or display much hostility. Your aggressiveness, although in excess, has still not evolved into free-floating rancor. You do not bristle with the barely governable rage that seethes so often just below the surface of the personality of the full Type A person.

Similarly, your impatience is not of towering proportions. You may attempt to squeeze more and more events into smaller and smaller pieces of time at work but often you can avoid this practice in off hours. You do not feel that you have to propel your "bicycle" faster and faster to keep your balance once your business or professional day has ended. At such times, like fire wagon horses unharnessed after returning from a fire, you may become almost torpid. But again like fire horses, who used to neigh and stomp their hooves just as soon as they heard the first peal of the fire alarm bell, so you, on hearing the alarm clock in the morning, shed your indolence and begin to hustle, bustle, and resume your strife with time.

Nor as a moderate Type A are you *obsessively* involved in the acquisition of sheer numbers. You are still aware of the many nonnumerate, charming aspects of full-bodied, full-souled living, even if you cannot completely enjoy and lose yourself in them.

YOU POSSESS TYPE B BEHAVIOR PATTERN:

1. If you are completely free of *all* the habits and exhibit none of the traits we have listed that harass the severely afflicted Type A person.
2. If you never suffer from a sense of time urgency with its accompanying impatience.
3. If you harbor no free-floating hostility, and you feel no need to display or discuss either your achievements or accomplishments unless such exposure is demanded by the situation.
4. If, when you play, you do so to find fun and relaxation, not to exhibit your superiority at any cost.
5. If you can relax without guilt, just as you can work without agitation.

The Type B person is far more aware of his capabilities than concerned about what peers and superiors may think of his actions. Unlike the Type A person, who really is never quite certain of his virtues and cannot ever quite face up to his deficiencies, you as a Type B know fairly well the value of your virtues and have resigned yourself to the restrictions that your deficiencies set upon you. You seek and succeed in finding your self-confidence by a process of candid self-appraisal. The Type A man seeks but never quite succeeds in finding self-confidence because he looks for it in the acquisition of an ever-increasing set of "numbers."

You, too, may strive for the things worth having. Indeed, as the "tortoise" (which the Type A "rabbit" more or less always believes you are) you may, in the final stretch, obtain a greater share of the things worth having than your Type A counterpart. But usually (if you have not been too critically wounded by the ethos of our times) you also attempt to become at least some of the things worth being. In any event, you do not build your life's ladder with rungs composed solely of numbers.

You may not be a completely-developed Type B, but if you are relatively free of all the habits enslaving the Type A subject, and if you exhibit relatively rarely any of his traits, then you may still be classed as a Type B. You may occasionally feel a sense of time urgency, but if you do, it will be associated exclusively with your vocational and never with your avocational activities. Also, even at work, you will not feel this stress except during those limited periods when the demands of your position make it logical to feel that time is short. For example, if you are an accountant, you may well feel a sense of time urgency during the first two weeks of April.

But precisely like a fully developed Type B person, you, too, never suffer from the presence of free-floating hostility nor do you habitually attempt to speed things up like a Type A. You, too, strive to acquire the things worth having, but again, you will not do so at the expense of totally disregarding the pursuit of the things worth being.

We have presumed to slice the spectrum of personality types rather sharply, and possibly, rather arbitrarily. Even in our increasingly standardized society, human beings possess personalities that cannot be nearly so precisely categorized as has been done here. Behavior types tend to run together to some extent.

Then, too, there are some people (but no more than about 10 percent of an urban population) who possess some habits and exhibit some traits that are Type A and some that are Type B. Ordinarily, though, it is not difficult to recognize and differentiate persons with Type A Behavior Pattern from persons with Type B.

Theologians and psychologists may object vigorously to the implication obviously inherent in this section that large numbers of human beings are "typable." They would insist (though the Harvard psychologist B. F. Skinner might not) that man has available to him, and frequently acts upon, myriads of different responses to identical challenges. This is so in respect to many Type B subjects. But it certainly is not true of a man whose personality has eroded to the point where his choice of responses is actually limited. Type A persons, having suffered such erosion, rarely vary in their responses to specific challenges of their milieu. Their original endowment of free choice has been supplanted by a sad enslavement and absorption in the acquisition of "numbers."

In attempting to assess yourself, we should again like to suggest that before you make your final decision whether you are a Type A or B person, you request the advice and opinion of your spouse, or a relative or friend who knows you well. We have observed that many Type A persons are totally unaware of either the presence or effects of their behavior pattern. They do not notice their restlessness, their tense facial muscles, their tics, or their strident-staccato manner of speaking. Nor are they always aware of their free-floating hostility—when it is present—if only because they can rationalize it so beautifully. Some Type A persons are not even aware of their sense of time urgency; it has been present so long that it seems a part of their personality. For that matter, they may be understandably reluctant to recognize, as enslaving and

spiritually devastating, habits and traits that only yesterday were held in high esteem by all—including
Horatio Alger and his prosperous friends.

Chapter 8

TWO CASES

William Osler, the true father of medicine in North America, always believed that merely presenting medical students with a bare body of fact about any disease was poor teaching. He felt the key to helping them understand and remember was to confront them with actual cases. He believed so strongly in this pedagogical device that once, when he was scheduled to give a lecture on typhoid fever and couldn't find an authentic typhoid fever patient, he nevertheless provided a fake.

Acting on Osler's principle, we now will present brief sketches of two actual acquaintances of ours, a typical Type A and a typical Type B. Both "Paul" and "Ralph" still live in our community, and we see them rather frequently. We have made a few trivial changes in their circumstances in order to forestall any possible embarrassment to them.

TYPE A—PAUL

Paul Crimmins is the successful manager of a California brewery, having begun with the company as a salesman twenty-five years ago. He is fifty-two years of age, of medium height, and approximately twenty-five pounds overweight (he carries the excess mostly around his waistline). He married in 1950 and has two sons, both of whom are now students at the University of California.

Paul is not merely an impatient man, he is also a harried man. A very disproportionate amount of his emotional energy is consumed in struggling against the normal constraints of time. "How can I move faster, and do more and more things in less and less time?" is the question that never ceases to torment him.

Paul hurries his thinking, his speech, and his movements. He also strives to hurry the thinking, speech, and movements of those about him; they must communicate rapidly and relevantly if they wish to avoid creating impatience in him. Planes must arrive and depart precisely on time for Paul, cars ahead of him on the highway must maintain a speed he approves of, and there must never be a queue of persons standing between him and a bank clerk, a restaurant table, or the interior of a theater. In fact, he is infuriated whenever people talk slowly or circuitously, when planes are late, cars dawdle on the highway, and queues form.

He also strives as often as he can to do several things at once. While driving his car to work, he sometimes dictates letters into his portable tape recorder, or he shaves himself with an electric razor. He also keeps his car radio on in order to hear the news.

Paul has learned the sly habit of automatically saying, "Hmm, very interesting," or "Is that so," or "How amusing," or "Right, right," during conversations—particularly with his wife and children—about subjects that don't interest him deeply; he believes that this maneuver shows that he has been listening. He is likely to take a trade journal to his dining room table or to the bathroom with him.

While no gourmet, Paul does eat foods rich in cholesterol and animal fats. For breakfast he usually takes fruit, toast, a pat of butter, two eggs, sometimes bacon, and at least two cups of coffee. For lunch he regularly selects a large meat serving, one starchy and one green vegetable, bread, a pat of butter, and again, two cups of coffee. He also likes to drink either one or two martinis before or a bottle of beer during his lunch. However, he regularly refuses a dessert.

In the evening he invariably drinks two more martinis before dinner. The latter consists of a very generous meat serving, one or two kinds of vegetables, a salad, a pat of butter, and several slices of bread. More and more frequently he has taken to drinking a glass of wine with his dinner. Again, he may refuse a dessert. If he is eating his dinner in a restaurant, he may request a brandy with his several cups of coffee. Sometimes in the evenings he eats snacks, not because he is especially hungry, but because he is restless or tense.

Paul smokes two packs of cigarettes a day, but is thoroughly ashamed of it. He has repeatedly promised himself that he would quit. He succeeded several years ago in quitting for eight months, but found that he had gained fourteen pounds, became "very nervous" and irritable, and wasn't able "to think as sharply as I used to do." He tried smoking a pipe, but "the damned thing made me nervous because I always had to fool with it, lighting it over and over, tamping it, cleaning it. I found I was inhaling the pipe smoke too. To hell with a pipe."

Paul rarely exercises more than an hour or two a week. "I'd like to play golf several times a week, but now I just can't find the time for it." Several times a year, however, he will go on a fishing trip lasting several days. He had also considered the idea of jogging, but his physician wisely counseled him to avoid this sort of exertion.

He has almost no hobbies. "I used to like to read, but I don't have time to now," he explains. He rarely visits a museum, library, or art gallery. Sometimes, to please his wife, he will attend a symphony, ballet, or opera. He is not averse to movies, however, and likes very much to watch sporting events on his television set.

He also likes to play poker or bridge or gin rummy, but here again he finds he doesn't have as much time as he would like. When he does play these games, he prefers that the stakes be relatively high. He also always plays with extreme competitive zeal.

He feels he is too busy and too tired to make minor repairs of his house, to dabble in woodworking or electronics, or to garden.

What, then, does Paul do when he returns nightly to his home? Well, he has his cocktails; eats his dinner; reads a newspaper, trade journal, or news magazine; or looks at television until 9:00 or 9:30 P.M. Then he goes to bed. In short, Paul employs the avocational phase of his twenty-four-hour day to fuel up and rest up for his vocational struggles.

Paul has scores, perhaps hundreds, of acquaintances, but they are almost all people whom he has met in business life. Indeed, he strives to know and to be known by as many persons as he possibly can. From this large group of acquaintances, he encounters no difficulty at all in finding men with whom he can go to lunch, go fishing, or play poker and bridge. Paul also chats easily with his barber, the waitresses at his favorite restaurants, the garage attendants, and the security guards at his place of business. But he possesses no real friends, nor does he perceive any disadvantage from not having any. *He associates persons with events, not events with persons.*

Paul has tried very hard to be a good husband to his wife, and a good father to his two sons. Certainly, he has always given them anything they have wished so long as he could afford it. Yet the family, while not an unhappy one, is nevertheless discontented.

His wife, who is now forty-seven years of age, interests herself in various community affairs such as the art museum, the symphony, and the ballet. When Paul comes home at night, he dutifully pretends to be absorbed in her rather long-winded accounts of her day's activities. As we have already said, Paul has developed the faculty of seeming to be listening to her as he thinks of other subjects. It is probable that his wife knows that he isn't really listening, but she is content to talk without a listener as long as she can at least listen to herself.

She abruptly and decisively discourages any attempt by Paul to talk about his business affairs. This, however, never annoys him, because he prefers to contemplate his business affairs by himself. Then he won't have to listen to her comments, most of which he believes would be irrelevant or silly.

In short, both manage to tolerate each other fairly well, although Paul finds his wife really rather dull.

Paul never found it difficult to communicate in an affectionate manner with his two sons when they were younger, but now he finds that communication is becoming increasingly difficult. He has little patience with their antiestablishment views, their mode of dress, and what he considers their strange unawareness of the "realities" of life.

Extremely sensitive as he is, Paul is often hurt when at the dinner table his visiting sons appear to take more pleasure in listening to his wife's chitchat than to his own conversation, which both boys increasingly appear to ignore. His very genuine love and affection for them may thus be swamped by a fierce wave of hostility. It is at such times that Paul feels he is running his life's course quite alone and unappreciated. Several times recently he has even asked himself, "I wonder if any of them would feel very deprived if I were to die?" As a consequence, he often blurts out cutting, hurtful remarks that further estrange his sons, making affectionate and fruitful communication between them increasingly difficult.

Although Paul calls himself an Episcopalian and donates liberally to his parish church, he has never sought aid or solace from God because he really doesn't believe that He exists. The origin of our universe and its creator are for Paul pointless questions. Yet sometimes, when on a Sunday morning he sees radiant young couples streaming from the portals of a church, he wishes wistfully that he, too, could be as naïve as he suspects they are, and believe also in a Divine Protector.

Paul has never succeeded in formulating a basic philosophy to guide his living. Yet he often recalls the time when his father once said to him, "Some day, Paul, I think you ought to sit down for a few minutes and ask yourself where you plan to go in life. And after you've answered that question, you might ask yourself why you want to go there." Although forty years have passed since his father made this suggestion, Paul never yet has found either the time or the inclination to find the answer to either of these questions.

When Paul was examined by his physician a few weeks ago, he was found to have a normal electrocardiogram. However, his blood pressure was moderately elevated (155/100), and his serum cholesterol was

considerably higher than normal (304 mg./100 ml.).
He did not, however, show any sign of diabetes.

Despite this rather equivocal medical report, Paul
may be lucky and escape having coronary heart disease in the next ten years. But he will have to be very,
very lucky. On the basis of our clinical and research
experiences, his chances of escaping will only be about
one out of twenty.

TYPE B—RALPH

Ralph Longly is the president of a California bank.
He entered the company thirty-four years ago, first
working as a teller. He is fifty-four years of age, tall,
and takes pride in the fact that he now weighs no more
than he did when he played on the baseball team of his
university.

Ralph graduated from the University of California
in 1939 and joined his present company immediately
after graduation. He married in 1943, and has two
daughters and one son, all of whom are now married.

Ralph is a very patient man. Indeed, sometimes he
feels that he is far too patient in his dealings with other
people. Certainly, he doesn't mind if his friends speak
reasonably slowly; he generally speaks in an unhurried
manner himself. Indeed, sometimes Ralph may break
off speaking in the middle of a sentence to think a bit
longer about the subject at hand before continuing.
When Ralph's plane departure is delayed, he simply
shrugs his shoulders, traipses indolently about the airport, inspects the racks of paperback novels, and
reads with pleasure as he sips a cup of coffee. Of
course, he doesn't like to stand in a line, but if he
must, he good-naturedly resigns himself to doing so,
observing closely and with interest the faces and conversations of others standing near him. "Then, too,"

he says, "it's as good a time as any other to daydream or meditate."

Ralph is so content with the pace at which he thinks and lives that he never indulges in the "polyphasic" activities so often resorted to by Paul. When he converses with other people he finds it almost impossible to think of anything else except what they are talking about; he had never trained his mind in the art of "polyphasic" thinking.

Similarly, when he drives a car, although he may occasionally scan the countryside, he sees no need to indulge in such activities as shaving or dictating letters. He enjoys listening to his car radio, but he abruptly turns it off if a friend or acquaintance enters his car.

Ralph likes to eat, but habitually restrains himself from eating too much of certain foods. For breakfast he takes fruit, toast, and coffee, but he eats eggs only on Sunday mornings. Of course he would like to eat eggs daily for breakfast, but his physician informed him that eggs were extravagantly rich in cholesterol. For lunch he usually orders only a salad (with French dressing) and rarely eats any bread and butter. He will drink one cup of coffee, but rarely takes any alcoholic beverage at lunch. "I become too drowsy in the afternoon if I do. But you go on and have a drink," he frequently tells a guest at lunch.

When he arrives home, he, too, will drink one, sometimes two, cocktails. If, however, he decides to drink wine with his dinner, he either forgoes the drinking of his cocktails or limits himself to only one drink.

His dinner qualitatively is about the same as that eaten by Paul, except that Ralph habitually eats a meat serving about half the weight of Paul's. Also, Ralph tends to eat sparingly of starches, but generously of the leafy vegetables and salad. He also sprinkles far less oil dressing upon his salad. Ralph also rarely eats a cooked dessert, but occasionally he finishes his dinner with some variety of fresh fruit.

Ralph has never smoked cigarettes. And while he does smoke a pipe, he limits himself to three pipefuls of tobacco a day.

He regularly exercises every day. Every morning and evening he indulges in about ten to fifteen minutes of calisthenics in his bedroom, and he plays several sets of tennis doubles twice a week with three friends of his own age. The game is conducted at a leisurely pace, and Ralph never strains himself to return a ball strategically placed. "I'm too old to chase balls," he explains.

Ralph also tries to walk at least forty minutes a day. He takes pride in the fact that he never uses an elevator to ascend a single floor in any building. He also prefers to park his car several blocks or more from any place he wishes to go in order to get the exercise of walking.

Ralph has a number of hobbies. His favorite one is book printing, which he accomplishes with an antique Columbian hand press. He also has a great affection for classical music. He finds time almost every evening to spend fifteen minutes or half an hour listening to some great piece of music. Another of his hobbies is collecting books. He has accumulated a fine but select library. He takes particular pride in the fact that the number and variety of its reference books allow him to find at least a bit of information about almost any subject.

Besides these hobbies, Ralph takes a great interest in the theater. He has read or seen the plays of most contemporary dramatists, and he is not at all reluctant to travel a considerable distance to see a favorite play performed.

Ralph has never attempted to know a large number

of people. While always courteous and gracious to the men he meets in his commercial life, he does not strive to share any of his avocational time with them unless he perceives that they possess qualities he particularly admires.

Ralph believes he has five real friends, and he is not at all ashamed of the fact that he goes far out of his way to preserve and enhance those friendships. He has no hesitation whatsoever in requesting legitimate favors of all kinds from these five friends because he in turn would not hesitate to bestow favors upon them.

Ralph has also tried very hard to be a good husband to his wife and a good father to his two daughters and son. He, too, has given them most of the things they desire. Yet his family, too, has its elements of discontent.

His wife, now fifty-one, has, in many of her attributes and habits, changed very little in the last twenty years. She still likes to golf several times a week, continues to read avidly, and still finds fun in her kitchen. She enjoys music and drama as much as Ralph does, and her opinions and views on many subjects remain fluid and subject to revision.

When Ralph returns to his home in the evening, his wife relates to him the events of her own day that she hopes may interest him, trying very hard to tell him about those matters which she thinks may surprise, amuse, or entertain him. Since he likes to listen to her, he sometimes finds these accounts interesting and often amusing. Ralph, on the other hand, infrequently discusses his business affairs with his wife, preferring to tell her about the actions or thoughts of various persons that have interested or intrigued him that day.

Ralph, unlike Paul, still has no difficulty in communicating with his two married daughters, or with his son. He can easily tolerate all their views, even when some of these appear naïve or downright immature, because he quickly reminds himself that as long as their views are neither evil nor selfish, it is best that time be allowed to correct them.

However, he frequently observes their sense of guilt about the fact that they have lived and still live in a luxurious manner that they received but did not earn for themselves. He feels this same sense of guilt himself. Although he tries to rationalize it away, nevertheless it persists and induces a certain melancholy in him.

Ralph calls himself an Episcopalian and contributes to his parish church. Like Paul, he, too, doubts the existence of a God to whom he can appeal for personal guidance and aid. Yet he has pondered many times about the source of the design and purpose he perceives in the universe.

He has, however, sketched a basic philosophy for himself that is half pragmatic, half metaphysical. Thus he believes that hard work of any kind forms the basic core of a satisfying existence. If it is avoided, deterioration of the spirit inevitably occurs.

He believes that the principles of honesty, humility, and altruism carry their own special reward, if only because he has never met or known of an honest, humble, and unselfish man who remained permanently unhappy or dissatisfied with his life. So believing, Ralph tries conscientiously to act honestly and unselfishly.

He quickly admits, however, that only too often he has failed to adhere to these principles. "But," he explains, "when I did act dishonestly or selfishly, I at least knew that I was being a son-of-a-bitch. Then, too, since I myself don't always follow these principles, I believe I'm much more apt to be tolerant of some other man in the same position. Mind you, though, I'm not interested in drawing up blueprints for other people to follow."

When Ralph was examined by his physician a few months ago, he was found to have a normal electro-cardiogram, a normal blood pressure, a serum choles-terol level of 208 mg./100 ml. and no sign of diabetes.

Ralph's totally negative medical report does not, of course, surprise us. Nor does he need to have any luck at all in order to avoid having coronary heart disease in the near future, because again, from our combined clinical and research studies, his chances of getting this disease even in the next twenty years will be far less than one out of twenty.

Chapter 9

SOME SURE CAUSES
OF CORONARY
ARTERY DISEASE

Our main purpose in this book is to suggest a reason why otherwise apparently healthy individuals suffer coronary artery disease, and may in time suffer coronary heart disease—a heart attack. There are, however, several conditions that we *know* cause coronary artery disease. While these must be mentioned, they may also be dealt with relatively briefly, as there is little real doubt about their connection with heart disease. They may be diagnosed with considerable ease. There is, in fact, no excuse for anyone following a sensible program of regular checkups to remain in ignorance of having one of these conditions. Treating them is another matter. The precise causal relationship between these symptoms and the ultimate danger of coronary artery disease continues to be a subject of debate among specialists.

1. Diabetes mellitus is beyond any doubt a cause of coronary artery disease. But though the superficial symptoms of diabetes—high blood sugar, plus a urinary leak of this same sugar—can and regularly are

treated by antidiabetic drugs such as insulin, a very acrimonious battle is now raging among biostatisticians about the possible harm these drugs may do to the heart. Apart from the question of immediate harmfulness to general living, it appears to be very doubtful that simply lowering the blood sugar level of a diabetic does anything at all to protect him from the advent of coronary artery disease. Excess blood sugar may, in fact, be merely a warning indicator of a more far-ranging disorder, and symptomatic treatment directed solely to regulate the blood sugar level may be of limited value. Nevertheless, while we await more substantial evidence, it makes sense to try to keep the blood sugar down, if only to enable the patient to function on a day-to-day basis. After all, coronary heart disease is only one of the complications of diabetes, and it is usually a relatively late one. So if you are diabetic and your doctor advises you to take insulin, for goodness' sake do so, and be thankful that this life-maintaining hormone is available to you.

2. Hypertension (or high blood pressure) is another widely—though not universally—accepted cause of coronary artery and heart disease. We know of several doctors who are loath to treat or reduce the hypertension of patients who exhibit an only moderately elevated blood pressure. But we are not impressed by their wisdom, and suspect that very few of our professional associates would disagree with the flat statement that hypertension (whether severe, moderate, or slight) *does* lead to premature development of severe coronary artery disease. And the prematurity of onset of such disease varies directly with the severity of the hypertension. In other words, if your blood pressure, let us say, is 275/120 and you allow it to remain untreated, you almost certainly will develop not only severe coronary artery disease but also some form of coronary heart disease (angina pectoris, for example) in the

next five years—if, that is, you manage to escape a stroke or uremia during this same interlude. On the other hand, if your blood pressure is only slightly elevated, to a level, let us say, of 165/100, you might well escape coronary heart disease for decades; but allowing it to remain untreated is a variant of prolonged Russian roulette.

We aren't precisely sure at this time why *untreated* hypertension leads so frequently to premature severe coronary artery disease. Some of us believe that the coronary arteries of the hypertensive person are injured far more frequently and more severely than those of normal subjects because they encounter two unusual sorts of strain. First, the coronary arteries of the hypertensive person are constantly subjected to an internal pressure that is much greater than normal. This might not only itself produce tiny or even large tears in an artery's lining, but also aggravate a tear arising from any other cause. Second, the heart laboring under the strain of pumping blood against a greater gradient of pressure probably contracts far more vigorously. Such exaggerated contraction probably bends and twists the coronary arteries clinging to its surface to a far greater extent than usual.

But hypertension can and frequently does lead to a second kind of heart disease. This we designate hypertensive heart disease. It results when the heart, having grown thicker and heavier to overcome its difficulties in pumping blood against the heightened pressure, finally begins to founder as a pump. When this happens, the patient may suffer breathlessness and his legs may puff up with stagnant fluid that has escaped from blood that, no longer being effectively circulated, begins to distend and weaken the blood vessels attempting to contain it. Not too infrequently, hypertensive patients may suffer both from this form of heart disease and a coronary heart attack. It is not a pleasant combination!

Fortunately, physicians now have at their immediate disposal a veritable arsenal of potent drugs with which they can not only lower a previously high blood pressure, they can also normalize it. This being the happy therapeutic state of affairs, we need only patients who are equally willing to be treated.

But too many hypertensive patients are not always willing to continue treatment, year in and year out. This is particularly true when their blood pressure is only moderately or slightly elevated and was discovered to be so during a routine checkup. Unlike uncontrolled diabetes, untreated hypertension—sometimes even very severe hypertension—may not evoke symptoms for years, even decades.

"Why should I take medicines for the rest of my life when I feel fine and my blood pressure isn't so very high?" This is the question thousands of doctors have had to answer hundreds of times. And unfortunately, only too often the doctors' answers have failed to convince their questioning patients of the need for continuance of medication that admittedly does provoke an occasional side reaction, usually of trivial import. Why aren't their answers always convincing? Because these answers consist only of predictions of what *may* happen a decade hence if the blood pressure isn't kept within normal limits. And most hypertensive patients are particularly prone to a singularly shortsighted refusal to worry about anything having to do with their health ten years off. This is due not to their intellectual unawareness of the future and its events, but rather to their total emotional absorption and preoccupation with matters other than those having to do with their bodily well-being. Such involvement, of course, is due to the fact that so many, if not most, hypertensive patients are also Type A persons. Type A Behavior Pattern captures most of these persons long before their blood pressure rises.

But the fact is that most hypertensive patients will need to take drugs of one kind or another for the rest of their lives. Even when, through painstaking work with drugs, a patient's blood pressure is finally reduced to a proper level, there must be no letup. Ideal therapy for hypertension, moreover, is not just the reduction, but the total normalization, of blood pressure throughout the day, every day. Too often blood pressure may be normal in the doctor's office, only to rise dangerously under stress or irritation. Thus a patient is well advised either to learn to take his own blood pressure frequently, or to arrange to have it done. Other protective steps include bringing one's weight down to the level it was in high school; eliminating the use of tobacco in all forms; following a low cholesterol, low animal fat diet (see page 69); getting regular exercise; and above all ameliorating Type A Behavior Pattern, so commonly associated with this condition. No one knows exactly what causes hypertension, though Russian scientists have suggested (in our view wisely) that it may stem from a derangement of one or more brain centers, and hence be of nervous origin. If so, the linkage with Type A behavior is even more logical.

3. Hereditary hypercholesterolemia is a relatively uncommon, genetically linked condition marked by a radically elevated serum cholesterol level. While there is a growing tendency among heart researchers to consider *all* types of hypercholesterolemia to be at least partly hereditary, this one is universally accepted as inheritable, as its common name indicates. It goes by a number of other names, the most fashionable one just now being familial hyperbetalipoproteinemia. Whatever you call it, however, it is a wretched disorder that may not be recognized in a child's early years unless he happens to have a cholesterol check, or perhaps if the parent from whom he inherited it has a heart at-

tack and is found to be suffering from the telltale
symptoms—a cholesterol level anywhere from 300 to
1,200 mg./100 ml., and a distinctive variety of
small, rather hard, and poorly defined lumps in certain tendons of the body. Occasionally, the ailment
may signal its presence in an adolescent by producing
chest pain or even a myocardial infarct. When this
happens, it is a sign that one or both of the two coronary arteries have been blocked. As a rule, however,
such a drastic development does not occur until after
the second decade of an afflicted person's life, but few
reach their sixties without some form of coronary
heart disease.

Anyone aware that he (or his children) suffers from
hereditary hypercholesterolemia requires the services
of a physician who devotes his working time mainly to
the study and treatment of cholesterol disturbances.
Such physicians can be found in most of our larger
medical complexes. The completely successful treatment of this condition is not too frequently accomplished. Nevertheless, enough persons have been
helped by skilled and knowledgeable specialists to
suggest that a guarded optimism appears warranted.
We are absolutely certain that time will brighten the
situation. But we cannot urge too strongly that those
concerned consult an expert without delay.

4. Hypothyroidism, or a deficiency in thyroid hormone production, if allowed to go untreated, will
undoubtedly lead to the premature occurrence of coronary artery disease. But it is almost pointless to mention it here. An untreated thyroid deficiency is virtually unknown today, primarily because of current
medical expertise in ferreting out even minor thyroid
malfunctions and the tendency of physicians to prescribe thyroid hormone preparations on the mere
suspicion that a thyroid deficiency may exist. It is
extremely unlikely that there are more than five hun-

dred Americans now who are not well supplied with this hormone. Next to aspirin, multivitamins, and tranquilizers, thyroid preparations are probably the most widely swallowed drugs in America. So though hypothyroidism is distinctly linked to coronary heart disease, in practice we can almost never point to it as a cause. A pity—how wonderful it would be if we could stop the progress of coronary heart disease simply by administering a pill that perhaps a quarter of all urban American white women are already taking with no bad effects!

Every individual who is presently suffering from one or more of the disorders we have labeled here as certain causes of coronary artery disease needs and will need for the rest of his life the *continuous* and *regular* supervision of his personal physician. Indeed, if you happen to have diabetes, hypertension, hereditary hypercholesterolemia, or hypothyroidism, supervision by a physician will do far more to extend your life than any number of books of this type.

This advice actually does not have to be given to a person suffering from severe diabetes; he knows only too well that in the absence of close professional medical scrutiny he may encounter disabling symptoms in a few days or few weeks. But the present admonition does have to be driven home to those individuals who do not *suffer* from but still possess either a high blood pressure or a high blood cholesterol level.

Neither of these two conditions, when medically uncontrolled, necessarily evokes symptoms immediately. In fact, they rarely do. Years and even decades of their medical neglect may elapse before the effects of their gradual erosion of arterial integrity "surfaces" as a vascular tragedy. Indeed, it is not unusual if, suffering from hypertension (that is, high blood pressure), you actually first encounter symptoms only after your blood pressure is reduced to a normal level. Then, too, the drugs we employ today to lower blood pressure or cholesterol levels sometimes do evoke side effects that may be slightly irksome but rarely disabling or perilous.

Why are we emphasizing so strongly that if you are a hypertensive or hypercholesterolemic subject you should continue to see your physician regularly and also continue to take the medicines he prescribes until he, the doctor, decides—without incessant prodding on your part—that you no longer require such medicines? Because we have good reason to suspect that the hypertensive or hypercholesterolemic patient (and of course the coronary patient, too), has a peculiar— indeed, almost diagnostic—aversion to medication, even though he knows that this medication has been effective in lowering his blood pressure or cholesterol level.

"Now that my blood pressure is normal, must I keep taking my pills?" hundreds of hypertensive patients have asked us. "Are they bothering you?" we then always ask. "No, but I hate to take medicine," they invariably reply. Sometimes, accustomed over the years to this question, we smile gently and reply, "But you use toothpaste every day and you don't mind that —but it too contains drugs." Yet even to this statement, a hypertensive patient will sometimes counter with, "But at least I don't have to swallow the toothpaste."

We venture to prophesy that when the true cause of high blood pressure is discovered, part and parcel of this cause will be the singular personality complex we call Type A, one of whose facets is a dislike of being dependent upon either a doctor or his "expensive" prescriptions. In this connection, we should again like to point out that most Russian physicians believe in and also treat high blood pressure as a disorder whose provenance lies in a disturbed personality complex. We suspect that they are correct in this belief, but few of our scientific colleagues will even tolerate the possibility. It is of interest in this connection that although some of our medical leaders have agreed to do cooperative medical studies with their Russian counterparts, it was decided that the time was not yet quite right for any "cooperative" study concerning the causes of hypertension. We feel certain that the Russian scientists will not mind this exception.

Chapter 10

SOME PROBABLE— BUT STILL DEBATED— CAUSES OF CORONARY ARTERY DISEASE

As we have pointed out before, heart researchers are still arguing about the causes of coronary heart disease for one simple reason—nobody really knows enough about the problem as a whole to assign blame with pinpoint accuracy. We are still feeling our way, exploring coincidences, analyzing apparent linkages, weighing apparent contradictions in the evidence. Surprises are frequent, the solution of mysteries too often merely creates more mysteries, but over a period of years research efforts have yielded a list of fairly well-founded suspicions that may be termed "probable causes." Each has its sometimes vociferous proponents. Personally, we believe that this list of probable causes is disastrously incomplete without inclusion of the Type A syndrome we ourselves discovered—but anyone concerned about avoiding a heart attack must pay careful attention to all these factors. There is no question but that each of them is implicated, even though we have yet to discover just how, and how much.

DIETARY IMPRUDENCES

There are few heart researchers who do not suspect that the dietary habits of Western man play some part in causing coronary artery disease. On the other hand, few of them are absolutely convinced that these habits play a major role. For each piece of data implicating the usual Western diet, another piece of evidence tends to confuse matters.

For example, the strongest indictment of diet arises from the fact that, as we have pointed out, it is possible to induce coronary artery disease in certain animals—rabbits, monkeys, pigs, pigeons, and chickens —simply by feeding them *excess* cholesterol. This has been known since the beginning of the century. Were it not for this finding, all the other evidence we have accumulated about the relationship between heart disease and the food we eat would have to be considered suggestive at best, chimerical at worst.

Nevertheless, it isn't hard proof. Certain other animals—rats and dogs, for instance—escape having coronary artery disease no matter how much cholesterol is added to their diet. Their blood cholesterol level can't be changed, and they don't exhibit arterial lesions. Moreover, even such susceptible animals as rabbits and monkeys don't get coronary artery disease unless they are fed prodigious quantities of cholesterol. If they receive only the tiny amount present in our diet, nothing is likely to happen. Further, these susceptible animals are being fed a substance they never ingest in nature, while the other species—dogs and rats—which *do* normally eat foods containing cholesterol, are relatively immune to the excessive doses fed them in the laboratory.

The second fact that makes a large number of scientists suspect that our diet may be playing a role in the production of coronary artery disease is that fully half of all persons who display symptoms of coronary heart disease show elevations in their serum cholesterol levels. Moreover, persons who do not yet have coronary heart disease but who show the same high serum levels of cholesterol are far more likely to go on to develop coronary heart disease than subjects exhibiting a normal serum cholesterol level. Since the serum cholesterol level is somewhat related to the amount of cholesterol ingested, you can easily understand why scientists once more must be suspicious of the American diet. However, other factors besides dietary cholesterol and fat intake can and do elevate the serum cholesterol level. Thus, attempts on the part of a few epidemiologists to attribute *total* responsibility of high serum cholesterol levels to the dietary intake of cholesterol, fat, or both must be regarded as evidence of overenthusiasm.

The third collection of data that strengthens the suspicions of scientists about the possible dangers of our Western diet is this: the incidence of coronary heart disease is high in almost *every nation* whose average intake of cholesterol and/or animal fat is high and—conversely—relatively low in every nation whose intake of cholesterol and/or animal fat is low. The Japanese, for example, have been found to ingest far less animal fat (and possibly cholesterol, too) than the inhabitants of most Western countries, and they suffer much less from coronary heart disease than the persons of any Western country. But once again scientists are confronted with some damaging statistical paradoxes.

Perhaps the data that most effectively subvert the enthusiastic claims of the dietary enthusiasts are those which they themselves first discovered but now prefer never to mention. For example, though persons of certain countries eat approximately the same diet as persons of certain other countries, they may show inexplicably different rates of coronary heart disease. The people of Finland ingest approximately as much cholesterol and animal fat as the people of Holland, but have almost two and a half times more coronary heart disease. Likewise the Swiss ingest just about the same amount of cholesterol and fat as the Scots, yet their rate of coronary heart disease is only half that of Scotland. Even more disconcerting to those enthusiasts who believe that coronary artery disease is chiefly due to a high cholesterol and animal fat intake is the case of the Finns living in the eastern half of Finland. They eat the same amount of cholesterol and fat as the Finns living in the western half of the country but they suffer almost twice as frequently from coronary heart disease. These discrepant data, of course, suggest that food just can't be the total or even the major answer to the question of what causes coronary artery disease.

But other, even more jolting data have been uncovered. For example, the Navajo Indians ingest as much—or more—cholesterol and animal fat as their Caucasian American neighbors, yet they rarely if ever suffer from coronary heart disease. "Why don't they?" so many heart researchers keep asking themselves. Likewise, the Masai tribesmen of Kenya, who ingest frighteningly huge amounts of cholesterol and animal fat, never suffer from coronary heart disease nor at autopsy are they found to have any coronary artery disease. "And why don't they?" again many heart rereachers keep asking.

Few serious heart researchers can be unaware of the study done by some Harvard nutritionists in which the diets and incidence of coronary heart disease of a large number of Bostonian Irishmen were compared with similar data obtained from their brothers who remained in Ireland. The results of this study indicated that although the brothers who remained on the Irish sod actually ate more cholesterol and animal fat than their emigrant Boston brothers, they suffered only half the heart attacks. What gave these stay-at-home Irishmen their protection?

The unavoidable fact is that both coronary artery disease and its end result, coronary heart disease, have increased at least fivefold in the United States during the past fifty years. If diet alone is truly guilty, then one would expect that the average dietary cholesterol and fat intake of Americans must also have increased fivefold in the same period. But as far as can be determined, the average individual consumption of cholesterol and animal fat does not appear to have increased at all since 1910. Certainly your grandparents knew what an egg was, or a pat of butter, a glass of milk, a piece of beef or pork. They recognized them as foods and consequently ate them. But most of these foods contain high quantities of cholesterol and animal fat. "Why didn't they suffer from coronary heart disease as we do?" is another question so many heart researchers keep asking themselves and also each other. It is a question most epidemiologists have avoided answering, and for a good reason—they can't!

There is a fourth observation about the Western diet that also tends to make most heart researchers view it with at least a modicum of suspicion. This has been the finding that the ingestion of excess simple sugars (and probably starches, too) can lead, in some but certainly not in all persons, to a rise in the fat level of their blood—and to a rise in their cholesterol-containing pre-beta lipoproteins. Then, too, some English investigators have published data that they believe suggest that a relatively high correlation exists both historically and demographically between the ingestion of simple sugars (that is, the sugar you use in your ordinary cooking, and which is also found in honey, syrups, fruits, and so on) and the incidence of coronary heart disease.

But once more, very few heart scientists are *convinced* that the sugar and starch components of our contemporary Western diet have been or are chiefly responsible for the swiftly rising incidence of coronary heart disease. The citizens of various Central and South American countries have been eating a diet high in sugar and starches for generations, yet manage to escape the ravages of coronary heart disease far more frequently than their North American neighbors. Furthermore, it is almost impossible to induce this disease in any experimental animal by adding even huge quantities of various kinds of sugars or starches to its diet. It is this last fact that more than any other bit of data prevents the acceptance of the dietary concept. Nevertheless, most scientists are aware of the fact that certain middle-aged American persons do seem to react to the presence of sugar in their diet with an increase in their blood pre-beta lipoprotein level. And since (as we previously observed) this particular lipoprotein is elevated in the blood of many persons suffering from coronary heart disease, it should produce little surprise that heart scientists have become wary of including too much carbohydrate in one's diet. We ourselves believe that subjects exhibiting Type A Behavior Pattern are particularly prone to developing a high level of cholesterol in their serum if they ingest an excess of simple sugars.

Finally, there is a fifth reason why some heart researchers implicate our dietary habits. Quite recently, it has been observed that most Americans now eat the greater part of their daily quota of food at the evening meal. This really is rather a new phenomenon. More often than not our grandparents ate a decent-sized breakfast (the antique "hearty breakfast"), a moderate lunch, and a light supper. Nowadays, it is gauche to refer to the evening meal as anything other than "dinner." Nor should it be called anything else—it's much too heavy to be termed a supper. In any event, it has been found that if we take most of our day's cholesterol and fat at the evening meal, the average cholesterol and fat content of our blood tends to increase.

These are very recent findings, and we have not yet had the opportunity of discovering the reaction of our research colleagues to them. But we would suspect that once again they would not be convinced of the overriding importance of this change in the eating habits of hundreds of thousands of Americans.

Many of the epidemiological studies concerned with the possible role of diet in the causation of coronary artery and heart disease have been executed with an almost unbelievable unawareness of the necessity of adequate controls. For example, in one of these studies jungle dwellers, most of whom were heavily infested with intestinal parasites and suffering from dozens of chronic infectious diseases, and all of whom belonged to a culture and socioeconomic milieu totally unlike that of our Western society, were compared with a group of American businessmen who were free of all parasitic and infectious diseases but who were immersed in and subject to the stresses and strains of modern American business life. Yet no regard at all was paid to these differences. Only the comparative dietary intake of cholesterol and fat, blood cholesterol levels, and the incidence of coronary heart disease were given attention. Is it any wonder that this study, which attributed the relative absence of heart disease in the natives to their low cholesterol and animal fat intake, met with a lukewarm reception?

In the press releases of dietary enthusiasts, laboratory scientists and physicians instinctively feel, there is not only exaggeration but bias. Not fully understanding the causes and reasons for this distrust of their results, the food epidemiologists continually strive to obtain new grants—totaling many millions of dollars—from Federal sources in order to repeat identical studies. Somehow they seem to hope that since they failed to convince their colleagues with the results of surveys involving mere hundreds, perhaps results obtained from exactly the same sort of studies done upon tens of thousands—at an approximate cost of a billion dollars—might so succeed.

It is time for our epidemiologists to realize that great medical discoveries are not dependent upon the number of animals or human beings being studied. It did not require the study of an army of smallpox victims, but only the marvelously close and precise scrutiny of several milkmaids' arms, for Jenner to discover his antismallpox vaccine. Pasteur also needed only one child bitten by a mad dog to work out his vaccine against rabies. In our own times, when Baron Howard Walter Florey and his associates saw twenty-four or twenty-five rats to whom they had given penicillin survive after being injected with a fatal strain of bacteria, they knew instantly that penicillin was a marvelously effective drug.

In short, after two decades in which scores of millions of dollars have been consumed in studying what Yemenites, Bantus, Serbs, Eskimos, Masai, Rendille, and scores of other groups eat, whatever of value that might be extracted from studies of this type has been extracted. Indeed, so many data have been extracted by so many different groups that now a veritable bedlam of statements and counterstatements blossom forth in medical journals and in the organs of mass media, leading to a state of confusion in our minds as well as in yours.

What then, if any, is the danger of our Western

diet? We believe that when *all* the laboratory, clinical, and epidemiological data are considered (and nothing is left out), it seems quite likely that it might be relatively difficult for you and for most other human beings to incur significant coronary artery disease if you never have ingested much more than 200 mg. of cholesterol a day (about the amount of cholesterol in about three teaspoons of egg yolk).

We say this because in the laboratory, no matter what means are employed to damage an artery, this same artery heals promptly and only a relatively tiny scar ensues—unless cholesterol is added to the diet. If, however, cholesterol is present in the diet, then what would have been an insignificant scar becomes a growing mass of cholesterol-filled cells that progressively narrows the lumen of the vessel. The danger of cholesterol entering into an injured area of an artery is not due to the fact that it simply accumulates in the repairing arterial tissue, but rather that its presence evokes a tumorlike increase in the number of new arterial cells. As we explained in Chapter 5, cholesterol is not an inert sort of arterial garbage; it is an irritating, growth-enhancing chemical. Its effect upon a damaged area of an artery is very similar to the effect of salt, which, when rubbed into a facial saber cut, doubles or triples the size of the resultant scar (as prewar Heidelberg University duelists knew quite well and indeed put to use).

It has been one of the unfortunate results of our excessive preoccupation with the diet's content of cholesterol and animal fat that we have paid—and still pay—so very little attention to the various kinds of traumas inflicted upon arteries and even less attention to those properties of an injured artery which make it turn into a tumorlike tissue when its injured cells are brought into intimate contact with cholesterol. If only we knew how to prevent or mitigate the intensity of these original injuries, or if we could dull the growth responses of the injured arteries to excess cholesterol, we wouldn't have to worry so much about the noxiousness of cholesterol and animal fat in our diet.

But until we do tackle these latter problems, you should restrict your intake of cholesterol and animal fat. At best, of course, you may only be feebly twisting the small tail of a very huge and awesome monster.

You must never forget that most of us Westerners now eat pretty much the same types and amounts of food. If these foods uniformly caused the early advent of serious coronary heart disease, all of us—and not just 5 to 10 percent of us—would fall prey to heart attacks. Obviously, other factors must be coming into play that either protect 90 percent of us or kill 10 percent of us. It is urgent, we believe, that these factors be uncovered. Meanwhile, you must not forget that one of the reasons dietary alterations are so fanatically advocated today is that many of us, still frustrated in our effective approaches to this disorder, sort of believe that doing something, no matter what, is better than doing nothing at all.

Have we been too critical in this section about the possible role of diet in producing coronary artery disease? Before you decide about this matter, may we request that you first read what the "task force"——composed of some of our leading heart scientists—assembled by our National Heart and Lung Institute, concluded in June 1971 about this subject:

Although there is some evidence to support the popular belief that blood lipids (i.e., blood fats and cholesterol) are *causally* related to arteriosclerosis, and that a decrease in total and saturated fats in diet may help to prevent . . . heart attack and stroke, the evidence is scientifically not entirely convincing. Therefore, recommendations concerning diet are based on *personal* impressions and *fragmentary* evidence rather than on *scientific* proof.*

Thus hath spoken our National Heart and Lung Institute—after several decades of spending millions of dollars to support dozens of epidemiological dietary studies!

CIGARETTE SMOKING

Although there is considerable controversy about whether America gave syphilis to Western society, there is universal agreement that she did confer tobacco upon the rest of the world sometime in the sixteenth century. And for several centuries afterward, the more thieves, bankrupts, and prostitutes England dumped upon America, the more tons of tobacco America dumped upon England. Just how devilishly attractive tobacco proved to be from the very first to many persons can be understood when it is recalled that only four years after Sir Francis Drake introduced pipe smoking into Queen Elizabeth's court circle, Edmund Spenser referred to tobacco as "divine" in his *Faerie Queene*.

But if tobacco has proved to be seductively attractive to some, it has also appeared to be a gift straight from hell to many others. From James I of England, who thundered in 1604 that tobacco was "a branch of the sins of drunkenness, which is the root of all sins," to Victorian essayist John Ruskin (who was certain that cigarette smoking was responsible for the demoralization he believed he was witnessing in the youngsters of continental Europe), political and literary figures have been attacking the use of tobacco for three and a half centuries—with, of course, little effect, be-

* The italics are our own.

cause, for every distinguished writer who condemned the smoking of tobacco, there were at least two others who extolled it. Charles Lamb wistfully wrote, "For thy sake, tobacco, I would do anything but die." Then there was Byron who described tobacco as "sublime" and Charles Kingsley who wrote that "there's no herb like unto it under the canopy of heaven."

A primary reason why the use of tobacco flourishes is its economic importance. Millions of persons owe their jobs to it. Perhaps even more important, like some other products a government is slightly embarrassed by, tobacco is taxed almost unmercifully. Governments of course rationalize that such high taxes will discourage the consumption of tobacco.

Unfortunately, however, they have become accustomed to the receipt of such taxes. Governments tend to be reluctant to do away with any product—even opium—when it provides such luscious, though sinful, revenues. If you believe this all fanciful thinking on our part, just try to name a senator from our South who has seen fit to indict cigarette smoking.

Historically speaking, the most serious development in the gloomy tale of Western man and his use of tobacco occurred during the Crimean War, when British and French troops were exposed to the Turkish fashion of smoking slender, short tubes of paper enclosing finely shredded tobacco—the cigarette. How rapidly since that time cigarette smoking has supplanted all other forms of tobacco consumption! It was not nauseating to witness or to smell; it seemed to offer a milder, gentler smoke; and it required so little mess and bother—just one flick of a match and then it took care of itself. Oscar Wilde summed up its advantages in 1891 when he wrote, "A cigarette is the perfect type of a perfect pleasure."

But this "perfect pleasure," because of the seeming mildness of its smoke, introduced Western man to a habit the pipe and cigar smoker had more or less avoided—the introduction of tobacco smoke directly into the lungs. Normally, the lungs act to remove, for the body's use, beneficial substances contained in the inhaled air, and to expel with the exhaled air all those impurities and waste products the body is well rid of. But when the cigarette smoker inhales smoke, his lungs remove the nicotine, carbon monoxide, and coal-tar products contained in the air coming in and then expel this same air relatively purified, at the body's expense. Crudely stated, the cigarette smoker uses his lungs as a sewer to rid the air he breathes of its pollutants.

Regardless of this ugly reversal of function brought about by cigarette smoking, the habit has enjoyed a frighteningly rapid growth in the United States. If statistics can impress you, then you might be interested to know that the smoking of cigarettes per person has increased over 8,000 percent in the United States during the last five decades!

You undoubtedly have already sensed that we do not aprove of this state of affairs. Like ninety-nine of every hundred physicians, we are *dead certain* that smoking is responsible for well over 95 percent of all lung, throat, and tongue cancers, as well as for a very great percentage of the crippling cases of emphysema. But what about the relationship between cigarette smoking and coronary artery disease? Certainly heavy cigarette smokers—persons smoking more than ten cigarettes a day—in America and in the United Kingdom are three or more times as likely to suffer the early onset of coronary heart disease as nonsmokers. We know of no American epidemiological study (including our own) which has failed to document this proclivity of the heavy cigarette user to coronary heart disease.

Given these statistics, why are some of us still rather

confused about the role of cigarette smoking in coronary artery disease? Why did a blue-ribbon committee, selected by the Surgeon General of the U.S. Public Health Service to study this relationship a few years ago, report after due deliberation that while male cigarette smokers did have a higher death rate from coronary heart disease than nonsmoking males, they were still not prepared to state that this statistical association had *causal* significance? There are several reasons.

First, the Surgeon General's committee—unlike the committee set up by the American Heart Association in 1960—noted clearly that the same studies that found the heavy cigarette smoker so vulnerable to heart disease also revealed that pipe smokers (and cigar smokers, too) did not appear to suffer from coronary heart disease any more frequently than nonsmokers. This seeming invulnerability of even the heavy pipe smoker moreover could not be due to his absorbing less nicotine. Pipe-tobacco smoke is even richer in this substance than cigarette smoke, and nicotine is about as easily absorbed from the mouth as from the lung. Indeed, long before sophisticated studies were done upon such matters, little boys attempting to smoke their father's pipe knew only too well how easy it was to become nauseated from the nicotine they absorbed from the pipe smoke that, in their case, went no further than their mouths and throats. In other words, if nicotine is the villain, then why shouldn't pipe smokers run the same risk? The Surgeon General's committee failed to find the answer to this question—perhaps one of the major reasons why the committee hesitated to brand cigarette smoking as a cause of coronary heart disease.

But the government committee, again far more discriminating and sapient than its counterpart committee of the American Heart Association, also noted that persons susceptible, and exposed, to emotional stress smoked far more than persons not so afflicted. It might be this stress that not only led to increased cigarette smoking but also to increased coronary heart disease. This, of course, was a rather daring thought to entertain, so the committee quickly retreated to a relatively mushy but far safer position. They concluded that their findings did not permit them to make any "definitive statements" with respect to the relative role of psychological factors and smoking in the causation of coronary heart disease. Later we shall discuss the matter of personality and cigarette smoking, and we *shall* make some "definitive statements."

But the government committee also probably refrained from indicting cigarette smoking as a cause of coronary heart disease because the members of the committee were well aware of the fact that a large fraction of patients suffering from coronary artery disease never smoked cigarettes during their entire lifetime. This fact alone proved that if cigarette smoking truly did lead to heart trouble, it certainly was not the only agent capable of doing so.

Even more baffling to this same committee were the Japanese statistics. Despite the fact that the Japanese smoke almost the same number of cigarettes as Westerners, they still escape the ravages of coronary disease with relative ease. For example, the Japanese smoke approximately 1,667 cigarettes per adult per year, about the same number (1,925 cigarettes per year) as the Finns smoke, yet for every nine Finns dying of coronary heart disease per year, only one Japanese dies. This discrepancy is also seen between the American and Japanese coronary mortality rates. Why does the cigarette appear to be so innocuous to the Japanese and so lethal to Westerners? Certainly it cannot be any racial immunity at play, because when the Japanese emigrate to and live in the United States, their coronary mortality rate rises to the same level as that of native-born Caucasian Americans.

These striking statistics have been and still are "being swept under the rug" by many of our current epidemiologists. Yet even if these epidemiologists believe that the airing of such discrepancies in public would serve only to "confuse and bewilder" the people, consider how *disillusioned*, besides being confused and bewildered, this same public will be when eventually it learns—as it will—that its trusted health leaders were lacking in candor? Isn't there the danger that in the future they might (as so many of our disillusioned youngsters do now) sneer at any advice, even though it might be perfectly sound?

There is also another reason why it is unwise for researchers to disregard this peculiar Japanese immunity to the reputed coronary artery-injuring property of cigarette smoking. It is that the close study of just such an exception to a general rule has, in the past, so frequently uncovered an even more important or relevant general rule or truth lying hidden beneath a currently accepted generality, one that may be of far more importance and pragmatic relevance.

Nicotine, one of the constituents of cigarette smoke (but certainly not the only and possibly not even the most noxious one), has been extensively studied in the laboratories. The drug is certainly a stimulant of the nervous system, including not only the brain but peripheral nerves as well. It particularly excites nerves that continue to perform their function whether you consciously wish or order them to do so or not, that is, that portion of your nervous system, which we call the *sympathetic nervous system*, whose function is to regulate and control your internal organs every single microsecond of your life. Such nicotine stimulation can and probably does lead to the overproduction by these nerves of two substances—epinephrine (or adrenalin) and norepinephrine (or noradrenalin). Either of these two substances, when circulating in excess in the blood, are not healthy at all for the delicate lining or wall of an artery. If an artery is exposed too long to too great a concentration of either or both of these two nerve-manufactured chemicals, the artery will definitely sustain serious damage. Indeed, if the blood concentration of these substances is high enough, the artery may be destroyed quite rapidly. As far as we can determine, however, the blood of even an avid smoker of cigarettes never contains such extremely high levels. But it is quite possible that the blood of these persons can contain a sufficiently high level of either epinephrine or norepinephrine to permit some slight arterial damage. Granted that this blood level may not be terribly high; nevertheless, if it is attained twenty to forty times a day (by the smoking of twenty to forty cigarettes), and this continues year after year, severe chronic arterial damage may very well ensue.

Have researchers been able to induce coronary artery disease in any experimental animal by the latter's chronic exposure to concentrated cigarette smoke or to injections of nicotine? No, not really. But if certain animals that are fed excessive cholesterol are also injected with nicotine, there has been obtained some rather middling evidence that suggests that coronary artery disease is worsened in these animals.

There also has been obtained some rather doubtful evidence that certain clotting elements in the blood of heavy cigarette smokers may be altered in such a fashion that they will deposit more readily upon the lining of their coronary arteries. Such evidence should not be airily dismissed; severe coronary artery disease develops, in man, not in a day, week, month, or even a year, but over several decades. Consequently, whatever the defects are that promote this disease, they are not too obvious when examined, let us say, on the

12,775th day of a man's expected 25,550-day biblical life span. Hence these defects, when observed in any given experimental period, may appear as almost insignificant, even though they most definitely are not.

The truly undisputed danger in smoking, of course, is its cancer-producing potential. Time after time, when treating patients with coronary heart disease, we gained at best a Pyrrhic victory. After forestalling a second bout of heart disease, we then saw our patients succumb to a far worse fate—lung cancer. Coronary artery and also coronary heart disease occur quite frequently in persons who have *never* smoked a cigarette, cigar, or pipe, but we cannot recall in our own experience having treated a single case of *primary* lung cancer occurring in a patient who had not smoked cigarettes. Yes, we know that a number of documented cases of primary cancer of the lung have been recorded in the medical literature as occurring in persons who have never smoked. But neither we nor most of our own intimate medical colleagues have seen many such cases!

We believe that cigarette smoking may injure your coronary as well as your other arteries, just as we have indicated that diabetes and hypertension probably directly injure arteries. But we believe that if cigarette smoking were the *only* insult you offered your coronary arteries, their degree of disease might be about as minimal as that shown by the coronary vasculature of the heavily smoking Japanese. But if you were to add to this moderate arterial insult a life-long custom of ingesting excess cholesterol and animal fat, such as so many Americans and other Westerners do, then the two habits acting together conceivably could triple or quadruple the evil effects of either acting alone.

But truthfully, we can't be absolutely certain even about this last statement. Subjects exhibiting Type A Behavior Pattern smoke inordinately more cigarettes than subjects exhibiting Type B Behavior Pattern, and we know that Type A subjects, whether they smoke or not, are far more susceptible to coronary artery and coronary heart disease than Type B subjects. So we may be attributing to only a characteristic (that is, cigarette smoking), which is part and parcel of a behavior pattern, responsibility for enhancing a disease, when it is the behavior pattern itself that is truly effecting the damage to the coronary artery. You might find it hard to believe that so many medical researchers could be this naïve—to confound the tail of a horse with the horse itself. But we have already referred to just such an error in our long-held belief that a high blood sugar was the overwhelmingly important derangement in diabetes. We also have pointed out that a high serum cholesterol may also not be the prime protagonist in coronary artery disease, but only an indication of the presence of other far more devastating agents at work.

PHYSICAL INACTIVITY

Right from the outset, we wish you to know that we believe, as every physician we have ever known believes, that physical activity of the proper kind and amount is an eminently salutary adjunct of a well-balanced life. Indeed, we have watched with fascination and growing dismay the ingenuity with which Western man is supplanting human muscle energy with fossil fuel, nuclear, and electrical power.

Because this machine-induced physical indolence has increased at about the same rate as the incidence of coronary heart disease in America, it is deeply suspect as a possible causal agent. There are a number of cardiologists who have become virtual zealots for this point of view. Some, having avoided heart disease, attribute their own immunity to their particular favorite form of exercise. Others, having suffered coronary heart disease after failing to exercise, are just as certain that exercise might have saved them. Both types, with almost messianic fervor, have gone to the organs of mass media to "enlighten" their fellow citizens about the virtues of exercise in general, and of their own favorite form of exercise in particular. Hundreds of other physicians and thousands of physical education directors have joined in this propaganda campaign. Dozens of books and hundreds of pamphlets have been published, and thousands of television and radio shows broadcast. As you might expect, plenty of nonmedical cranks have also tried to preach their views on exercise.

As a result, thousands of Americans now walk, jog, sprint, run in marathon contests, bicycle, swim, climb mountains, and hit, kick, or throw all sorts of balls ranging from Ping-Pong balls to volley balls. At this writing, however, few persons seem to be playing marbles.

But again, the question is whether the absence of physical activity (that is, physical indolence) leads to coronary artery disease. What solid, incontrovertible evidence do we have that indicates that physical activity may provide you with protection against coronary artery disease? We have almost none whatsoever. This may come as a surprise, so we had better review some of the studies done on the subject.

It has been an extraordinarily difficult feat for medical investigators in the past to assess the effects of exercise on coronary arteries, because until just a few years ago we had no instrument by which we could measure or even estimate their interior diameter. Even now, although we do have such instrumentation, its use carries a bit of risk (see page 37). No medical investigator can subject healthy volunteers to a test that carries even the slightest risk. As a consequence, we still have no studies that show beyond any doubt the relationship between exercise, the condition of normal coronary arteries, and coronary artery disease. There is nothing to indicate directly that any form of exercise modifies the structure of the coronary arteries! And mind you, if physical activity is to protect against coronary artery disease, it must prevent these arteries from becoming narrowed by atherosclerosis. In other words, no matter how good exercise may be for the muscular element of your heart, if it doesn't specifically prevent your coronary arteries from narrowing, it cannot stave off early coronary artery disease. We wish to emphasize again that coronary heart disease never *begins* with the muscles of the heart.

Thus when Chuck Hughes, the Detroit Lion star, collapsed and died October 24, 1971, on the football field after having received a forward pass, it was not his fine, healthy, superbly trained and conditioned heart muscle that felled him, but a blood clot that had formed in a severely diseased coronary artery.

This football catastrophe dramatically disproves the widespread belief that because exercise "trains" the heart to beat more slowly and more vigorously, it must also be good for the coronary arteries. No such thing at all! The exercise is simply enhancing the vigor of the heart muscle and its subjection to nervous control, which has absolutely no bearing on the state of the coronary arteries. If you happen to begin a daily series of exercises and observe that you can do these same exercises later with less breathlessness and with a smaller elevation of your pulse rate, you may take what pleasure you can from the fact that your heart muscle may be functioning more efficiently. But *never* assume that your coronary arteries have changed one iota, either in their size or in the amount of cholesterol/fat debris that they initially possessed.

Remember that many old ladies of eighty years of age possess heart muscle almost as fragile as the lace some of them love to wear about their necks. But just as long as their coronary arteries remain sufficiently open, their fragile heart muscle will never get them into any difficulties, even after the passage of several more decades.

In other words, allow physical education directors, retired coaches, and even doctors—who should know better—to enjoy their achievements in terms of a pulse and breathing rate gradually decreased by exercise, but don't allow yourself ever to be misled into thinking that these phenomena necessarily demonstrate an improvement in the condition of your coronary arteries. Perhaps sometime in the future we will be able safely to check the coronary arteries of subjects before, during, and after various types of exercise. Then, and only then, will we be able to state that exercise has been demonstrated to afford some protection to the coronary vasculature.

This may never happen. Medical investigators *have* been able to study the effects of exercise upon the coronary arteries of various animals, to find out whether exercise promotes the growth of new coronary artery branches (that is, collateral vessels) to "bypass" those areas of the original coronary arteries which have been severely narrowed. Most of these studies have failed to show that exercise does anything of the kind. This has been crushing news to those who had and perhaps still do hope that exercise may open new vessels in the hearts of those patients who have suffered a complete closure of one or more of their three major coronary arteries.

Nor have the studies done on such creatures as the dog, rabbit, rat, or chicken given us much reason for believing that exercise may alter the blood cholesterol level or prevent the atherosclerotic process responsible for the narrowing of the original coronary arteries. Indeed, one investigator found the average blood choles-

terol level and the degree of coronary atherosclerosis
of his exercised dogs to be much worse than those of
his unexercised dogs. Admittedly, however, there are
a few reports that suggest at least that in other species
(for example, the rabbit and chicken) perhaps exercise
can hold their blood cholesterol down and impede the
rate of narrowing in their coronary arteries when these
animals are fed excess cholesterol. All in all, however,
the experimental results are at best flimsy.

Epidemiologists have also tackled the problem of
the effect of exercise upon your coronary arteries. But
they have succeeded only in contradicting each other,
or even worse, have drawn conclusions that are at
variance with their own data.

Quite a few years ago, a seemingly beautifully designed study was done on drivers and conductors on
London's double-decker buses and trams. The results
at first glance suggested that the conductors, who presumably had to climb frequently (hence exercise) during their tour of duty, incurred coronary heart disease
significantly less often than the drivers who engaged in
no exercise during their work period. But when we
ourselves critically examined the data of this study, it
became clear that the original investigators had not
taken into account the fact that the drivers of the bus
or tram, unlike the conductors, were constantly exposed to another factor—the acute emotional stress of
driving itself.

The possible importance of this type of stress became quite clear when we separated the drivers and
the conductors of the buses traversing only the inner,
heavily congested central area of London from their
counterparts on buses and trams that traversed the peripheral regions of London. When such a separation
was made, we found that the drivers of the buses of
the periphery of London—the least physically active
group of all—actually incurred coronary heart disease

less often than the conductors of the buses traversing central London, the group that got the most exercise and should have been most immune. This analysis, of course, reduced the final conclusions of the authors to nonsense.

When we published our analysis of their published data, the senior investigator of the original London study wrote a protesting letter to the editor of the medical journal. While he admitted that our analyses were correct and that he couldn't explain them, nevertheless he insisted that traffic was just as congested in the suburbs of London as it was in its inner central zone. We were amused a few weeks later when the British Parliament appointed a committee to investigate what could be done to ease the traffic congestion in the inner central square mile of London. Some day —although it may not be soon—investigators may realize that in trying to find the causes of diseases by studying large population groups, they must take into account *all* the possible variables that may be present. Without hazard to their own reputation and also that of medicine itself, researchers cannot go on blithely ignoring or rationalizing away any possible variant they find too inconvenient or "messy" to take into account.

We again stress this last danger, which always presents itself to the epidemiologist, in connection with the Harvard-sponsored study of Boston Irishmen and their brothers in Ireland we have mentioned before. Repeatedly, the investigators concerned with this study had been advised of the necessity of taking into account a *specific* emotional complex that might or might not be operating in either of the two population growths. This advice was not heeded. As a result, despite the expenditure of time (at least seven years) and money (probably hundreds of thousands of dollars), and despite the statistical sophistication with which the researchers treated their raw data, their published reports end by merely *assuming*, without demonstrating, that the greater amounts of physical activity indulged in by the brothers in Ireland was possibly responsible for their comparatively marked immunity to coronary heart disease. It would be interesting to see how these same Harvard investigators might go about explaining the terribly high incidence of coronary heart disease in the rural Finns, who probably indulge in just as much exercise as the Irish.

Perhaps the best epidemiological study concerning physical activity and coronary heart disease was one done on thousands of American railwaymen. The results of this study have indicated that those who must do physical labor in performing their jobs (brakemen, for example) incur coronary heart disease just as frequently as those who do no physical labor (clerks, for example). Again, how carefully other variables were controlled in this study we cannot know.

Finally, in Georgia an ongoing study is attempting to discover a relationship between income level and susceptibility to coronary heart disease. Once again, however, there has been a failure to take *all* variables into account. The unbiased observer can only conclude at this point that the study's finding of relative immunity for the low-income group is no more useful than the findings of the Harvard group. Whatever it is that is protecting the low-income group from coronary heart disease, it does not appear to be any difference in their diet, in their blood cholesterol level, or in their smoking habits.

A third method of studying the possible effects of exercise upon the state of the coronary arteries has been postmortem examination. Several studies have been done on the coronary vasculature of persons who have indulged in considerable physical activity and of those who had been physically indolent during their lifetime. The results suggest that there is just as much coronary artery and heart disease in those who were active as in those who were not. But there is considerable question in our minds about the reliability of the data obtained in these several studies. We suspect that a definitive study has yet to be undertaken.

Certainly those doctors who enthusiastically jog or otherwise exert themselves are not at all convinced of the reliability of the pathological studies. Almost to a man, they will point out that a certain Mr. De Mar, who had been a marathon runner for fifty years, was found at his death to possess lovely coronary arteries, almost three times wider than the coronary arteries observed in most normal subjects. Mr. De Mar died well over a decade ago, but we suspect that jogging and running enthusiasts in 1990 will still remember Mr. De Mar's huge coronary arteries and argue that they know what caused them to become so huge.

If jogging ever requires a patron saint, certainly Mr. De Mar will be chosen. Well and good; but let our enthusiastically exercising medical colleagues also keep in mind the late Paavo Nurmi, the Finnish athlete whose skill in long-distance running half a century ago catapulted him into repeated Olympic championships and athletic immortality. Such grueling physical activity did not prevent Mr. Nurmi from suffering a coronary in his sixties. Several years ago in Helsinki, when we had the pleasure of dining with him, he asked us what we thought was the chief cause of coronary heart disease. We replied, "Type A Behavior Pattern," and proceeded by means of our interpreter to explain to him precisely what this pattern was. He listened carefully to us. Then he said tersely, "I agree. That's what probably caused my first heart attack."

If scientific evidence tends to discourage complete confidence in the prophylactic virtues of exercise, then clinical studies designed to determine the possible effect of exercise upon blood cholesterol and fat levels are even less confidence-inspiring. At best, the various reports are vague, at worst directly contradictory. For example, the Masai tribesman's low blood cholesterol has been attributed by several investigators to his physical activity, despite the fact that after forty years of age the average tribesman simply sits about—but his blood cholesterol nevertheless still remains low. Also, we are not convinced that just because men tend cattle every day they necessarily engage in exhausting physical activity. Then, too, the most recent scientific observers of the Masai play down the possible role of exercise in his immunity to coronary heart disease. These latest observers attribute such immunity to hereditary factors.

Then there have been various volunteer groups of American students and businessmen who have agreed to exercise a given amount of time each day and to eat a standard diet. The results of some of these studies suggest that the blood cholesterol is lowered by the exercise regimen, but the results of other, similar studies show no such effect. Therefore, anyone reading these articles is left vaguely confused. At least that is how we have felt after perusing them.

There is no good solid evidence that physical indolence leads to coronary artery disease or that physical activity protects against the same disorder. Yet, like most physicians, we cannot help believing that despite the paucity and inadequacy of the data now available to us, moderate physical activity somehow or other may help to delay the actual onset of coronary heart disease, even if it does not prevent or even slow down the underlying coronary artery disease. We suspect that if a coronary artery is growing narrower because of the arterial disease it harbors, physical activity conceivably could enhance nature's attempts to circumvent this narrowing by encouraging the development of collateral vessels. And if you were to ask us how much of this belief of ours is founded on wishful thinking, we would be forced to reply, "Quite a bit."

Beyond this, we realize only too well that physical exercise can be, at best, only a moderately effective prophylactic measure. For example, if you suffer from one of the certain causes of coronary artery disease (described in Chapter 10) or if you possess a Type A Behavior Pattern, any real faith in the prophylactic potential of physical activity might be dangerously illusory. Under certain circumstances, which we will discuss later, some kinds of physical activity can actually bring on acute attacks of coronary heart disease. This is a ghastly possibility to which some of our exercise-addicted medical colleagues still resolutely refuse to face up.

HEREDITARY FACTORS

This summer in America, 1887, I began to think that my time was really coming to an end. I had so much pain in my chest, the sign of a malady which had suddenly struck down in middle life, long before they came to my present age, both my father and grandfather.

So wrote Matthew Arnold, the distinguished English poet and essayist, in a letter to a friend. He must thus be considered the first person—lay or medical—to note the suspected role of heredity in the occurrence of coronary heart disease. Now almost all physicians and medical scientists agree that heredity can and often does play a part in bringing on coronary artery disease.

Despite such near medical unanimity concerning the probable influences of heredity upon the course of coronary artery disease, considerable uncertainty still exists concerning the specific mechanisms altered, or set into motion, by hereditary factors. Certainly all physicians would agree that one of these mechanisms involves the control of cholesterol metabolism. As we have already discussed, certain types of hypercholesterolemia are inheritable, and when present invariably lead first to coronary artery and then to coronary heart disease. Similarly, hypertension and diabetes may be inheritable, and as we previously pointed out, both these diseases can hasten and aggravate the course of coronary artery disease.

However, even in the absence of hereditary hypercholesterolemia, hypertension, or diabetes, those whose parents (either of them) suffered from coronary heart disease still exhibit a significantly greater incidence of coronary heart disease than the offspring of parents who have been free of this disease. Are they vulnerable to coronary heart disease because they first develop a more severe degree of coronary artery disease? Or is it because they are far more prone to injure or narrow their coronary arteries in other ways in addition to their basic coronary artery atherosclerosis? Or are they more liable to suffer from heart disease because they have inherited coronary arteries that lack the usual potential of such arteries to enlarge and carry more blood if one or more of the three of them narrows too greatly or too abruptly? Or, perhaps, are they more prone to form clots upon their coronary artery plaques, thus greatly or even completely obstructing the remaining flow of coronary blood? Medical scientists are still not able to answer these questions.

In other words, excepting hereditary hypercholesterolemia and hypertension and diabetes, medical scientists frankly do not know just what frailties these particular offspring inherit. It is well within the realm of possibility that only too often they inherit from one or both of their afflicted parents a specific type of personality, one that may give rise to a behavior pattern —which in turn leads to diseased coronary arteries.

Obviously, medical scientists at this juncture should not content themselves solely with repeatedly collecting statistics that demonstrate hereditarily transmitted susceptibility to coronary heart disease. It now is urgently necessary that the *specific* mechanisms or factors that are being hereditarily transmitted be identified with precision and certainty. We have been "wringing our hands" helplessly about this matter for more than five decades. Now we need to use our hands to "dig" and discover the processes-at-play.

If one or both of your parents have suffered from coronary heart disease, are you inevitably doomed to suffer from the same disease? Not at all! Statistics only indicate that your *chance*s of incurring this disease may be about twice those of your friends whose parents have remained free of it. You might then ask whether you can feel fairly confident that you won't incur this disease if neither of your parents has or had incurred it? Yes, you can feel slightly more secure, but not really very much more so. As we shall point out later, you are being exposed to—and reacting to—a milieu totally different from that which confronted your parents.

There do appear to be hereditary influences at work in the pathogenesis of coronary artery disease. Certainly, if both your parents have hypertension or hypercholesterolemia or diabetes, your chances of escaping serious coronary artery disease are only fair. If but one of your parents has one or more of these three diseases, you still should certainly take advantage of every possible *effective* prophylactic measure that is or will be available in the future.

Unfortunately, abnormalities other than the above three disorders may also be inheritable and play a very decisive role in determining either the degree of coronary artery disease or heart disease that may develop in various persons. It is quite likely that certain hereditary factors influence solely the basic or initial disease (coronary atherosclerosis), whereas other hereditary factors, given the presence of the basic coronary artery disease, lead to serious complications, thus evoking coronary heart disease itself. Therefore, one person may easily live out a life span of seventy-five years without symptoms, even though his coronary *artery* disease is relatively far advanced, whereas another person may suffer severely from coronary heart disease at thirty-five years of age, having no greater degree of basic coronary artery disease than the former. It remains for us medical researchers to identify the nature of these factors and the mechanisms they employ to bring about such catastrophes.

OBESITY

If you were to sit in the reception room of a busy cardiologist for several afternoons and observe his patients, you would not be struck by their obesity. While it is possible that one or two out of thirty to fifty persons were a bit roly-poly, few of them would appear to be downright fat. Well-nourished, yes; perhaps a bit on the burly side; but not grossly overweight. You also would probably not see a single, quite tall (over six feet), very lean or almost gaunt individual. Certainly, neither of us can ever remember detecting coronary heart or artery disease in a six-foot person (under sixty-five years of age) weighing normally less than 160 pounds. Undoubtedly there probably are such very lean individuals suffering from heart disease, but we just haven't managed to see one yet.

Now if the cardiologist invited you into one of his examining rooms to observe these same persons in the undressed state, you would then note that most but not all the male and female patients were carrying about ten to twenty pounds of excess fatty tissue about their abdomens, flanks and thighs. This moderate amount of excess body weight was not observed in the reception room because it was concealed to a large extent by the skill of modern tailoring. But though these coronary patients do carry some excess fat-ridden flesh, so do most middle-aged or elderly Americans and Europeans. The slight to moderate overweight of the average coronary patient, then, is not a signature of his disease, but rather of his status as a citizen of Western society.

This last reality is the chief reason why there is so much confusion and contradiction about the role of obesity in the causation of coronary artery disease. In various studies, the average person not afflicted with coronary heart disease exhibits as much overweight as his counterpart who does have coronary artery or heart disease. Even so, most well-executed epidemiological studies do suggest that obese persons are more prone to the occurrence of severe coronary artery disease. Possibly the greater tendency of obese individuals to diabetes accounts for the greater incidence of coronary disease in the ranks of the obese. If, however, we were to study only those obese persons who show no tendencies whatsoever to later develop diabetes, it is highly unlikely that we would find such individuals any more susceptible than their slimmer counterparts to coronary artery disease. If obesity, then, is to bring on coronary disease, it must first bring on diabetes, and although most diabetics are overweight, relatively few overweight persons become diabetic.

If this last is true, why was simple and uncomplicated obesity ever thought to bear an important relationship to coronary artery and heart disease? Because a number of years ago life insurance actuaries published statistics relating the mortality rates of their policy holders according to their body weights. Such statistics did show a moderate relationship of body weight to coronary mortality. But body weight is determined not just by the fat of the body, but also by the weight of the skeleton and muscle mass. Taken as a whole, men prone to coronary heart disease are better muscled (the anthropologists label such heavily muscled persons *mesomorphs*) and probably do possess a heavier bone structure. Indeed, several cardiologists have been deeply impressed with the possibility that the burliness of a man may lead to his having early heart disease. We believe that the enthusiasm of these particular cardiologists far transcends their ability to derive valid conclusions from the data they have collected. We say this because if some cardiologists believe that the more muscle a man carries the more liable he is to incur heart disease, such cardiologists should not encourage (as at least some are doing now) Americans to develop a greater muscle mass by indulgence in vigorous physical activity. The American people have no right to expect all their doctors to be Pasteurs, but they do have the right to expect them to possess common sense.

If no clear-cut relationship exists between moderate degrees of obesity (uncomplicated by diabetes) and coronary artery disease, there may well be such a relationship between extreme obesity and the disorder. After all, very few professional "fat ladies" become septuagenarians. We ourselves haven't treated any obese persons. However, one of our friends, who in his earlier years had acted as the agent for a side show "fat lady," reported to us that she died at the age of thirty-five years. And while he was not certain that she died of heart disease, he does remember that, weighing well over four hundred pounds, she resisted any sort of physical exercise.

If food does play a part in bringing on coronary artery disease—and we are fairly sure that it does—it would appear that the critical issue is not how much you eat, but rather what you eat, and possibly how frequently you eat. If obesity does increase the incidence of coronary artery disease, it probably does so by first bringing on diabetes. But even if we could make every American slim, we still would not reduce the incidence of coronary artery disease very much. Regardless of all the other illnesses that have been attributed to obesity, you will probably be well advised not to put too much blame on this product of human frailty as a cause of coronary artery disease.

Chapter 11

EAT? SMOKE?
EXERCISE?

Assuming that you are not suffering from one of the certain causes of coronary artery and heart disease (and luckily most of you aren't), and also assuming that you are a youngish man (that is, under forty years of age), we can declare categorically that if *all* our instructions in this chapter and in the rest of the book are *meticulously* heeded and followed, your chances of suffering a heart attack before you are in your seventies or eighties will be very slim indeed!

This is a rather cocksure statement. What proof can we present for its validity? Simply this: in writing the next two chapters we shall assume that not only are *our* ideas of the precipitating causes of coronary heart disease correct, but also that all those of our colleagues are similarly correct. Therefore, regardless of how important in the total frame of causes we personally believe such-and-such a scientist's "pet cause" may be, if its attempted eradication can do no harm to a subject, we shall give instructions for its eradication.

But might there still be causes yet undiscovered, rendering all your efforts fruitless? In short, no. We believe that medical scientists do know *all* the causes of this disease, even though we still argue bitterly amongst ourselves about the relative importance of each. The difficulty surrounding the treatment of coronary heart disease is not that we don't know its causes, it is that there are so many causes!

DIETARY ADVICE THAT CAN'T POSSIBLY HARM AND MIGHT DO YOU QUITE A BIT OF GOOD

If all Americans from birth had *never* smoked cigarettes, and if they had never succumbed to Type A Behavior Pattern, this chapter would be superfluous. There is not one bit of evidence now available to indicate that a nondiabetic, nonhypertensive individual who has *never* smoked cigarettes and who always has been and remains a Type B subject, will ever get coronary heart disease just by ingesting a diet rich in cholesterol and animal fat.

What we are saying is that dietary cholesterol and animal fat *by themselves* probably do not cause coronary heart disease, but if they are teamed up with excess cigarette smoking (that is, over ten cigarettes per day), or severe Type A Behavior Pattern, they may become deadly. Indeed, in our own personal experience we cannot remember more than a handful of persons who ever reached the age of sixty years without suffering from coronary heart disease, hypertension, or cancer of the lung if they (1) had smoked more than twenty cigarettes a day, (2) had exhibited the *severe* form of Type A behavior, and (3) ingested a diet rich in cholesterol and animal fat.

Since well over half of all urban Americans either smoke excessively, or exhibit Type A Behavior Pattern, it seems to us to make good sense to advocate food habits that will ensure that these addicted or afflicted persons will not be compounding the insults to their coronary arteries.

But you may ask, "Suppose I quit smoking and rid myself of my Type A behavior. Need I still change my food habits?" We believe that you still must make the change because your arteries have probably already been injured by the tobacco or behavior pattern. We have described the unfaltering ease with which dietary-excess cholesterol, once it is taken up in the blood, seeks out previously damaged arteries to accumulate and derange the healing process. We've known patients who developed coronary heart disease as much as a decade after they gave up excessive cigarette smoking, just as we've known many patients who have died of lung cancer many years after they gave up the habit that caused the cancer, namely that same smoking of cigarettes.

The first objective of any dietary regimen for the prevention of coronary heart disease is to keep the serum cholesterol level of a person *as low as possible*, not just at the so-called American "normal" level. We again stress this point because whereas the so-called "normal" serum cholesterol level of the average adult American is generally considered to be any value under 275 mg./100 ml., and that of the person under twenty-one years of age any value under 200 mg./100 ml., these levels are probably not low enough to be safe. Ideally, an adult's cholesterol level should be the same as that of persons of other races who never get coronary heart disease. Such a value would be approximately 150-175 mg./100 ml.

The second objective is to furnish a sufficient amount of not only protein, fat, and carbohydrate, but also of the necessary minerals and vitamins. The third objective of any dietary regimen is that the regimen be one that is simple to follow and doesn't require a slide rule or a computer to understand.

The fourth objective is to present foods that are as attractive and as tempting as the ones they are replacing. It is this last objective that scores of dietitians, having satisfied themselves of the accuracy of their calorie and vitamin requirements, completely ignore. The food presented to a hospital patient is dietetically elegant, but only too often abominable in aesthetic and sensuous terms. This, fortunately, is happening less and less these days, as master chefs take over the direction of hospital kitchens.

First, let us look at foods you usually eat and see how much cholesterol, fat, protein, carbohydrates, and simple sugars they contain. Table 1 gives the approximate amount of these various constituents, and also their approximate caloric values. Obviously, some vegetables and fruits will have more protein, fat, or carbohydrates than others, but for purposes of simplification we have calculated the *average* composition of commonly eaten foods. Of course, if you only eat avocados, our "fruit" values will not be of much help to you. On the other hand, if endives are your vegetable, our "vegetable" values will also be misleading.*

Table 2 depicts the composition and caloric value of a typical serving of various foods (some admittedly on the spare side). If you are willing to follow our recommendation of a low cholesterol, low animal fat diet, you can see that some of these foods—for example animal organs, shellfish, and eggs—just won't do for you.

Table 2 gives a general daily food regimen that is low in cholesterol and animal fat. It calls for two serv-

* For those of our readers who wish an exhaustive, very detailed, and beautifully meticulous handbook of food values, we recommend that they purchase Agriculture Handbook No. 8, *Composition of Foods,* for $1.50 from the Superintendent of Documents, U.S. Government Printing Office, Washington, D.C. 20402. This is truly a treasure for the person who wishes to know the energy-producing components and mineral and vitamin composition of each specific foodstuff.

ings of trimmed lean meat, fish, or fowl each day. Admittedly a meat, fowl, or fish serving weighing five ounces uncooked isn't large, but it is moderately appeasing. Preferably seven or more of these fourteen servings per week should be of any kind of fish except shellfish. Fish contains polyunsaturated fats while meat contains the possibly dangerous saturated fats.

And while we are on the subject of fats, we would like you to know that no vegetable fat—that is, polyunsaturated fat—ever *lowers* your blood cholesterol. The best that can be said for it—and this is not negligible—is that it does not *elevate* your blood cholesterol. Animal fats do. Also, when you eat any animal fat, you also consume the cholesterol dissolved in it. Vegetable fats, on the other hand, contain not even the slightest trace of cholesterol. But you cannot counteract the possibly harmful effects of eating either cholesterol or animal fats by swallowing extra corn or safflower oil. Please remember that. We have had more than one patient who believed that if he fried his eggs in corn oil, the corn oil would protect him against the cholesterol in the egg yolks. We wish that such protection was a fact, but unfortunately it is a fantasy.

If you take seven or more of your fourteen meat, fish, or fowl servings in the form of some variety of fish, we would recommend further that several of the seven remaining allotted servings be of fowl, prepared any way that pleases you.

As you can see from the daily food plan, you can have four servings of any type of vegetable, two salad servings, two glasses of skim milk, two slices of bread, a generous serving of fruit, and a breakfast cereal in the morning, as well as sufficient oleomargarine to "butter" your bread and to use in the preparation of your other allowable foods.

At first glance you will undoubtedly be surprised at this suggested diet because it *seemingly* differs so little

Table 1 APPROXIMATE COMPOSITION OF VARIOUS FOODS*

Type of Food	Cholesterol (mg. per oz.)	Fat (g. per oz.)	Protein (g. per oz.)	Carbohydrates (g. per oz.)	Simple Sugars (g. per oz.)	Calories (per oz.)
A. Meats (lean)						
Pork	24	7	7	0	0	91
Beef	27	6	6	0	0	78
Lamb	20	6	6	0	0	78
Veal	30	3	9	0	0	63
Organs (e.g., liver)	91	1	8	0	0	41
B. Most fish†	24	2	5	0	0	38
C. Shellfish						
Crab	42	0.5	5	0	0	25
Lobster	66	0.5	6	0	0	29
Clams	50	0.5	6	0	0	29
Shrimp	50	0.5	6	0.5	0	31
D. Fowl (Chicken & turkey)	20	1	8	0	0	41

* All values given represent those for raw foods.
† Certain fish (e.g., salmon and cod) contain more fat and cholesterol.

E. Dairy Products						
Whole milk	3	1.5	1	2	1	17
Low-fat (2%) milk	2	1	1	1	1	8
Skim milk	0	0	1	1	1	8
Buttermilk	0	0	1	1	1	8
Cream	34	14	1	1	1	134
Butter	83	24	0.2	0	0	180
Cottage cheese (uncreamed)	1	0.5	2	0	0.	12
F. Egg (1 whole)	275	6	3.5	0	0	68
G. Vegetables‡	0	0.2	0.8	3	1	16
H. Fruits	0	0.1	0.2	4	2	17
I. Nuts	0	18	7	6	2	214
J. Cereals						
Breakfast cereals	0	0	0.4	26	1	105
Bread	10	1	2.2	16	2	82
Cake	25	5	1.5	20	15	131
Cookies	35	7	2	22	15	159
Waffles	55	4	2.5	12	8	94

‡ The avocado and olive are much richer in fat than most other vegetables.

Table 2　A Daily Diet Plan Sufficiently Low in Cholesterol*

Type of Food	Total Daily Amount (oz.)	Approx. Cholesterol (mg. per day)	Approx. Fat (g. per day)	Approx. Protein (g. per day)	Approx. Carbohydrates (g. per day)	Approx. Calories per day
A. 2 servings lean meat, fish or fowl	10	240	70	70	0	910
B. 4 servings vegetables	16	0	3	13	48	271
C. 2 servings salad†	8	0	0	4	12	334
D. 2 glasses skim milk	16	0	0	16	16	128
E. 2 slices bread	2	20	2	4.4	32	164
F. Oleomargarine‡	2	0	53	0	0	477
G. Fruits	6	0	0	1	24	160
H. One serving of cereal	2	0	0	1	52	212
Daily Total	62	260	158	109.4	184	2,596

* All values given represent weight as raw foods.
† Includes 2 tablespoons of oil dressing.
‡ Includes margarine in foods.

A. *Never Eat These Foods*

  1. Egg yolks
  2. Any animal organs, including roe
  3. All sausages, including wieners
  4. All shellfish, particularly shrimp
  5. Butter, cream, ice cream, or foods containing these
  6. Cheeseburgers, pizza
  7. All cheeses except uncreamed cottage cheese and cheeses specially processed to be cholesterol free
  8. Almost all cooked hors d'oeuvres

B. *Restrict Your Intake of These Foods as Much as Possible*

  1. Sugars, syrups, jelly, honey
  2. Candy
  3. Cookies
  4. Cakes, except angel food cake

C. *Eat as Much as You Like If Your Bathroom Scales Approve*

  1. All vegetables
  2. All vegetable oils
  3. All nuts, except coconut
  4. Egg whites
  5. Skim milk, buttermilk, yogurt

from what you usually eat. Indeed it appears to allow you to make all the choices. However, as you will detect from the list of forbidden foods shown in Table 2, certain foods that you have been eating are eliminated. For example, the egg yolk is forbidden not only in the form of an egg serving but also as a constituent of any food. Note, too, the absolute elimination of butter, cream, and ice cream and all cheeses except uncreamed cottage cheese. And note that all animal organs such as liver, sweetbreads, kidney, brains, and caviar are also forbidden. Nor does the diet permit *excess* sugar, syrups, jellies, honey, cakes, or cookies.

Many of you will object to our recommendation of two glasses of skim milk per day. Many of you have already given up fresh milk; besides, you may not like skim milk. But it is difficult to find a better food than skim milk, which so well provides protein, minerals, and the most essential vitamins. If you prefer milk with the fatty taste of whole milk, pour a teaspoon or two of corn oil into a glass of skim milk and then put the mixture into a blender for a minute or so before you drink it. You might be surprised at how rich the milk tastes then.

Most men—particularly Type A men—eventually resent any diet that takes away their favorite meat, fish, and fowl foods. And no matter what sort of ingeniously contrived substitute is placed before them, sooner or later their irritation at being deprived of those accustomed foods will erupt in frank bad humor. Ashamed at the real cause of their irritation, they are likely to express their anger in some other way, perhaps over some subject brought up during the dinner conversation. It is only after a series of such eruptions that the puzzled and sometimes deeply hurt wife finally begins to see that her husband's irritability is really caused by deprivation. No spice, herb, or condiment can, in the long run, substitute for an habitually eaten and enjoyed piece of meat.

The present dietary plan takes this into account. The dieter is not deprived of meat, fish, or fowl, and is subjected to only one restriction—he can't eat *as much* of his favorites as before. Thus, each cooked meat serving weighs only about four ounces, perhaps only two-thirds or one-half as much as before. Who has ever been reduced to fury by such moderate restraints? A full understanding of this bit of dining psychology transcends in value the line-by-line memorization of at least a hundred diet schedules. Of course every successful restaurateur must learn this truth— his guests never will desert him because of the small quantity of food he serves them, but if the quality falls off, how quickly they will forget his address. Nor will any wife ever be deserted by her husband if she serves him his accustomed foods, as beautifully prepared as ever but just a bit on the modest side.

Our dietary regimen will help you ingest less cholesterol and more vegetable than animal fat. A second objective is for you to regain or maintain the body weight that you possessed as a high school senior.

As Table 2 indicates, the proposed diet will provide approximately 2,600 calories. This amount will be too great for those of you who must slim down and who exercise very little. It may even be too great for those of you who, already sufficiently slim, hope to remain so. In such circumstances, you must use your bathroom scales as a *daily* monitor. If you want to lose weight, and following this diet do not, then you must alter the quantities of food allotted. The first items that should be eliminated or cut down are bread and cereals. If the elimination of both these foods still does not prevent you from losing your excess weight (or keep you from gaining), then the amount of oleomargarine and salad oil should be reduced. If this latter cut still does not allow you to approach or to maintain your desired slimness, then the milk quota should be halved. But the meat, fish, and fowl servings should never be cut down. You require their protein content.

For those of you whose physical activities are such that the diet's caloric intake will not maintain your ideal weight, or being overweight, caused you to lose more than two pounds a week, you will obviously have to eat a bit more. Try a third glass of skim milk (fortified with corn oil) first. If you still lose weight too quickly, use more margarine and salad oil in your salad and vegetable servings. Finally, you may wish to eat several ounces of nuts a day. But never change your meat, fish, and fowl servings.

For those of you who know you are Type A, we suggest that this diet be followed very closely. We should further emphasize that you take particular care to avoid all but small quantities of sugar, syrups, honey, jellies, and foods such as candy, pies, and cakes. There is considerable evidence suggesting that the excess ingestion of various types of simple sugars is particularly apt to elevate the serum cholesterol of Type A subjects. So whenever you can substitute saccharine for sugar, please do so.

What about children? Should they be given this diet? We believe that except for slight modifications in certain individual cases, a diet of this sort should be given to all American children unless there are specific medical reasons for not doing so. Undoubtedly, depending on their physical activities and age, many children will require greater quantities than those suggested in Table 2.

For example, they should receive twenty-four rather than sixteen ounces of skim milk. They can increase the quantity of any of the proposed servings except the meat, fish, and fowl. They can eat as many nuts as they wish. And candies, cakes, and cookies, provided they do not contain egg yolk, may be eaten —in moderation.

Ice cream we believe deserves special attention as a culprit. If our usual American diet is partially responsible for our present flurry of heart attacks, the reason cannot be solely the milk or butter it contains. The consumption of these items has not increased during the last thirty years; it has actually decreased markedly. But the consumption of ice cream, relatively low up to 1930, has increased greatly among our youngsters. We who were children in the twenties ate ice cream several times a month at most, while those who grew up in the subsequent decades only too often ate some ice cream three or four times a week. Given the freezing compartment of our refrigerators and the reluctance of modern mothers to concoct homemade desserts, ice cream in one form or another has become the preadolescent—and only too often adolescent—pacifier. And it is, of course, rich in cholesterol and animal fat.

Then, too, forty years ago adolescents and teenagers never ate commercially prepared cheeseburgers (made out of very fatty meats and cholesterol-rich cheese), hot dogs, pizzas, French fries, or chili. They rarely drank rich milk shakes. If we are indeed eating ourselves into heart disease, it is probably because of the availability and wide consumption of these foods. By making such between-meal "snacks" possible for our youngsters, our affluent society may be the real villain in the matter.

We do not know how parents can cajole their children into avoiding the foods that now are being presented to them by commercial purveyors, but it is well worth trying. Certainly, it will do your children good to warn them of the dangers that a cholesterol-rich diet may lead to later in their lives. Few children take dangerous, habit-forming drugs without an awareness that some day they will have to pay heavily for such a habit. But unfortunately, too many children today believe that the "here and now" is infinitely more important than the "there and later." It is not ignorance of consequences but a strange disregard for them that now plagues so many of the young of this country. We are fortunately not obliged to write a book about how to handle children.

Need all adults adopt our suggested dietary regimen? No. If you have never smoked cigarettes and if you are very, very *sure* you are a *very* unstressed Type B sort of person, this diet probably isn't necessary. But if you ever have smoked or are now smoking cigarettes heavily, and if you even suspect that you may possess or have possessed Type A Behavior Pattern, you will be well advised to adhere to this plan. Also, if your cholesterol level is over 225 mg./100 ml., even if you don't smoke and are absolutely positive that you do not possess the Type A Behavior Pattern, you had better follow it.

Those of you who already know that your serum cholesterol level is too high may wonder if our recommended diet is satisfactory for you. In this case, you should be under a doctor's care. Although he probably will not fault our diet, he may find that you also require specific medication to normalize your serum cholesterol.

How religiously should you follow the diet we have presented? You should follow it moderately conscientiously, but never to the point of fanaticism. The most important goal to keep in mind is the *total* amount of cholesterol consumed daily, rather than any particular food ingested. For example, if you should desire on any particular day to eat some ice cream or butter or wish to drink a glass of whole milk, then do so. But then cut down your meat or fish ration so that your total intake of cholesterol on that day still falls below 300 milligrams.

One additional bit of advice: do not discuss your diet and its changes with anyone except your doctor. Remember that no matter how fascinated and even proud you may be of your strict adherence to the diet plan and of your weight loss, these details invariably induce pure boredom in others. Your friends have been eating food all their lives, and the only phenomenon concerning food that truly interests them, for the most part, is the taste of food in their own mouths.

Nor is it necessary to make a miserable bore of yourself when you have been invited to a dinner party. Your hostess will not notice or care whether you drink all your soup or eat all your salad. She likewise will not care whether you eat her bread, rolls, or butter, nor will she care how much of her vegetables you put on your plate. But the odds are that she will observe whether you enjoy the meat or fish serving. In such cases, forget your diet and eat most or all of the entire entree (after all, she will not be serving you brains, liver, or kidney and probably not sweetbreads) but eschew the sauce or gravy. Then when dessert is offered, smile and say nonchalantly, "Just coffee, thanks. The meal was delicious and I ate far too much to have a dessert."

This, then, is our plan whereby you can achieve or maintain your high school slimness and avoid an oversupply of cholesterol and animal fats. The regimen, by the way, should be followed for the rest of your life.

YOUR CIGARETTE MUST BE QUENCHED

We have expressed our opinion that heavy cigarette smoking probably does accelerate the course of coronary artery disease and in so doing leads to the premature emergence of coronary heart disease. Approximately six months have elapsed since we finished writing that chapter, and we are now even more inclined to suspect the cigarette as a not-so-slow destroyer of coronary arteries. During these six months, we have been studying the life histories of persons who had died suddenly of coronary heart disease in the San Francisco Bay area. This study has already indicated that most of these heart victims had smoked twenty to eighty cigarettes a day for years.

Admittedly, half of all adult men smoke cigarettes, and admittedly, too, heavy cigarette smoking is one of the characteristic traits of the Type A man. Nevertheless, the monotonous regularity of the relationship of heavy cigarette smoking to the sudden coronary deaths we have seen and are continuing to see more and more convinces us that this "weed" itself may be a killer.

An especially pathetic aspect of the problem is the fact that once the coronary artery is damaged severely, it never totally recovers. This means, of course, that even if a person eventually does succeed in freeing himself from "nicotine slavery," his coronary arteries may always carry the scars from exposure to the nicotine and coal tar that once circulated in his blood.

No addiction is easy to escape, and if you happen to smoke a pack or more of cigarettes a day, your addiction may be almost as difficult to overcome as addiction to heroin or morphine. You are not just addicted to the nicotine in the smoke of your cigarettes; you also have been habituated and indeed heavily dependent upon the emotional satisfaction you *immediately* obtain from the contact of the smoke with your lung's lining cells. It is the loss of this "smoke-lung contact" that you will feel most keenly during the first few weeks of total abstinence from cigarettes.

Peculiarly, almost no psychological studies have been done on this key phenomenon of cigarette smoking. It is also unfortunate that few if any pathophysiological studies have been made. It is remotely possible that the chronic repetition of this "smoke-lung contact" and its subsequent far-flung reflex nervous stimuli could even play a part in accelerating the course of coronary artery disease.

Certainly, the apparent relative immunity of the heavy cigar or pipe smoker to coronary disease cannot be laid to the fact that he doesn't get as much nicotine in his system as the cigarette smoker. It may also not be due entirely to his behavior pattern, either. His protection may actually be due in part to the fact that he infrequently inhales, and hence is not exposed to the baleful effects of the "smoke-lung contact." Incidentally, it is the immense emotional sustenance that this "smoke-lung contact" gives to the chronic cigarette smoker that makes him wonder what possible pleasure a cigar or pipe smoker receives in taking smoke into his mouth and throat only to blow it out again immediately.

If the withdrawal symptoms due to the absence of nicotine and the "smoke-lung contact" are not bad enough, you also, in giving up cigarettes, will discover that you miss handling the cigarette, inserting it between your lips, even the process of lighting it. These discomforts are trivial indeed, however, compared with those brought on by the loss of "smoke-lung contact" and nicotine.

Is there any easy, painless way to lose your addiction? We don't know of any. Nevertheless, hundreds of thousands of adult Americans have managed to quit smoking during the past five years. The alarming increase in lung cancer due solely to cigarette smoking is being dinned into the American consciousness by all branches of the mass media, and this exposure is beginning to bear fruit. Thousands more would also quit smoking if, when a man dies of lung cancer, the newspaper account in reporting his death revealed that he died of lung cancer, instead of merely stating that he died after a "long illness." You will not be too far from the truth if you always substitute "lung cancer" for "long illness," when reading such accounts.

Of course, all sorts of devices, ranging from chewing gum to hypnotism and "encounter" sessions have been and are still being presented as aids in breaking the cigarette habit. Since few if any of these nostrums are downright harmful, you might experiment. But to free yourself from tobacco you must first nourish the *intent* to do so, then having this incentive, you then must search for the *will* to achieve the intent.

Finally, just this word of advice. If you do decide to quit, don't taper off. Quit completely! As you know, an old truism states that if you must strike a king, strike to kill him. Well, cigarette smoking is a "king-sized" addiction!

EXERCISE—BUT MODERATELY

If the evidence that might incriminate physical indolence in the "crime" of coronary artery and heart disease is flimsy—and it is—certainly there is absolutely no evidence whatsoever that *moderate* exercise accelerates the conversion of a small, nonsymptom-producing plaque in a human coronary artery into a lumen-occluding, symptom-producing thrombus that marks the advent of coronary heart disease. But please note that we have underlined the word "moderate." Severe exercise, as we shall explain, may very well kill instantaneously. It may even kill a person supposedly suffering from no coronary heart disease at all.

But persons of all ages, if they do not suffer already from crippling coronary heart disease, should indulge in as much moderate physical activity as they possibly can. Certainly, at least one hour a day and preferably more time should be spent in moving your legs and arms.

By moderate physical activity, we mean any form of exercise whose execution does not cause panting, excessive acceleration of your heartbeat (that is, above 120 beats per minute), or leave you unduly fatigued. Walking on the flat, up very gentle hills, up one flight of steps or down as many flights of steps as you wish, swimming (noncompetitive), golfing, bicycling, tennis (but only doubles, and preferably mixed doubles), fishing, hunting (but not deer hunting at high altitudes or wading after fallen ducks), skeet shooting, horseshoe playing, croquet, billiards, and so forth, are the forms of exercise we recommend.

Persons over thirty-five years of age should not indulge in severe forms of exercise, regardless of how long and how often they indulged in such exercise previously, or how healthy they may think that they are, unless they first have undergone an electrocardiographic checkup while walking or jogging on a treadmill at a top speed of five miles per hour.

Almost all large hospitals are equipped with these treadmill-electrocardiograph examining units. The test can be taken in just a few minutes. If your electrocardiogram remains completely normal during your treadmill exercise, it probably will be reasonably—but not entirely—safe for you to indulge in various forms of even severe exercise.

But please note—the ordinary electrocardiogram taken as you lie supine on a cot just won't do. Fully half of those persons who have one or more of their three coronary arteries totally occluded still exhibit a normal electrocardiogram at rest. However, the electrocardiogram taken during a treadmill test *probably* would indicate the presence of such obstruction.

In short, if you're over thirty-five, seemingly healthy and absolutely determined to continue or begin a program of strenuous physical activity, please first spend about fifty dollars to get a treadmill-electrocardiographic surveillance. The latter may well save your life!

Approximately 200,000 American men who had never experienced a single symptom of coronary heart disease died suddenly last year. From our own studies of scores of these cases, we have learned two facts. First, even if these men had no symptoms of heart disease before death, in each case postmortem studies revealed coronary artery disease of sufficient severity that a treadmill electrocardiogram may very well have shown its presence. Second, more than a third of these men died during or a few minutes after indulging in strenuous activity. In many cases, moreover, the men had been exercising strenuously, regularly, and for years prior to their demise.

Again we wish to emphasize that coronary arteries aren't heart muscles—they don't get "accustomed" to regular exercise even if it is severe. No one ever made a diseased coronary artery more "physically fit." If this seems odd, look at a scar you may have and see if it has grown smaller because you have become more physically active. Remember that a diseased coronary artery is considered diseased because of the obstructing scars it bears, and becomes dangerous only when they deteriorate and rupture.

What are these severe or strenuous exercises which we are cautioning every American past thirty-five years of age to avoid as if they were a plague? First on our blacklist is jogging. This miserable postcollegiate athletic travesty has already killed at least scores, possibly hundreds, of Americans. We believe the following letter and the death it describes speaks for itself. Unfortunately, it is not the first letter of this kind that we have received, and equally unfortunately, we know it will not be the last one.

Dear Dr. Friedman:

As you know, I have been a confirmed jogger for a number of years. A recent event has caused me to reevaluate the merits of jogging and decide in favor of some other form of exercise.

After I had recovered from the acute phases of my recent coronary event, my jogging companion expressed hope that I would soon return to the track. Following your advice, I declined, but Dr. Louis Rothenberg, age 48, a superb research chemist, continued to run alone as he had done regularly during my illness. Louis, who had recently had a complete physical, including an ECG and found in good health and who had no previous cardiovascular involvement, died on the track while jogging just last week.

Jogging did not prevent me from having a heart attack, and it certainly did precipitate his. Knowing your concern for my personal well-being and your research into sudden death, I thought these events would be of interest to you.

> Your now confirmed swimming friend,
> Al Brown

Jogging is a form of exercise in which man transforms himself into a machine. Chug-chug-chugging along, looking neither to the right nor left, panting, the "man machine" chugs along. And what is "its" goal? To see if "it" can chug-chug faster today than yesterday. And what is "its" only joy? The soothing miraculous feeling of *relief* when the chug-chugging is finished. If ever an exercise was custom made for the Type A person, jogging is that exercise. Yes, some of our best friends are joggers!

Competitive handball, tennis singles, and squash rank next to jogging in potential lethality for the middle-aged American who plays these games—whether once a month or every day—without first having had his heart checked at least by the treadmill-electrocardiographic test (which, incidentally, is certainly not foolproof). And fully as dangerous as any of these violent sports may be speed ice skating and playing touch football or basketball with your teen-aged sons, particularly after even a moderate-sized meal.

Of course, you might be tempted to ask why we bother to recommend even moderate exercise in view of our doubt about its efficacy in preventing coronary artery disease, and our belief in the evident danger of violent exercise. We would reply that man has always felt better physically and psychologically after indulging in bodily exercise.

This observation has been noted and accepted as a fact by physicians and laymen for many centuries. We don't believe you will be harming the coronary arteries of your heart if you exercise relatively gently. And there is always the possibility—although it still remains to be demonstrated—that such gentle exercise might eventually favor the widening and new growth of some healthy small branches of your coronary vessels.

Chapter 12

THE MISSING
CONNECTION

It might seem incredible that very few medical investigators in the past have believed that your brain and its
functions could influence the state of your heart and
its own arteries. Yet even now very few cardiac researchers are focusing upon this possible relationship.
Even worse, there is still active resistance to this sort
of approach. Some investigators indeed have an almost hostile reaction to anyone who does dare to
"poke about" in the "never-never lands" where mind
and body come face to face to communicate with and
influence each other.

Why has there been this prejudice on the part of so
many of our colleagues? And why have so many of
our colleagues been even more reluctant to accept as
true, or even possibly true, the information brought
back to them by those very few who have attempted to
invade the many shadowy areas where mind meets
body? There are a number of reasons for this medical
and scientific (?) chariness. Let us look at some of
them.

First, almost all scientists share the desire to measure phenomena and to express such measurements in solid, understandable, and repeatable units—pounds, grams, volts, ergs, degrees of color changes, radioactive emissions, and so on. An unquantifiable phenomenon or process upsets many scientists deeply. Even worse, only too often their first reaction to such an irritating confrontation is to ignore the phenomenon or process altogether.

It is not just medical scientists who react in this manner, of course. Thus Walter Laqueur, the distinguished director of the Institute of Contemporary History in London, trying to explain the social scientist's neglect of political violence, remarked recently in *Encounter* that "violence is not the most attractive of subjects and that it is not ideally suited for the application of *quantitative* techniques and other social science methods." As the English novelist Goronwy Rees wrote, "the particular characteristic of our own age is that no evidence is regarded as acceptable unless it is statistical, that is to say, that it is of a kind which can be expressed in numbers. Nothing counts, we might say, unless it can be counted."

But all of us know nevertheless that political violence is not just about ready to disappear simply because our social scientists carry on as if it does not exist. Similarly, a man's lust for his neighbor's wife can be real enough even if the sociologist can't express its degree of intensity in quantitative units.

But do we exaggerate this reluctance of scientists to consider seriously what cannot be expressed in numbers? In an impressive study issued in 1971 by a specially designated committee of the Royal Society of New Zealand concerning the causes of coronary heart disease, a single sentence is allotted to the factor that we believe to be the major one. "Some members of the

Committee feel," it said, "that *until more satisfactory means of measuring stress* are developed that no firm conclusions should be drawn concerning this risk in CHD [coronary heart disease]."* Please note that the committee is not *recommending* as a measure of the highest urgency that more satisfactory means of measuring stress be sought and developed. What they are really implying is that emotional stress as a possible causative factor can be safely disregarded for the present and indefinite future. What they instead urged, incidentally, was that New Zealand's medical and scientific fraternity investigate immediately the possible role of the softness of drinking water in New Zealand's terribly high incidence of coronary heart disease.

In any event, emotional stress of any variety, because of its resistance to precise measurement, has been shamefully neglected by quantitatively oriented cardiac researchers. If the smoking of cigarettes could not be measured by the *number* of cigarettes smoked per day, if the ingestion of saturated fats could not be measured by the *number* of calories ingested, and if physical exercise were similarly incapable of being measured by the *number* of hours employed in this activity, none of these factors today would be considered as lethal as they are now (see Chapter 10). Nature unfortunately cares very little if man can or cannot measure some phenomena in terms that are acceptable to him. But let us not obscure the issue by reference to vague generalizations. Hundred of thousands of Americans have died, are dying, and will continue to die of the tragic complex of nervous factors we have designated Type A Behavior Pattern. Yet its existence has been largely overlooked because it still cannot be described in quantitatively acceptable terms.

---

* The italics are our own.

A second reason for the failure of past cardiac investigators to study the role of man's personality in the genesis of coronary artery disease is that they lacked knowledge of or interest in the mental or emotional processes of mankind. As a consequence, the various facts these men have accumulated, the machines and techniques they laboriously learned to master, even their individual scientific philosophies, all are relatively useless in this sort of approach to the problems of coronary artery disease.

No man, no matter how wise and saintly he may be, relishes discarding all his past experience, his training, and even his previously held concepts to begin afresh and in a field bearing few signs for his orientation. Dr. Harvey Brooks, the eminent Harvard physicist, stressed this universal reluctance in his C. P. Snow Lecture recently when he said, "It is very difficult for anyone to accept criticism of his brain children, and this may be particularly so in the case of engineers or technologists who may have committed a large slice of their careers to a single goal." Dr. Brooks could easily have included medical experts in this criticism. At the beginning, we ourselves did not relish abandoning the precision of our biochemical and physiological techniques—and the security they had provided us—to penetrate that area, half jungle, half desert, where mind and body communicate and influence each other.

In their search for some reason to account for the epidemic-like increase in coronary artery disease in the past half century, most scientists sought for such possible changes in only those substances which man ate, drank, or inhaled. They were not acutely aware of any changes taking place in Western man's spiritual ambiance, even though their own scientific colleagues were chiefly responsible for them.

Like the rest of us, they were able to "adjust" to

such changes because they occurred gradually. Although consciously we have managed to "adjust" to the emotional strains of modern life, the real question is whether we have managed to adjust our subconscious mental and our unconscious body process to these emotional strains.

Several extraordinarily acute and percipient scholars of Western society were not at all certain that we would ever be able to adjust to the changes in our ambiance. De Tocqueville, Thoreau, Henry Adams, and Sir William Osler, among many others both in the last century and in this one, warned of the dangers of the increasing pace of living that was afflicting Western man in general and Americans in particular.

Most of us are already aware of the fact that various environmental and societal agents are forcing us to live and work continuously faster. We must learn how to accept the continuous changes taking place in our ways of working, eating, playing, loving, and even dying.

After majestically reviewing man's cyclic progressions and retrogressions during the five thousand years of his historical existence, Arnold Toynbee, the great English historian, concluded:

At the earliest moment at which we catch our first glimpse of Man on earth we find him not only on the move but already moving at an accelerating pace. This crescendo of acceleration is continuing today. In our generation it is perhaps the most difficult and dangerous of all the current problems of the race.

Although Toynbee wrote this well over a decade ago, not a single academician—be he economist, sociologist, psychologist, or psychiatrist—has yet addressed himself to the problem it poses.

A partial explanation for the persistent hesitation of heart researchers to include man's personality in the ambit of their studies was the inability of most psychiatrists to detect any peculiarity or identifying quirk in the personality of the coronary patient. This diagnostic inability was due almost solely, however, to the simple fact that in the past very few coronary patients ever found it necessary to visit a psychiatrist, either before or after they experienced their first heart symptoms. Indeed, most of them not only thought it unnecessary to visit a psychiatrist, they violently protested any suggestion that they should do so. Indeed, when a group of Harvard cardiologists urged a hundred young coronary patients to take advantage of the free services offered to them by well-trained psychiatrists, almost to a man they refused to make more than one visit.

Given this reluctance of the coronary patients in the past to see psychiatrists—and such reluctance still exists—one could not expect these specialists to find diagnostic or causal traits in persons they had never met, except perhaps socially. Of course, now we realize we should have suspected something odd about the behavior of coronary patients, if only because so few of them ever thought it worth their while to consult a psychiatrist. After all, psychiatrists now see hundreds of thousands of patients annually. By chance alone, one would expect them to see thousands of potential or actual coronary patients, unless such patients characteristically avoid psychiatric help—which they do!

This last point, the positive resistance of the potential coronary patient to visit a psychiatrist, is due, of course, to his absolute confidence in the total integrity of his emotional faculties. Self-assurance on the patient's part bears much responsibility for the failure of the internist to suspect that the coronary patient's behavior pattern might bear a close causal relationship to his heart disease. Nor can the patient be faulted for his confidence in the healthy state of his behavior, because the Type A pattern has until quite recently been considered—certainly in its less intensely developed state—not only to be a perfectly normal *American* way of thinking and living, but an ideal state toward which every young man and woman should strive. This being so, you then may be able to understand how a Type A heart patient can visit his cardiologist— who is often a Type A, too—without either of them noticing anything at all wrong with each other's behavior. The Type A pattern is so deeply ingrained in our society today as to be almost a characteristic of it; and this fact in turn suggests an answer to the question posed in the next chapter—where did Type A Behavior Pattern come from?

Chapter 13

WHERE DID TYPE A BEHAVIOR PATTERN COME FROM?

In the past, even in the prehistoric past, some men were probably engaged in a continuous struggle to achieve more "numbers." Some, no doubt, were so beset with hostility that they fought constantly with members of their families, their neighbors, or their enemies. Such persons thus probably did suffer from what we have designated Type A Behavior Pattern.

But in the past people like this were the exception, and today they are ubiquitous. What happened to bring this about? Why is Type A Behavior Pattern so exclusively a disease of our times?

Perhaps the most important single reason, at least in the United States, is the transformation of nineteenth-century Yankee pragmatism into an unbridled drive to acquire more and more of the world's material benefits. As early as 1835, Tocqueville was struck by the American's search for mundane goods:

In the United States a man builds a house to spend his latter years in it and he sells it before the roof is on: he plants a garden and lets it just as the trees are coming into bearing. If his private affairs leave him any leisure, he instantly plunges into the vortex of politics; if at the end of a year of unremitting labor he finds he has a few days' vacation, his eager curiosity whirls him over the vast extent of the United States and he will travel fifteen hundred miles in a few days to shake off his happiness. . . . He who has set his heart exclusively upon the pursuit of worldly welfare is always in a hurry for he has but a limited time at his disposal to reach it, to grasp it, and to enjoy it.

Even then, it is clear, Americans were gearing up for more speed and greater acquisition. Industrial development in the twentieth century has simply driven the process to its logical conclusion, tempting the offspring of those earlier Yankees with the belief that almost any object perceived by their senses can be captured. When greed of this sort becomes indiscriminate, and cannot be sated by quality but only by numeration, the person involved has become a Type A.

Another aspect of the phenomenon is our present infatuation with speed. Having invented objects that can travel, communicate, or fabricate other objects at a greater and greater rate, we now seem willing to subject ourselves to their demands.

Your great-grandfather, for example, trotting along in his horse-drawn buggy at a leisurely pace, might very well have stopped to chat with a passing neighbor for ten minutes or so. Encased in your car, you will be fortunate even to glimpse your neighbor as you each hurtle by. That both of you might stop and pass the times of day is wholly unthinkable. It is as if your automobiles might resent the interruption. If that sounds silly, think about it. Isn't there truth in the idea that the faster a machine is made to operate, the faster the operator feels *he* must think and act?

Our urge toward acceleration is intensified by the increasing urbanization of society, which inevitably makes us more dependent on the actions and services of others. We take turns selling each other our services, always hoping that the exchange will somehow save us a bit of time. But since we are ourselves serving persons whom we know to be time conscious, we consistently try to do our work a little faster, both to satisfy them and to save some time for ourselves. When this practice takes on a minute-to-minute cadence, the result is Type A behavior.

America's open economy means that while opportunity is at least theoretically available to all, the absolute need to compete is also universal. An older society, built on a class system, could be exceedingly unpleasant for many of those trapped within it. But by relieving many people of the need to struggle for precedence, it did not encourage the development of Type A behavior.

Many observers, from Tocqueville to Thoreau and Adams, noted the pressure of competition that marked nineteenth-century American society. In our century, the struggle has become stronger with each succeeding decade. Today, with the ownership of almost all large corporations in the hands of shareholders and foundations, management jobs go to the able. It is performance, not pedigree, that achieves high economic status. But awareness of this state of affairs has led many millions of Americans to "overrespond" to the challenge it poses. They have become competitive in *all* aspects of their lives—not only their business and professional activities, but also in their avocational time. And such an attitude is as sure a route to Type A Behavior Pattern as any other. In fact, an excess of competitive spirit generally goes hand in hand with a continuous struggle against time.

There is another characteristic of modern society that has apparently contributed to the increase in Type A's: it is our tendency to reduce men to numbers, to strip them of their uniquely human characteristics and standardize them. To your bank you are already a number—look at the computer digits that identify you on your checks and deposit slips. The same goes for the government, your insurance man and stockbroker, even the companies that feed and clothe you and try to discover your television-watching habits.

Of course, a society would have little luck in trying to reduce humans to numerals or statistics if it were not for a companion tendency—the tendency of the people themselves to forget their individual identity, and the emotional linkages that draw them together. In times past, belief in the protective presence of a powerful God (or group of gods) allowed man to feel that he was being singled out and protected as a unique personage. Trust and pride in his particular group of fellow men, living and dead, gave him a feeling of emotional unity with them. These forces of religion and—for want of a better term—patriotism, supported by myth and ritual, have been waning relentlessly even as the forces making for automaton-man have been waxing.

Admittedly, millions of Americans are churchgoers, but fewer and fewer of them "live with their God" in any meaningful way. The myths and rituals of all religions in America have suffered disastrously from the destructive forces of secularization and so-called scientific raionalism. J. B. Priestley, the English writer, was dismally correct when he recently wrote that no matter what our Western society professes, it is not merely irreligious, it is powerfully antireligious.

We cannot say positively that the increase in Type A Behavior Pattern has been directly influenced by the continuing loss of religious faith and other sustaining myths and rituals. We can declare, however, with considerable certainty, that we have rarely encountered this behavior pattern in any person whose religious and patriotic beliefs take precedence over his preoccupation with the accumulation of "numbers" or the acquisition of personal power. We are certain, for example, that it is not solely because of their antipathy to medicine that so few Christian Scientists come to cardiologists for treatment for coronary heart disease. It could well be that the Christian Scientist's preoccupation with the ideals and aims of his religion shields him from Type A Behavior Pattern—and also from coronary heart disease.

We have already referred to the effects of the many new labor-saving devices upon your physical activities. These same devices may also be fostering various psychological tensions, tensions that may arise when large portions of your brain, evolutionally designed and developed solely to employ and guide muscle movements, are no longer needed, and function either less regularly or not at all.

We are not neurophysiologists. We are quite aware that experts in the field might be loath to believe that such alteration or abolition of particular cerebral activities might lead to emotional tensions and stresses. And yet there are few persons, even professionals, who do not believe that they can rid themselves of these tensions simply by indulgence in brief exercise. Even Emerson admitted that when he felt himself becoming emotionally balked in his writing, a short excursion to his garden, pulling up carrots, usually sufficed to restore his equanimity.

We have described many of the influences present in our Western society that we believe may have played a part in fostering the amazing increase in incidence of Type A Behavior Pattern. But is our society totally responsible? If so, why do close to half of the exposed members of this society withstand these influences and fail to exhibit this pattern even in its milder forms? Psychiatrists and psychologists may claim—influenced by their formal training in other types of emotional disorders—that various traumas in the past lives of individual sufferers played an important, perhaps decisive, role. They may even attempt to alleviate or eradicate the potential ravages of the behavior pattern by therapy. We hope that they will not focus so narrowly upon supposed infantile, prepubertal or even postadolescent traumas, however, that they will neglect the contemporary influences discussed above.

Repeatedly, we have been asked by our fellow cardiologists whether there may not be hereditary or genetic influences at play in the emergence of this behavior pattern. We believe in some cases, perhaps in many, hereditary forces have played a part. What is being inherited in such cases, we suspect, is an aggressive drive to achieve. This possibly inherited trait varies, of course, in its intensity. But only when the environment or milieu presents suitable challenges or enticements does trouble ensue. And Type A Behavior Pattern is defined neither by the inherited trait alone nor any single environmental influence; it is defined by the struggle that develops when an individual possessing this trait and confronted with several environmental influences decides to do battle.

Chapter 14

HOW TYPE A BEHAVIOR WREAKS DAMAGE

Before we get into what we consider to be the most important part of this book—pointed suggestions about how to alter Type A behavior—let us consider just how this behavior pattern encourages the development of coronary heart disease. Much of what follows is necessarily speculative, but (we feel) sound enough to help answer the question: How does an "error in spirit" lead finally to a catastrophic "failure in matter"?

No bacterium, no virus, and no tumor has or ever will be found to be responsible for the coronary artery disease that at least 100 million Americans now harbor in some degree. The arterial degeneration is caused, without question, by one or more of the certain or probable factors listed and described in earlier chapters.

As it happens, most Type A subjects sooner or later develop or exhibit many of these factors. As a group, Type A subjects show a higher serum cholesterol, a higher serum fat, more diabetic-like traits or precursors, smoke more cigarettes, exercise less (because they can't find time to do so), are "overdriving" certain of their endocrine glands in a manner that can be expected to damage their coronary arteries, eat meals rich in cholesterol and animal fat, and also suffer more from high blood pressure than Type B subjects.

As we have intimated before, the presence of one or of all these risk factors in a person would not lead to his becoming a Type A individual. Whatever cholesterol, for example, can and may do, its excess accumulation in your blood could never force you to *wish* to accomplish more and more in less and less time, nor could it ever make you any more aggressive and hostile than you are right now. On the other hand, such striving on your part—as we have repeatedly shown experimentally—does lead to a rise in your serum cholesterol and blood fat. Such striving may also evoke the other risk factors described above, and in so doing bring on coronary artery disease. That is why so many Type A and so very few Type B subjects suffer from this disease.

Consider first the somatic and biochemical results of emotional upset. Any form of emotion is experienced in certain well-circumscribed parts of our brains—the neocortex and the limbic system. Almost immediately after receiving and acting upon the proper sensory or intellectual signals, these areas of the brain send their own meticulously coded instructions to another very complex portion of your brain, the hypothalamus. This area lies at the base of the brain, directly over and intimately in contact with your pituitary gland. It is the prime function of your hypothalamus to supply a "body" to any emotion perceived higher up in the brain, but it also has something to do with the quality of an emotion, too. For example, if all connections between an animal's hypothalamus and the higher areas of the brain are sev-

ered, thus freeing the hypothalamus from all con-
straint, the animal becomes hopelessly maniacal and
deadly dangerous.

As a rule, the stimulated hypothalamus sends out
stereotyped coded signals whose precise character depends upon the particular emotion perceived. For example, if you are suddenly confronted with a sorrow-
inducing situation, the hypothalamus will send signals
to your tear glands, to the blood vessels in your face,
and to nerve complexes governing your lungs and
heart. You will turn pale, burst into tears, begin to
sob, and your heart probably will slow down.

On the other hand, if you become intensely angered
by some phenomenon, your hypothalamus will almost
instantaneously send signals to all or almost all the
nerve endings of your sympathetic nervous system
(that portion of your nervous system not directly
under your control), causing them to secrete relatively
large amounts of epinephrine and norepinephrine
(otherwise known as adrenalin and nonadrenalin, or
as a group, as catecholamines). In addition, this same
fit of anger will probably also induce the hypothalamus to send additional messages to the pituitary
gland, the master of all endocrine glands, urging it to
discharge some of its own exclusively manufactured
hormones (such as growth hormone) and also to send
out chemical signals to the adrenal, sex, and thyroid
glands and the pancreas as well, so that they in turn
may secrete excess amounts of *their* exclusively manufactured hormones. As a consequence, not only will
your tissues be bathed by an excess of catecholamines
when you become angry, they may also be exposed to
exceedingly large amounts of various pituitary and
adrenal hormones, testosterone (or estrogen), thyrox-
ine, and insulin.

Again, when a man or an animal is engaged in any
sort of struggle, the emotional repercussions of this

struggle induce the hypothalamus to send out the same series of signals. Roughly, the same complex of nervous and endocrine gland hormones are secreted as by the angry man. But after all, more often than not, a struggling man is also an angry man.

Now if the struggle becomes a *chronic* one, then a *chronic* excess discharge of these various hormones also occurs. It is, of course, obvious that the Type A man is engaged in a chronic, more or less continuous, minute-by-minute struggle. It was no surprise to us to find that most Type A subjects not only discharge more norepinephrine and epinephrine (the nerve hormones or catecholamines), but also "overdrive" their pituitary glands to secrete too much ACTH (a hormone that stimulates the adrenal glands to discharge cortisol and other hormones) and growth hormone. Further, most Type A subjects exhibit an excess of the pancreatic hormone insulin in their blood—a sign generally believed to indicate that something is seriously wrong with the disposition of fat and sugar in the body. As a result of these abnormal discharges of catecholamines from the nerve endings and hormones from the pituitary, adrenal, and pancreatic glands, most Type A subjects exhibit (1) an increased blood level of cholesterol and fat, (2) a marked lag in ridding their blood of the cholesterol added to it by the food ingested, (3) a prediabetic state, and (4) an increased tendency for the clotting elements of the blood (the platelets and fibrinogen) to precipitate out. In a sense, Type A subjects too often are exposing their arteries to "high voltage" chemicals even during the "low voltage" periods of their daily living.

Because we had observed that most of our severely affected Type A subjects exhibited these changes, and because we knew that they were hypothalamus-induced phenomena, we suspected that we could duplicate this entire syndrome in a rat if we altered its hypothalamic function. As we already have described, this was accomplished several years ago. Afterward, the operated-upon rat not only exhibited a behavior pattern resembling that of the Type A subject, it also exhibited most of the above hormonal and biochemical abnormalities.

Given these abnormalities, it is easy enough to envision the advent of coronary artery disease. What is difficult to determine, however, is the *proportionate* culpability of each agent.

For example, most Type A subjects not only exhibit a higher serum cholesterol level (as do our rats suffering from experimentally induced Type A Behavior Pattern) than Type B subjects, they also take three to four times longer ridding their blood of dietary cholesterol after each meal than Type B subjects. Thus, the inner lining of their coronary arteries is exposed continuously to large amounts of cholesterol in its most dangerous form. Ordinarily, the artery's inner lining allows the entrance of only very small quantities of cholesterol from the blood into the interior of the artery's wall. Of course, the more cholesterol present in the blood, the more eventually will seep in. And once having entered the artery wall, dietary cholesterol doesn't easily depart again, but remains perhaps for from weeks to months to damage and cause cellular overgrowth or plaque formation. When this process is allowed to take place over a few decades, the wonder is not that an artery finally closes but rather why it doesn't do so more rapidly. Of course, in those unfortunate children whose serum cholesterol level is grotesquely high (1,000 mg./100 ml.), the coronary arteries often thicken and close long before puberty.

But it isn't the behavior pattern-induced cholesterol changes alone that present a danger to the coronary arteries of Type A subjects. As we have stated above, these persons are also manufacturing and discharging too much epinephrine and norepinephrine. Unfortunately, an excess of either of these catecholamines leads, for one thing, to increased intravascular deposition of the clotting elements of the blood. Such deposition particularly occurs on the internal surface of a coronary artery plaque, thus leading to its enlargement as the clotted elements gradually change into tissue indistinguishable from that making up the initial plaque. Not only is there general agreement among cardiac scientists that plaques are made larger by the precipitation upon them of blood-clotting elements, but most English pathologists believe that this is the chief, perhaps the only, way by which plaques (otherwise remaining small and harmless) can become life threatening. Thus, the Type A subject may have arterial plaques being enlarged, not only from within, by the entrance therein of cholesterol, but also from without, by the deposition of clotting agents caused by the excess catecholamines injected into his bloodstream as he carries on his struggles against either time, other people, or both. When we examined the coronary arteries of scores of Type A subjects, that is precisely what we found to have happened.

The coronary arteries of many Type A subjects may also suffer from a third insult, which stems from the excess circulating catecholamines they possess. These excess catecholamines, besides encouraging the precipitation of clotting elements as noted above, may also cause serious narrowing of the small capillaries nourishing the coronary blood vessels and the plaques appended thereto. Such narrowing, if chronically continued, would seriously interfere not only with the nourishment of the still intact parts of the coronary arteries, but even more important, would threaten the viability of the internal areas of the plaques that may be present. This last is an ever-threatening eventuality, because the growth of a plaque is rarely accompanied by a sufficient growth of new blood vessels to nourish it properly. Hence, any further reduction in an already inadequate flow would lead to the death or necrosis of large parts of the plaque. As we've already emphasized, the real danger of a plaque is not just its size but rather its state of internal decay and ulceration. It is these last characteristics that so often turn symptomless and relatively harmless coronary artery disease into potentially lethal coronary heart disease.

As if these three potential artery-wrecking processes of excess catecholamines were not serious enough, the coronary arteries of most Type A subjects are subjected to a fourth peril. Apparently because of the hypothalamus-induced overstimulation of the sympathetic nervous system, excess insulin begins to accumulate in the blood. Now, of all known conditions that may lead to the disease of the coronary arteries, none is recognized as more devastating than any state associated with an excess of insulin in the blood. Is it the insulin accumulation in the blood or is it the abnormal metabolism of fat and sugar that may precede and cause the accumulation of excess insulin that so surely and quickly leads to the deterioration in the artery's structure? No investigator can be positive. Unfortunately, however, too many Type A subjects exhibit both abnormalities, so the distinction is purely academic. Such destruction of arteries inevitably takes place when both conditions are present.

Of all these known abnormal mechanisms set in motion by the chronic presence of Type A Behavior Pattern, which do we suspect is the most lethal destroyer of an artery's integrity? This is an extraordinarily difficult question to answer at this juncture, particularly when we are not absolutely sure that Type A behavior does not also produce some other biochemical and biophysical abnormalities that still have not been detected. But if we were forced now to choose the worst chemical insult, the guess is that it is the chronic excess discharge and circulation of the catecholamines. This may be the chief factor in the total process of arterial decay and thrombosis. We have seen coronary heart disease erupt in many subjects whose blood insulin level and metabolism of cholesterol, fat, and sugar were quite normal. But rarely have we ever witnessed the onset of this disease in a person whose rate of manufacture and secretion of catecholamines we did not know or suspect to have been increased.

It is possible that in the future we may find out how to neutralize the excess catecholamines secreted by Type A men, using some newly discovered chemical or drug. It is possible, too, that the excess fat, cholesterol, insulin, and ACTH secreted in excess by Type A persons may be similarly controlled. But this will not happen in 1975, in 1976, or even in 1980. Meanwhile, since it is Type A behavior that breeds these hydra-headed biochemical abnormalities, it is this root cause that deserves our attention right now. Thus our next section—contending with Type A Behavior Pattern.

Chapter 15

WHAT TO DO
IF YOU'RE TYPE A:
GUIDELINES

We have spoken on scores of occasions during these past ten years to many thousands of physicians in the United States, Canada, the United Kingdom, and Europe. The great majority of these physicians, presented with the clinical and scientific data that we have described in Chapter 6, have been quite ready to accept the probability that there is something about Type A Behavior Pattern that makes it a major factor in intensifying coronary artery disease and bringing on coronary heart disease prematurely.

But then they frequently ask us a question that neither we nor anyone else can yet answer: Can you prevent the onset of coronary heart disease in a Type A person if he changes or markedly ameliorates his behavior pattern? It is the same question asked of cancer specialists: Can a heavy cigarette smoker avoid suffering from lung cancer in the future if he gives up cigarette smoking *now*?

What is really being asked is this: Is it *too late* to prevent coronary heart disease (or lung cancer) by eliminating the agents that have been fairly well demonstrated to be inducing these disorders? The answer has been the same since the days of Hippocrates. If you find the cause or one of the causes of a disease, and are able to remove that cause without serious harm to the patient, remove it, no matter what the stage of the disease. This is the principle that makes physicians plead with alcoholics to quit drinking even if their liver is already enlarged. It is the same principle that makes lung specialists urge even those of their patients who have already had a cancerous lung removed not to smoke. Acting on this same principle, we strive just as hard to alter the Type A Behavior Pattern of a sixty-year-old patient who has already suffered one or more heart attacks as we do the Type A Behavior Pattern of an otherwise seemingly healthy individual thirty-five years old. *We will never, never believe that it is ever too late to aid such a person by taking away one of the major causes of his disorder.*

In the next few years, large groups of Type A subjects will probably engage in tests during which half will be given therapy and counsel in order to ameliorate or abolish their Type A Behavior Pattern. The other half will not be treated, and will serve as a control. This experiment will furnish the scientific proof many of our colleagues have insisted upon. These subjects then will be studied frequently over the years. We are already confident results will show that those persons who do alter their Type A Behavior Pattern will invariably be the better for it. It will never be too late to do them some good. We are sure that they will prove to be far more resistant to the future onset of coronary heart disease than their untreated, unchanged Type A counterparts. In our own private practice during the past few decades, those who suffered a heart attack or who died suddenly were not the coronary patients who reformed, but rather the patients who either could not or would not alter their Type A Behavior Pattern. Most physicians reviewing their own experience agree with us that it is probably never really too late to try to rid a coronary patient of his sense of time urgency or of his free-floating hostility.

Before getting too far in this chapter, let us be candid about certain matters. First, in the majority of cases, Type A Behavior Pattern can be altered and altered drastically; and it is a terribly dangerous delusion to believe otherwise. Certainly any phenomenon that flourishes as does this pattern in certain milieus (the United States, Finland, and England, for example) and is almost nonexistent in others (Yemen, southern Italy, and Africa, for example) cannot be ascribed solely to genetic predestination.

Second, it is probably a symptom of the disorder itself that induces many subjects suffering from Type A Behavior Pattern to believe that, regardless of their habits, they will still be lucky enough to escape the results. "Yes, I know that many of my habits are bad and they probably do cause heart disease in a lot of fellows, but I'm probably not going to be one of those fellows." That is the sort of head-in-the-sand philosophy with which hundreds of thousands of middle-aged Type A subjects now delude themselves.

In fact, for every five men who exhibit unquestioned Type A behavior, perhaps four will deny or underplay the intensity of the syndrome. The Type A person will particularly deny the existence of this pattern in himself if it carries the slightest pejorative connotations. It must be remembered that Type A subjects do not easily admit—even to themselves—the existence of any defect or emotional stigma. Certainly the most difficult Type A man of all to convince about his possession of this behavior pattern is that one who not only suffers from a sense of time urgency but also from free-floating hostility. We ourselves have been ridiculed more than once by the latter type of individual because of our attempts to demonstrate to him his possession of the behavior pattern.

Then, too, whereas many Type A subjects would admit (sometimes grudgingly) to their physician the presence of this behavior pattern, they would be most loath to do so to their wives or their peers and certainly not to their subordinates.

Third, no mass attack can be effectively launched against Type A Behavior Pattern until a major proportion of our medical colleagues not only recognize its overriding importance in hastening the onset of coronary heart disease but are willing to work to convince their patients of it. We do not mean to imply that most internists are not suspicious of the possible dangers of Type A Behavior Pattern. Most of them do suspect that it probably plays a part in bringing on or at least worsening the degree of coronary artery disease already present. But usually they content themselves with just advising their patients to "slow down" or "relax."

Nor is an internist necessarily helping his Type A patient, if becoming aware of his struggles with time and/or other persons, he refers him to a psychiatrist. Usually the patient will refuse to go, and even if he does, few psychiatrists will be prepared to help him. Ideally, it is the general practitioner or the internist who should cope with this problem. But in order to do so, he first must be able to recognize all facets of the behavior pattern, and he must be *emotionally*, and not just intellectually, convinced of its quintessential importance in the causation of coronary heart disease.

The physician who attempts to alter Type A Behavior Pattern will simply fail if the afflicted subject even scents the possibility that the physician himself is doubtful of the pattern's relationship to the disease. It is difficult enough for a Type A subject to alter his behavior even when his doctor is sure about the harm it is doing him. He would never do so if he even suspected that his physician wasn't really absolutely convinced of the necessity.

Similarly, heavy cigarette smokers quit smoking only when they finally accept data that make it virtually impossible for them to believe that they can continue to smoke and escape serious consequences. But even then, if one of these reformed tobacco addicts should happen to meet a healthy oldster of eighty years or more who has smoked cigarettes throughout his life, only too often he again wonders if he may not have been rather precipitate in giving up the habit.

In the last analysis, it is you, the Type A subject, who must accept the major responsibility in wrenching yourself loose from the habits you may have learned to view as virtues. Of course we will try very hard in succeeding paragraphs to offer guidance and techniques of a kind that have helped others and can help you in freeing yourself from the thralldom of Type A Behavior Pattern. *But neither we nor your own doctor can force you to seek this freedom. It is you who must take the steps to liberate yourself.*

PHILOSOPHICAL GUIDELINES

Many of you who now suffer from Type A Behavior Pattern have probably always considered that it was doing you good in the sense that it was directly responsible for whatever successes you achieved. To point out that, on the contrary, you have become enslaved to a rigid complex of stereotyped thoughts and habits that actually *impeded* your progress in life may at first glance seem absurd. But let us look a bit more closely at your life.

First, review your successes. How often were they

really due to impatience? Were you ever promoted or did you achieve success in your job, position, business, or profession because you did things *faster* than anyone else? Or because you easily became hostile or belligerent? We have questioned hundreds of men who have been successful in various economic or professional positions. Not a single one of these men, when asked to deliberate a bit about the causes of their success, ever concluded that any component of Type A Behavior Pattern had been significantly responsible.

Thus no executive of an advertising agency ever told us that he lost a client because a deadline was missed (as sometimes they had been missed) or because the client decided that the executive took too much time to accomplish his tasks. Similarly, no attorney ever told us that he lost a client because he took too long in bringing the client's case to court. Indeed, as one attorney once said to us, "No matter how long one of my clients must wait for juridical action, if I win the case, he always will return to my office if he again needs an attorney. But no matter how rapidly I may get court action for another client, if I lose his case, then I'll never see that client again." Nor have we ever found a banker, physician, truck driver, florist, haberdasher, carpenter, or plumber who could think of any person, group of persons or company who failed *because they managed to do a job too well, too slowly*. On the other hand, they were able to recall dozens of persons or companies who had failed *because they did a job too rapidly and too poorly*.

Actually, a *continuous* frenzied pace almost ensures later disaster in every field of human activity. Almost all successful ventures, whether or not they are initiated by excellent creative decisions and judgments, must be sustained by such processes. Even the most harried Type A person will admit, regretfully perhaps, that the surest way of causing almost any project to fail eventually is to substitute hurried, stereotyped thinking and action for relatively leisurely deliberation and meditation. If there is one prime principle that should never be forgotten it is this: The thrust of creative energy is always weakened by repetitive urgency.

So what we are saying is this: if you have been successful, it is not *because* of your Type A Behavior Pattern, but *despite* it. Admittedly, the *Queen Elizabeth*, even with its anchor still only half raised and dragging through the water, could still easily outdistance a rowboat. But what would you think of its captain if he claimed that his dragging anchor had been responsible for this victory and insisted on dragging it on all future voyages? Not a single one of your friends, fellow workers, employees, or superiors respects or admires you because you attempt to "hurry" hurry itself. If they do respect and admire you, they probably do so in spite of this "hurry sickness."

You may argue that if you didn't have the drive to succeed or accomplish, you would not have arrived at your present level of success or prosperity. This may well be correct, but such a drive need not be a pellmell, frenzied race to acquire as many things in as little time as possible. Many Type B men have drive, loads of it; *but they monitor it with a calendar, not a stopwatch*.

We believe that you will agree with us when we state that it is desirable to eliminate or alter this nonessential, potentially destructive behavior pattern. Let us now examine some of the additional philosophical aids that may make the job easier.

YOU CAN CHANGE YOUR
BEHAVIOR PATTERN

A number of physicians have gloomily generalized to us that "once a Type A person, always a Type A person." But this need not be so, as these doctors would easily discover if they studied the waning intensity of Type A behavior in certain of their own patients after they had survived a very severe myocardial infarction. These survivors may shed many of their Type A traits. For example, they no longer appear to be harried by their former sense of time urgency. They no longer hurry the speech of others, nor flagellate themselves attempting to think about or to perform two or more things simultaneously; no longer do they fret if they must wait in line for service, or for a delayed plane departure, or for an automobile, in front of their own, that may be moving too slowly for their taste; and no longer do they estimate life and its enjoyment in terms of acquired "numbers."

Having ventured so very close to the "other country" where there is neither time nor numbers, these survivors demonstrate an awareness of the only truly important "number" in their life, namely, the one indicating the number of days that have been allotted to them to remain on this planet.

Let us listen to a distinguished New York physician tell how he changed his behavior pattern after suffering a heart attack at the age of forty-nine. He decided that he would have to reform because he couldn't think of any other possible causes for his cardiac debacle. (His blood pressure, blood sugar, and serum cholesterol levels had been normal prior to his attack.)

"For the first six months after my heart attack, I lacked the stamina to return to any of my former activities. I believe I had to muster up all the reserves I possessed just to survive. But during this period, I also had the chance to review many of my pre-attack activities and beliefs.

"I began to appreciate how severe my sense of time urgency had been and how much of it was due to my aggressive overdrive to be too many things to too many people. I began to see too that various persons whom I considered giants in relation to my medical career were really dwarfs. I knew finally that my first aim had to be to survive and to survive in terms of beauty, life's beauty.

"Now five years have passed since I had my heart attack. What have I changed, you ask? Well for one thing, I no longer remain at my office after 5:30 P.M. Before the attack, I frequently worked there until midnight. Now, my evening phone calls are censored and I accept only the truly urgent or important messages. Before, I was available to every neurotic patient who just got lonesome and wanted to talk to me.

"Now I restrict by over half the number of lectures I give either at my own medical school or elsewhere. I rarely attend medical meetings unless I feel I have something terribly important to learn or to contribute. Now I have a home on Long Island, not in Manhattan, and I have learned to garden, to spend more time with my wife and children, and most important of all, to *enjoy* spending my time in this fashion. I did not do so before my attack.

"I know I haven't changed my basic personality just as a leopard doesn't really change his spots nor does a sow's ear ever serve as good material for a silk purse. But I have learned I can make various adjustments in my milieu so that my personality isn't challenged or aroused—it simply slumbers. After all, a sleeping tiger is as gentle as a sleeping rabbit; just don't challenge him by awakening him. And so I play a game with my basically hostile personality: I try to keep it 'asleep.' That isn't always easy, and I admit that it amounts to a conscious and constant surveillance of everything that I am doing and what I must stop doing. But what a small price to pay for the fun of living this new sort of life, these past five years."

There are many persons like this doctor who, having suffered an infarction, have managed to shed some or even all their Type A traits without any help from their physician. One cannot persist in believing that the generalization "once a Type A, always a Type A" has validity. Actually, many Type A subjects hesitate even to begin to change their behavior pattern, but not because they feel it is a hopeless task; they fear that without this pattern, they will encounter economic or professional disaster. Yet as we have already explained, this is a silly and needless fear. Or if we can quote the doctor above once more: "Neither the heart attack nor my changed behavior pattern has hurt my medical career in any way. I have been asked since my heart attack to assume positions carrying much more distinction than the positions offered to me prior to this attack."

Certainly we can agree, from our own experience, with the connotations implicit in this last remark. We have observed the careers of a number of persons who have altered their behavior pattern and we cannot recall a single one whose financial or social status deteriorated following the change in their Type A Behavior Pattern.

THERE IS A NEED FOR SELF-APPRAISAL

Robert Browning once wrote that "a man's reach should exceed his grasp." Almost all Type A individuals would agree most enthusiastically with this concept. Indeed, most of them throughout their lives have consistently attempted to act upon it. Certainly, no great harm can come to any man who consistently strives to seize what his fingertips can barely touch. But a man should know the limits of his reach, otherwise he can never know when he is simply creating frustrations. Unfortunately, few if any Type A subjects have any clear idea of the extent of their reach or the "firmness" of their grasp. They never have succeeded in gauging their intrinsic intellectual and emotional capacities.

As a consequence, few Type A subjects possess a continuous and basic sense of security. Whatever sense of security they do manage to have is ephemeral, maintained only by the continuously successful completions of more and more tasks or challenges. This is probably the chief reason why the Type A person so desperately strives to accomplish more and more things in less and less time. He is forever trying—and failing, except briefly—to appease a gnawing sense of insecurity with an ever-increasing number of socioeconomic victories or conquests.

It is this *deep* sense of insecurity that so often impels Type A persons to attempt to dominate all situations in which they are involved. In a peculiar sort of subconscious reasoning, Type A persons believe that if they can do this, and always win at everything they undertake, somehow or other they will finally achieve a lasting state of security. It never seems to occur to them that true security always depends upon an accurate self-evaluation of one's capacities and qualities, an evaluation Type A persons appear to shun as if it were the plague itself.

If you are a Type A person, therefore, it is more than likely that you have never submitted your basic capacities and qualities to a rigorous self-appraisal. If you wish to diminish the intensity of the behavior pattern, you must try. Until such an appraisal is made, you never will know just how strong or weak your intellectual and emotional processes really are. Lacking such self-knowledge, you cannot help feeling insecure. Your basic security does not depend upon, nor can it be safeguarded by, the opinions of your friends and associates; it depends upon your own precise awareness not only of your positive qualities and capacities but also of your inadequacies. Facing up to the latter may well *increase* your sense of security rather than diminish it.

If you possess an absolutely unbiased picture of yourself, you will become far less dependent upon the opinions of other persons, and far less inclined toward a frenzied career of acquiring more and more numbers. You will begin to understand that you have harried yourself mercilessly and needlessly in the past in an essentially vain effort to gain security from outside events and persons, when the only real hope for such security lay in frank self-evaluations.

1. In a meaningful self-appraisal, you must first attempt to determine just how intelligent, how percipient, and how creative you have been in your job.
2. You must examine your sense of humor to determine how it has served you. Is it chiefly a repository for jokes and anecdotes? Or does it function—as it should—to help you perceive your own occasionally ludicrous aspects?
3. You must assess your capacity for flexibility, for change of pace, and for rapid adaptability to change.
4. You must look at your leadership qualities and determine their worth.
5. You must examine all the activities that now absorb your intellectual, emotional, and spiritual interests. How many of these activities have to do with your concern with art, literature, music, drama, philosophy, history, science, and the wonders of the natural world that envelop you?
6. You must seek out and assess the intensity of your free-floating hostilities. As you do so, don't allow either rationalization or sophistry to blind you to their possible presence.

7. You must try to estimate the ease with which you can receive and give loyalty and affection.

8. You must attempt to determine the amount of sheer courage you possess. And if in this assay you detect some very large yellow splotches of frank fear in your personality, don't overlook them. Treasure them, just as you will treasure the steel-gray masses of frank courage you are likely to find there, too.

9. You must dare to examine critically your ethical and moral principles. How honest have I been in my life, how often and under what circumstances have I cheated, lied, and borne false witness against my neighbor? are questions you must not fail to present to yourself. And painful as it may be in the beginning, stubbornly persist in providing yourself with true answers.

10. Finally, you must not be afraid to ask, and to persist in asking yourself over and over, until you have answered the question: *What apart from the eternal clutter of my everyday living should be the essence of my life?*

But you may ask, "What scale can I use to evaluate these intrinsic qualities, capacities and deficits of mine?" All you have to do is to assess the same qualities, capacities and deficits of a number of your friends and associates. Then compare yourself. But take care when selecting those who are to serve as "scales." Choose as many persons that you feel may be superior to you in their possession of various qualities as persons whose attributes you have good reason to believe may be quite inferior to yours. After all, the object of this self-appraisal is to give you, perhaps for the first time in your life, a truthfully derived estimate of your basic worth.

And as you make this self-appraisal, you must of course review again the powerful hold that a sense of time urgency has obtained upon your personality. You must recognize that more likely than not you feel the need to hurry no matter what action you indulge in. You will probably discover that the growth of your sense of time urgency has been so unbridled and irrational that it cannot be abolished simply by an understanding of its provenance and the factors sustaining it. Rather, it will have to be subdued by instituting the drill-like program we describe in the next chapter.

Finally, assuming you have recognized the presence of free-floating hostility in yourself, you should remember that this destructive emotional force is only one side of a coin whose other side is love. The fierceness of your hostility can best be assuaged by affection and love. However, it is not at all easy for Type A individuals to accept affection and love. Acceptance of affection requires an element of passivity and dependency, traits most Type A subjects have rejected. Nevertheless, it is never really too late to begin to learn how to accept affection and love. And since such acceptance is perhaps the only effective way of diminishing the fury of free-floating hostility, you would be well advised to begin learning now.

Having made this self-appraisal, don't be too surprised if you begin to attain the sort of equanimity you never experienced before. For example, having determined in your self-appraisal that your intelligence is not that of a genius but about average, you are far less likely to become irritated and cantankerous when you confront a person whose intelligence is higher than yours; you will accept the discrepancy. (Recently, having observed an extraordinarily charming and relaxed doctor, one of us asked him how he avoided Type A behavior. He smiled and said, "A few years ago, I faced up to the truth that I always had been and always will be a second-rate physician. After I realized this, it was quite easy to begin to relax.") Conversely, you will find it less necessary to challenge other persons having a lower intelligence than you do. You will no longer need to use these persons as whipping dogs for the purpose of sating the demands of your former insecurity.

You may also be very pleasantly surprised to discover that when you meet persons who exhibit the sort of free-floating hostility that you found and detested in yourself, you no longer wish to parry their hostile thrusts. You may even surprise them, and yourself, too, by responding to their aggressive challenge with an act of affection half compounded (as it should be) of pity for the suffering the presence of their hostility imposes upon them.

YOU MUST TRY TO RETRIEVE YOUR TOTAL PERSONALITY

It is characteristic of the Type A personality to lack interest in the broader satisfactions of life and human culture. Those activities which are generally considered humane and edifying—the great works and achievements in art, music, drama, philosophy, history, science, and indeed the charms of nature itself—only too often tend to bore him. This sort of person eventually becomes so caught up in the process of acquiring more and more things in less and less time that he has little desire or need to interest himself in any other intellectual or spiritual process.

If your self-appraisal has made it clear to you that you no longer care much about the humanities, about art or science or the works of the mind, and that you also find less and less time to devote to your friends, then you cannot fail to see that you are rapidly dehumanizing yourself and in a most dangerous manner. What will there be left of your personality in a few short years if this spoilage continues unchecked? In a very real way, you are buying your way through life by selling yourself.

Obviously it is not easy to retrieve a personality, half of whose initial basic components may already have eroded away. It is particularly difficult to do so when the components of the personality that do remain continue to be almost exclusively absorbed in acquisitive activities. Yet no real change in Type A Behavior Pattern can be achieved until certain parts of the personality are at least partially restored. And no such restoration is possible until the Type A subject not only becomes aware of his atrophied personality, but determines to do something positive about it.

How is this to be accomplished? First of all, you must be deliberate. Set aside a portion of each day for pursuits that have nothing to do with your normal vocation. Use this time to expand your fields of interest and enjoyment. The subject matter is less important than your attitude toward it; the critical point is that you somehow detach yourself from the narrow pattern of work and short-circuited emotion. Most suitable of all, perhaps, is an attempt to widen your cultural and intellectual horizons, though you may find this difficult given your years of neglect. It may be weeks or months before these attempts begin to yield pleasure, although the effort cannot help but do you good from the start.

A reviving personality must be nourished with another kind of new communication—communication with people. Besides opening yourself to the riches of art and knowledge, you must also open yourself to new friendships, particularly to those which can reinforce your newly expanded interests. How long has it been since you noticed yourself warming to someone new, how long since you made even the mildest effort to bring a new person into your life and affections?

Do not underestimate the difficulty of this process: the Italian novelist Ignazio Silone was probably only too accurate in remarking that "the true revolution of our times is the disappearance of friendship." Most of us are so far out of the habit of searching for friends and retaining them that we feel it awkward and painful to begin. But there is nothing so satisfying as success in this regard, and nothing so basic to the problem of subduing the Type A's free-floating hostility.

Another form of emotional sustenance crucial to the reviving personality is a stock of fulfilling and pleasant memories. You must make a very conscious effort each day to choose from among the passing events and experiences those which yield pleasure. Enjoy them as you live through them; indeed, *concentrate* on savoring them. And then file them away mentally, to be called up at leisure. In this way you will not only live each moment more fully, but you will also be able to look backwards at your life with a new and special sense of satisfaction. What your personality needs is latitude—for fantasies, dreams, fresh hopes. Only you can provide it. In short, you are being urged to inject "unexpectedness" in your life if only because it is the key element of true humanity.

YOU MUST ESTABLISH LIFE GOALS

Ideally, you should establish two sets of life goals. The first set should embrace the accomplishments that you wish to achieve in your economic or professional career. The second set should include those that you wish to fulfill in your private life. These goals should serve not only to give purpose and meaning to your life, but perhaps almost as important, prevent you from embarking upon a career in which sheer hyperactivity replaces well-monitored progress.

So you must ask yourself precisely what you wish to accomplish in your job—it certainly will do no harm to commit these aims to paper—and then take a long, tranquil look at yourself as a private human being. What do you want out of life? Try to remember, as you begin to formulate your aims and goals, how little one really requires to live well and happily. Especially as you pass sixty-five, and family responsibilities decrease, you may find yourself satisfied with little more than adequate shelter, food, and clothing; sufficient funds to buy an occasional book or theater ticket or to take a short vacation; and enough friends to stave off loneliness.

After you have established life goals for yourself, don't fail to review them frequently. If you discover, as you probably will, that the aims of your life are really rather modest, knowing this can make gentle your passage through life.

MAKE SOME GESTURES TOWARD MYTH, RITUAL, AND TRADITION

One of the characteristics of modern times is the rapid disappearance of myth, ritual, and tradition from the lives of most of us. Soon, perhaps, you'll have no more need of such abstractions than a moose or sloth does. Yet for millennia they were important, exclusively human concepts that demanded and deserved much of mankind's attention. Apparently, however, we are now tiring in our efforts to keep them viable.

Some of you, particularly when your children were much younger, probably made valiant efforts to establish some ritual traditions in your own family. Unfortunately, however, the institution and maintenance of even rather trivial family traditions (such as the family reading of Dickens's *A Christmas Carol* on Christmas Eve) require a certain steadfastness, and a very strong belief in the spiritual value of sustained social or cultural continuities. And just as the common community has already faltered in its appreciation of traditions, so also have too many of you ceased to concern yourselves with patterned remembrances.

Perhaps you may think it absurd, in a book dedicated to the problem of coronary heart disease, that we as doctors bring in such seeming irrelevancies as myth, ritual, and tradition—particularly when our contemporary society is shedding itself as rapidly as it can of all three. Absurd we may be, perhaps irrelevant, too. Perhaps our Western society will prove to have acted in a supremely wise fashion when it began to replace them with mechanization, automation, and total bureaucratic social security. Except for one thing: this is the first time in the experience of man on earth that a large group of individuals is attempting to live in so absolute a spiritual void.

So far, our machines and computers still click conscientiously away. Yet how strangely sad we have become, as we search without hope for the color, the glory, and the grandeur that we think life should sometimes shed upon us.

It is for you to recognize the rituals and traditions that may still exist in your life. It is for you, too, to add new rituals and traditions. These need not be pompously contrived, grandiose social artifices carrying joy and fun to absolutely no one. Indeed, they should not be. Rather, they can be simple, regular repetitions of certain small, even trivial events in the past that were uniquely pleasant or truly enjoyed.

We have a friend who yearly takes his wife to a particular hotel in Arizona, which just happened twenty-eight years ago to be completely filled up and unable to accept our friend and his new bride on their honeymoon. Admittedly, this "ritual" is not earth-shattering in its importance, but it is to them. By observing it they live in two eras, now and the past, and the echoes of time enrich their whole existence.

But all traditions do not have to be based on ancient lineage or need be of gravity or importance. Any event enjoyed or appreciated in the past that is regularly repeated automatically turns into a tradition. For example, those of you who regularly attend the theater, symphony, opera, or various sporting events with the same persons or groups of persons are indulging in a tradition. The same is true if you annually give or attend the same Easter, Thanksgiving, or Christmas "family" dinner. Or you might give a Christmas Eve or pre-Lent cocktail party each year. Again you are nurturing a tradition.

Unfortunately, however, too many of you who are severely afflicted with Type A Behavior Pattern are inwardly annoyed by such activities, even though you go through with them. Instead of viewing these repetitive social activities as carrying a soft charm in their own right, only too often they seem almost insufferable to you. They appear to be "wasting" your time and to be "accomplishing" so little. It would be well to remember that the degree of irritation such traditional activities produce in you might serve as an index of the seriousness of your own emotional and spiritual disorientation.

Study your social relationship with people who do not play a direct part in your vocational life. If you conclude after such study that these social relationships have never truly flourished; that they have always played a very distant secondary role to your economic endeavors; and that they are increasingly becoming more boring and irritating, you can be very certain of one truth—you are rapidly dehumanizing yourself.

And the way back? First, at each of the future social activities (traditional or otherwise) you attend, you should not fail to remind yourself *consciously* of the fact that you suffer from an emotional illness by which people are made subservient to the acquisition of numbers. Of course, the first score or more times you remind yourself of this truth, it really won't help very much, because you still will not be able to believe it.

Second, try studying the faces of your friends and relatives to see what you can discover about them as individuals. You might find it interesting also to recall their past as you may have known it a decade or two before. How did they look then, what has life done to them? Could things have come out differently?

Third, you should ask yourself why *they* still appear willing to share traditional activities with *you*. Do they go to the theater or the opera with you because they find you appealing and interesting? Or is it because they know of almost no one else whom they could ask to accompany them?

But a final note of caution. Up to this point, we have assumed that it is only you that has to change your attitude to and regard for social relationships. However, it is quite likely that your friends have become as delinquent as you in safeguarding the finer nuances of meaningful friendship. We emphasize this because Type A individuals do tend to seek each other out socially, despite the fact that only too often their free-floating hostility and excessive competitiveness sometimes convert their social meetings into war games.

If, then, your friends have also lost their way, is it worthwhile to try keeping them as friends? Of course! Type A subjects may have the serious emotional difficulties we have described in this book, but they also possess beguiling and admirable traits. Honesty, loyalty, and the capacity to give a rough, unmitigated sort of affection are qualities that are encountered as often —perhaps possibly even more often—in Type A as in Type B subjects. We would be grossly unfair if we failed to note that the Type A person often has an air of animation that makes him an exciting person to know.

Nor will we deny that the Type A subject often— particularly early in his career—can be astoundingly creative. He usually manages quite adroitly to gather and direct the forces that will convert his creative ideas into real achievements. It is only later, when he has been seduced by the quantitative components of his life, and has begun to neglect its quality, that he becomes a true Type A. But even then he can still be a pleasant friend.

Also, if most of your friends are Type A individuals, you can't help beginning to recognize that many of their traits, which you have now begun to observe and attempt to understand, are precisely the same as yours. Perhaps nothing can help you rid yourself of an objectionable trait faster than your recognition of the presence of this same trait in a friend or acquaintance. And in this process of discovery you will learn to develop a sense of tolerance and pity. Unlike you, they remain unaware of, and committed to, a behavior pattern that in fact goads them mercilessly.

STOP USING YOUR RIGHT HAND TO DO THE WORK YOUR LEFT HAND SHOULD BE DOING

There are a considerable number of very important, perhaps even life-important, processes and transactions that will demand your attention in the future. Also, myriads of relatively unimportant matters will present themselves. These, the ephemera and the trivia, can be called the "left-hand activities" of your life.

Unfortunately, the Type A person often fails to distinguish between these categories. He is quite apt to devote as much or even more of his energy and attention to a trifling task as he does to a truly major problem.

For example, recently a friend of ours, having become board chairman of his food corporation, found himself "tutoring" his successor as president of the corporation. This new president was a Type A person, while our friend was not. It came as no surprise to us when our friend noted with dismay that his successor was spending far too much time correcting the grammatical mistakes in interoffice memoranda. "He must learn," complained our friend, "to separate the wheat from the chaff."

We, of course, hope that this new president will learn that correcting grammar is work at best for his left hand, not his right hand. But until he does learn, he will continue to harry himself subconsciously.

One does not need to be a corporate executive to make the mistake of doing left-hand work with the right hand. The plumber, the brick mason, and the electrician who spend evening after evening poring over their income tax forms when a single visit to an accountant and the expenditure of a few dollars would take care of it, are just as guilty.

The great difficulty the Type A subject experiences in delegating work to others is only in part due to his "hurry sickness." It is also due to his belief that *all* his activities require his right hand and only *his* right hand. Nothing can be delegated to anyone else. This chronic refusal grows out of the basic insecurity of the Type A subject. He fears that even the slightest error in performing a task may topple his total structure of past achievements. Each task to be done appears to be too important to risk failure—and trusting an associate or subordinate simply increases the risk to an unacceptable point.

LET YOUR MEANS JUSTIFY YOUR END

Sophocles in his play *Electra* had Orestes remark that "the end excuses any evil," and the early Jesuits insisted that their ends justified their means. Many people tend to rationalize the wretchedness of the means they use to reach their own ends.

Now, the ordinary Type A person is no more evil than anyone else, but he is extremely apt to excuse many of his daily errors in living by pointing to his hoped for end. The real tragedy, of course, is that the Type A person's fundamental immaturity never allows him to discern two basic truths, the first one being that the end of man is always the same, whether he has been a galley slave or a Moorish prince; and the second, that life is not a particular cluster of days that made up his childhood or that will envelop him in his senescence. Rather, life is a series of single days. Certain days, of course, become more important than others. But the Type A man, not realizing the real composition of his life as a whole, allows thousands of days to pass by unnoticed, and even worse, not enjoyed, always believing that there will be some sort of "end" that will finally explain and justify his time on earth.

If he manages to escape a heart attack or cancer and reaches sixty-five years of age, he may begin to wonder where this marvelous "end" is and when it will begin to cast its golden glow upon his waning years. Then the soul-crushing truth falls upon him. There is to be no great "end" but only a slow petering out, a period during which he must watch his mental and physical prowess fade gradually away. He learns that disease and disappointment are no longer his distant relatives; they become his regular house guests. Only now, so very late, does he realize that his real life had been composed of days that had already passed away long ago.

It is for you, who are still young enough, to free yourself of this illusion that somewhere far ahead there lies an "end" that can justify your stumbling through your present days, scattering them thoughtlessly like dull, dry leaves.

If, then, you are to live a beautiful life, you first must begin to live beautiful days. And to live beautiful days, you also must think of beautiful things and events, even if these things and events should seem silly to your business associates. After all, they don't have to be told all that you think. We know a rather staid-appearing banker who almost daily walks in San Francisco's Golden Gate Park and amuses himself by private speculations about whether the flowers he sees there can dream, and if they do, just what do they dream about. Admittedly, he might not be asked to stay on several boards of directors if his colleagues were aware of his notions. But they are his own closely guarded ideas!

And to be certain that you are living a day-to-day life, be brave enough to pen your own obituary at intervals. Then you may judge what you have been, and what you have done. The practice might suggest some changes to be made before it is too late.

A SUCCESSFUL LIFE IS ALWAYS UNFINISHED

No one truly enjoys having all his affairs in a state of flux. Without question all of us daydream of that time when all our pursuits are crowned with success. Realistically, most of us do look forward to the time when our car will be paid for and the mortgage retired. We also can't help looking forward almost impatiently to the time when our high-school-age children will have matriculated at a university. As human beings, we were not only cursed at our birth with original sin but also with the inexplicable desire to finish as fast as possible everything we begin. Unfortunately, if you are a Type A person you harbor more than just a desire to finish every project you take on. You are seized by what justly might be called a frenzy to finish everything in which you have involved yourself in as brief a period of time as possible and are willing to go to extreme lengths to do so. Thus your bent for acquisition, when tied to your "hurry sickness," leads invariably into a self-harassing state in which you chronically are confronted by dozens or even scores of processes at various stages of completion. And completion itself is the only stage that possibly can soothe or satisfy you. You habitually persist in striving to bring about a situation in which you will be able to sit back and say to yourself, "Well, everything now has been completed."

But since life itself is a series of unfinished events, your dream of achieving or reaching a state where everything will have been completed to your satisfaction is totally unrealizable. Moreover, it is particularly unrealizable in your case because as a Type A person you habitually involve yourself in or take on far more projects than anyone could finish.

It may seem to you a very sad, almost intolerable acquiescence, but part of the process of liberating yourself from the enslavement of Type A behavior is to recognize and to accept the fact that your life must be structured upon and maintained by uncompleted processes, tasks, and events. You must begin to accept your life as a melange of activities in which only some of many processes manage to get finished. And you should not cavil at the fact that perhaps the majority of your activities at any given point in time appear to be in a state of flux; you must begin to take pride in this unfinishedness. It is your reassurance that you are living. Repeat over and over to yourself this statement until finally you realize its truth: "Life is an unfinishedness."

And try to remember, when it irks you that something hasn't been finished as rapidly as you thought it would or should be finished, it may be a hint that you are trying to run a race with death itself. After all, as a wise man once remarked, only a corpse is completely finished!

Chapter 16

WHAT TO DO
IF YOU'RE TYPE A:
REENGINEERING

In the previous chapter we established some philosophical guidelines we believe must be followed if you are to succeed in mitigating Type A Behavior Pattern. In this chapter we propose some practical procedures, ways in which you can "reengineer" your daily life; in the next chapter we give "drills" to help replace old, harmful habits.

It would be unfair of us to suggest that this reengineering will be an easy process or a painless one. It must go on for a period of years. Often, you may find it necessary to refer back to the philosophical guidelines to reinforce your will to change. You will find that it requires great persistence rather than a dramatic sort of courage; the measures to be adopted frequently run directly counter to impulses that have become natural to you. Tyrannizing habits that have been in command of you for decades will not yield to mere armchair resolutions or a few days of desultory attention. In our experience, the battle of new habits against old may have to continue indefinitely.

The procedures outlined below have for convenience been framed in terms of those who work in offices. But let us emphasize again that Type A behavior is found among persons of every class and profession. It originates within the person himself, not in his environment, and must be fought on home ground.

REENGINEERING "HURRY SICKNESS"

If you could free yourself of "hurry sickness," at least 50 percent or more of your Type A Behavior Pattern would disappear. As we have repeatedly pointed out in this book, although the Type A person frequently struggles against various challenges presented to him by his milieu, it is his battle against time that we suspect is the chief component sustaining his behavior pattern.

The very first step you must take is to revise your usual daily schedule of activities so as to eliminate as many events and activities as possible that do not contribute directly to your socioeconomic well being. Previously, you worked to crowd in events; now you must work to shed events, even if those events are closely linked to your business or profession.

For example, let's assume that you are a dentist and that you previously scheduled yourself to treat a patient every thirty minutes, allowing yourself a five- to ten-minute interval of rest and relaxation every several hours (an interval, incidentally, that few Type A dentists allow). Under your new anti-Type A program, you will plan to see and treat a patient every forty-five minutes, even though his therapy will require only twenty-five or thirty minutes. What change will this make in your life? Only this: you might make a little less money and feel strangely relaxed and carefree for part of every hour of your working days for the rest of your professional life.

Similarly, if you are a business executive, you will stop cluttering your appointment schedule so badly that try as you might to hurry each of your visitors, you invariably fall behind and know that you are keeping your next appointment waiting. One of the surest ways of intensifying the stress of Type A behavior is for you to keep someone else waiting. Allot more time to various events than you believe they will require! What can you lose? At worst, you may find that you have a bit of time during some lull to sit back in your chair, to daydream, to recall some happy moment from your past. You may even have the time to brood about, and perhaps solve, some heretofore stubborn problem.

Whether you are a dentist, attorney, architect, physician, or business executive, your secretary at first may not willingly cooperate in this slowdown. The probability is that she, too, is a Type A person, since you hired her. As such, she likes "action" in the office, and "action" to her means a schedule overflowing with patients, clients, or customers. No Type A secretary easily permits her employer to steer a Type B course. But if she cannot live with a Type B office, she should be dismissed!

Other activities in your life may require revisions if you are to recover from "hurry sickness." For example, you may be one of those thousands of suburbanites who for years have arisen *just in time* to dress, eat breakfast, scan the newspaper, reach the station, and board your train. Such a daily schedule, which never makes any time allowance for a protracted inspection of your garden, a chance conversation with your neighbor, or even a changed shirt in case you spill some coffee, carries with it, whether you will admit it or not, a note of regimentation. Though it's early in the day, you have already begun to fight time.

Why not arise fifteen minutes earlier than you

usually do? If you wish a second cup of coffee or want to dawdle a bit more over your newspaper, you will be able to do so. If you wish to take a stroll in your yard or garden, or even talk to a neighbor, you will have time without forever having to consult your watch. And let us remind you, incidentally, that the more frequently during the day you look at this monster on your left wrist, the more serious your "hurry sickness."

You must also reengineer your telephone habits if any person can telephone your office or your store and be directly connected with you, regardless of what you may be doing or with whom you may be talking. Unfortunately, most Type A persons instruct their secretaries or subordinates to put anyone through.

The only reason why Type A persons allow themselves to be interrupted this way is that they are basically insecure. They always fear that a terribly important client or customer may telephone and become furiously upset were he denied immediate access. If you have this fear, and permit yourself to be interrupted continually, you are aggravating your "hurry sickness." Unconsciously, you are likely to hasten the pace of your conversation with business associates in anticipation of a summons from the telephone.

And by allowing all telephone messages to reach you, you cannot avoid ending up with a visitor in your office sitting idly and restlessly as you talk. The telephone interloper may possibly be your best friend, but more likely he is a stranger who desires to sell you something, perhaps insurance or stocks. Whoever he is, you become tense and stressed as you try to hurry his message so as not to anger the visitor already in your office. The odds are, of course, that he has already lost a bit of respect for you because you run your affairs in such a fashion.

You should stop such nonsense immediately. Your

aides should be instructed that no one be allowed to interrupt you, even when you are alone in your office, until your direct permission has been gained. Furthermore, when you have a visitor or a business colleague in your office, you should not even be informed of incoming calls unless they are of transcendent urgency or from one of your superiors who wishes to speak to you immediately. Each caller may be told in splendidly courteous language that you presently are in conference or otherwise occupied and that you will return his call as soon as possible. If under such circumstances the caller is insulted, then he is probably a bit sick himself with Type A Behavior Pattern.

It is only after this sort of telephone screening has been in effect for several weeks or more that you will begin to feel a good deal more relaxed and less nervously expectant of telephone interruptions in your office. Your office conceivably might become a protected retreat in which you feel able even to muse or daydream.

TRY TO WORK IN A MILIEU THAT PROMOTES PEACE

If you are like most Type A persons, you are not much concerned about your everyday working surroundings. Unconsciously, however, these same surroundings and their disorderly jangle may play a very important part in nourishing your sense of time urgency.

If you work at a desk, for every unanswered letter or unfiled fragment of data, for every brochure and every memorandum to yourself that now clutters your desk or working space, there exists that much more "hurry sickness" in you. All these items have one thing in common—they continually remind you of the fact that you are behind. And no matter how intriguing, important, or interesting any office visitor may prove to be, when your eye is ensnared by this sort of debris lying on your desk, your sense of time urgency is enhanced.

Peculiarly, it is precisely your original sense of time urgency that creates the desk mess, and thus further intensifies your sense of time urgency. In your single-track, goal-oriented intent to push certain things through with incredible rapidity, you allow less important matters to hang fire. They usually do so at the four corners of your desk, eventually moving in to take over the center.

First, if only to convince you of the possibility of change, we would urge you to visit the executive offices of any large bank or corporation at noontime. Inspect the orderliness and neatness of all the desks. Usually they are completely devoid of loosely strewn papers and pamphlets and glisten in their simple emptiness. Only an ashtray and an inkstand, and sometimes a personal photograph, lie on these desks. Most of the incoming mail and memoranda of that morning have already been answered, and those that have not yet been acknowledged are probably neatly ensconced in appropriate folders. They are never allowed to turn into litter.

If the top executives of giant corporations can view their desks with placidity for the greater part of each day, so can you. You need only sort all your mail and other messages each morning into three categories—messages requiring prompt replies, those allowing a delay in response, and those requiring no reply.

After such sorting, immediately answer the messages requiring a quick response. Then if you have a secretary, give her your dictated or written responses and advise her to hold the second category of messages for later answering and to file the third category

—or even better, toss them in the wastebasket. She leaves and your desk is clear.

Remember, too, the rule about never doing left-handed work with your right hand. In this case it means never wasting time responding to a letter if your secretary or someone else can do it for you. If you receive crank mail, allow it to drift harmlessly and unanswered into your wastebasket. It would not be gentlemanly or gracious of you to enslave yourself to the task of responding to it. It would be a capitulation to your obsessive desire that everyone think well of you.

And one thing more about responding to personal letters. If you can't find time to read and then sign your name to your typewritten responses, don't dictate a letter in the first place. Nothing is so unpardonably rude and inane as to allow your secretary to sign your name to a letter, or even worse to permit a letter to leave your office with the silly comment: "dictated but not read." Recently, a curator of a museum wrote a letter to one of us requesting the loan of a painting for a show he planned to put together. His letter of request did not carry his signature but only the words, "dictated but not read." Do you suppose the requested painting was sent?

Do not allow yourself to be satisfied with a working environment simply because it does not encourage "hurry sickness." If humanly possible, bring objects into it that also allow beauty and elegance to accompany you in your commercial, industrial, or professional life. Certainly you have visited enough of your economic peers—and superiors, too!—to know that a beautiful Persian rug gracing their floor or a haunting abstract painting adorning one of their walls has not weakened their commercial acumen.

CONSIDER YOUR WORDS

If you are like most Type A persons, you not only talk far too much but you talk far too narrowly, and repetitiously as well, about your own few interests. In conferences with your business associates, it is you who does most of the talking. Of course, if what you are saying moves your audience and accomplishes a tangible objective, well and good. But too often it serves only as an idle vent to internal pressures you have allowed to accumulate.

If you are the top man in your group, try to let the others do most of the talking. All you have to do is to select one or more of your subordinates to carry on the conversation or discourse. A smile, a scowl, or a shrug of your shoulders during such conversations will signal your message to your followers as effectively as dozens of spoken words. Remember that part of Type A illness is the inability to refrain from repeating that which both you and your listener have heard not once but possibly scores of times before.

Only too frequently also, as a Type A person, you may talk so much about your own interests that you fall hopelessly behind in your office schedule. You have thus intensified your own sense of time urgency for that day by erasing so much of the time that had been available to you. You have talked yourself into a time shortage.

But the problem doesn't lie only with your own talkativeness. Since you probably see many persons who wish to communicate with you each day, you must learn the fine art of discerning quickly and accurately those whose words have no value of any kind for you. Such persons, of course, waste your time, again adding to the intensity of your sense of time urgency.

You may try desperately to hurry such people

along, but you rarely possess enough of the Type B's sangfroid to terminate such conversations or interviews quickly. And why won't you quickly terminate such interviews, even though you feel your tension and ire rising to astronomical heights? Sensitive yourself, you believe your visitors would be hurt if you directly terminated their conversation. So thinking, you don't even realize that anger and irritation are already showing in your voice.

In "reengineering" your life, you must begin to cut short your visits with those who waste your time. Then you can begin to lengthen your visits with those who can and will enhance either the opportunities or the worthwhileness of your life.

EACH DAY AT NOON, TRY TO FIND YOURSELF

If you are a severely afflicted Type A, at noon you tend to substitute a restaurant table for your own desk. Indeed, sometimes you scribble numbers on the napkins and the blank spaces of the restaurant's menu cards, as if they were your own office pads. Only the martini or the beer serves as a signal that a small change in your activities has taken place, except that the change is purely geographic. Luncheons, some of our patients have told us, allow "outside" committee meetings, as opposed to the normal "inside" committee meetings conducted during the rest of the day. Often too, lunchtime serves as the place where Type A persons launch their campaigns against competitors.

How dreadful the scene is at a typical club or restaurant each weekday noon! Look at those two men over there, each one leaning toward the other blowing cigarette smoke and martini fumes, each pushing forkfuls of gravy-covered goop into their mouths, yet still miraculously able to grunt words at each other. Their faces are furrowed in strange, tense, frowns which we can only hope their mothers never saw.

In reengineering your life, you should seek to eliminate luncheons at which you continue to talk and think about the same things you do the rest of the day. Obviously, such luncheons cannot be completely eliminated—situations will arise when it will be necessary for you to mix your bread with your business. But up to now you have probably regarded your lunch period as an extension of working hours.

We have already insisted that if you are a Type A person and are to break loose from your thralldom, you must begin to explore yourself, and you must allot some time for such contemplation. Your lunch period probably offers you the first true opportunity to consider yourself objectively.

During this period, having escaped from your office, you can amble in a park, sit in a noontime-deserted church, visit a museum, browse in a bookstore, or just watch fellow human beings pass by. This is the period of the day when you can have lunch with an old friend or classmate; we have already urged upon you the importance of friendship in your battle against Type A Behavior Pattern. And your lunchtime probably offers you your first opportunity of the day to indulge in some sort of physical activity. Exercise is, of course, being emphasized as a possible anticoronary measure.

But let us urge again that you use your lunch period as an opportunity to meet yourself. Until you try seriously to discover what is the *essence* of your life, and find out how to disengage it from the garbage of the days and years, your life will not be graced by peace—or your heart (most literally) with tranquillity.

FORGET FIVE O'CLOCK FRENZY

Many Type A persons take considerable pride in the fact that they can almost always finish all their day's work by 4:30 or 5:00 P.M., an accomplishment that is quite often managed by spurts of pressure and tension beginning between 3:00 and 4:00 P.M. Such spurts themselves may intensify your already severe sense of time urgency. Of course, there are times when it is eminently desirable to finish a piece of work at the end of a day, but far too often Type A persons do it simply because of the pleasure, and a rather inane pride, they find in completing any sort of task. Such pride underlines again the chronic fascination that battles against time hold for Type A persons.

We suggest that you no longer go into a dither as the evening hour approaches. No great harm will be done if you leave your office somewhat later than usual. Nor is it necessary for you to battle crowds of people in buses, subways, or automobiles because of your frantic desire to reach home in record time. What is there awaiting you at your home each evening that can possibly be worth the bustling, bruising, and battling? Are you really that anxious to see your wife, children, dog, or cat?

We, of course, are not seriously implying that your family is not worth coming home to. We are only suggesting that the return need not be a forced march!

SEARCH FOR ALONENESS

We already have emphasized that in combatting your Type A behavior pattern, you must retrieve as much of your total personality as possible. You must begin to find the things worth being, a search you neglected for so long while striving to obtain the things worth having.

But the things worth having are not necessarily the same for all of us. For example, you might believe it exceedingly worthwhile to become adept in reading contemporary French poetry, whereas another person might consider it eminently worthwhile to be able to bind books in fine leathers. What is common to you both is that you will have to expend energy in an altogether new direction—to form fresh thought processes and habits.

A habit, after all, is only a shortcut for your brain, a method of executing a complicated process automatically with an absolute minimum of conscious thought. To alter a habit may take weeks, months, or even years. If your brain is like most people's, it doesn't particularly enjoy this tedious task. But to achieve anything really worth being requires this alteration and the effort associated with it.

Unlike achieving things worth having, to achieve things worth being usually requires long periods of solitude. If you are not alone it is almost impossible for you to memorize new facts, begin to think, meditate, or philosophize in new ways. The only exception to this rule is your possible need for a teacher. Even so, you will still require a good deal of solitude, if only to take full advantage of your instructor's advice.

So you must begin to scan each coming week in advance to find and reserve periods of time during which you can be alone. We have already said that to find such free time will force you to curtail some of your "number-building" activities; if you continue to participate in as many things as you are now, and also attempt to squeeze in these new activities, you will simply be aggravating your "hurry sickness."

Another reason for you to seek out periods of the week when you can be totally alone is the need for privacy for self-analysis. Such a critique of your personality can never be successfully undertaken in company with others.

To be alone requires a place that will allow you to be alone. How strange it is that so few persons, even incredibly rich ones, possess a room they can truly call their own. We have a very good Texas friend who occupies an extraordinarily plush office, and lives in a mansion that is wondrous even for a Texan. In order to find solitude, however, he regularly visits a mausoleum that he had built for himself and his wife. "I just like to go there and think out some of my problems," he explains. "I'm never interrupted out there, not even by a telephone call."

It should not be necessary for you to construct a mausoleum in order to find a place to be alone. You might have a room or a section of a room or even a part of your yard that you could call your own, to which you could retire and know that you will not be disturbed.

REENGINEERING YOUR HOSTILITY

Although not all Type A persons are plagued with a sense of free-floating hostility, the majority, as we've already said, do harbor varying amounts of this destructive emotion. We have met some Type A's so severely afflicted that they almost never enjoy a moment of tranquillity. One sees the darting, hateful, belligerent sparks escaping from their eyes even when they are merely asking the time of day. One also sees the strange twist of their mouths as they laugh—as if a scar had reluctantly broken open.

Almost demented by their unbridled hostility, such persons are likely to believe that the core of our society is essentially evil. It is impossible to convince them that true goodness actually exists. Luckily, these ultra-hostile persons form only a tiny fraction of the population. We say luckily because neither the reading of this book nor any other human agency can probably change them. If they serve any purpose at all, it may be that of a horrible example to other Type A's who might be inclined to dismiss or undervalue the perniciousness of the behavior pattern.

If you are to reengineer your life so as to subdue whatever degree of hostility you already have, you first must understand just what this hostility is and what can aggravate it.

First, it is inextricably connected with aggression. A completely passive person is usually completely devoid of hostility. Of course, there are very few such passive persons. Even Jesus lost his temper when confronted by the money changers in the temple. Hostility also has a component of fear in it, fear of what other persons may do to hurt you. Further, it reflects a frustrated longing for love and affection, and a conviction that most other people, faced with the alternatives of doing good or evil usually choose the latter. And finally, it is a sign of emotional immaturity.

If the above general description is a correct one, then even a moderately hostile Type A person would be unlikely to react to any creature whose own aggression does not threaten him, who causes no fear, who will offer love or affection, and whose motives are above suspicion.

Let us test this hypothesis. An affectionate puppy gaily approaches a truly hostile Type A prototype and licks his hand. Does our Type A man curse the dog, slap, or kick him? Not at all. He smiles—admittedly a bit uneasily—perhaps even chuckles as he pets the puppy, lifts him to his lap, and cuddles him. Hardly Type A, you say? Yet even Adolf Hitler acted like this whenever his dog approached, as Albert Speer revealed in his autobiography.

Say a small child laughingly approaches a Type A man afflicted with a great amount of hostility and throws his small arms about the man's legs in a gesture of sheer affection. The Type A will not be angry unless perhaps he suspects that the child's display of affection was motivated by a desire to receive a reward of some kind. If he does have reason to suspect the child of this, then his hostility may surge to the fore.

Affectionate puppies and nondesigning children are certainly not the only creatures that a Type A subject can meet without stirring up whatever hostility he harbors. Anyone approaching with obviously sincere affection and no underlying thoughts of self-aggrandizement has a reasonably good chance of eliciting warmth and affection.

Yet let an office colleague or a fellow worker slightly sneer at him or even tease him in a fashion that intimates that the colleague's respect for him is less than overwhelming and the Type A's sense of hostility instantly spreads like wildfire through his brain, making his heart pound with hate and his hands tremble in sheer fury. Gone in a millisecond is the influence of all those signs of love, good will, respect, and admiration he had received earlier that same day from his pets, his children, his friends, nature itself. Now in the full grip of his hostility, he should understand how one "hate" may overshadow a dozen "loves." What is the power of affection when compared to the evil intent of this colleague who could not possibly wish him well in his career?

We need not remind you of the times you've had to wait in a restaurant, despite having a reservation, and watch others enter and be seated immediately by the head waiter. Your anger rises not only because of this obvious injustice but also because the head waiter thinks so little of your dignity as a human being that he makes no attempt to excuse the unfair maneuvers he boldly executes in your presence. Perhaps if some of our head waiters knew how many Type A persons they had to encounter every day and how many of these find it barely possible to keep their hostility under control, they might act more discreetly, if only to forestall mayhem.

Now, how are you to reengineer your daily living to keep your degree of hostility at its absolute minimum? First and foremost, you must recognize that you do harbor flaws in your personality, and that they are not virtues but defects. It is not easy for Type A persons to admit that they have any free-floating hostility, although some will admit that they "tend to be quick tempered." So for our purposes, let us also assume that all "quick-tempered" people do possess a varying amount of hostility. The best time for you to recognize its presence and label it for what it really is, is when you are under no stress and there is nothing in your milieu that threatens to incite it.

Once you have admitted to yourself that you do possess hostility, then you can seek help from two of your other mental attributes in trying to hold it in check or even eradicate it. There are two methods. First, use your reasoning powers to check your tendency to see every situation as a challenge, designed to upset and annoy you. Second, use your sense of humor. Even if a provocative or irritating event does succeed in breaking through your first line of defense, your sense of humor still may serve to defuse your anger. Almost all of us are able to laugh at the other fellow, but it may require a little doing to develop a sense of humor exquisite and brave enough to permit us to laugh at ourselves. Your reengineered behavior will allow your free-floating hostility to emerge only after your power of reasoning has recognized the delivery of an insult worthy of being noticed—and your sense of humor agrees.

But you cannot depend solely upon your reason and sense of humor to control your tendency toward hostility. Only too often, your hostility will flare up long before controls can be brought into action. It is well for you to avoid personal contact with those persons who in the past have caused your hackles to rise merely by entering your presence.

No doubt you have frequently resolved beforehand to make yourself pleasing to some of these individuals in spite of the fact that they always had succeeded in "churning up your guts" (an accurate expression from a patient of ours). But this miracle of agreeability never has taken place, and it never will. They sense your free-floating hostility instantly, and this ignites their own arsenal.

The reason, of course, that you feel hostile almost instantaneously on meeting another hostile person is that you are probably mirror images of each other. Each of you competes to be the talker, not the listener, each of you competes not to learn from the other, but to teach and "correct." Each of you strives so hard to receive the *verbalized* respect of the other that you both quite forget to exhibit any verbalized respect for each other. There is always the possibility, too, that since you are both Type A's, you unconsciously irritate each other by interrupting or hurrying the speech of the other. These conversations abound in such remarks as "But you're not listening to me," "Yes, yes, you've already said that," or "If you would just let me get a word in edgewise." These are not conversations, they are battles—silly, needless battles.

Persons who have almost never failed to arouse your ire must be stricken from your list of acquaintances. They never have and probably never will benefit you spiritually and very few of them ever will qualify as your material benefactors. Perhaps after a space of several years, during which time you can cool down the flames of your own hostility and smooth out some of the more abrasive facets of your behavior pattern, you may revisit these mirror images of yourself. If they then no longer irritate you but elicit your sympathy and tolerance, then you have made marvelous progress in "rehumanizing" yourself. But if hostility quickly rises up and chokes your gullet, then you've done a poor job of rehabilitating yourself. You will also probably be just as coronary prone then as you are right now.

Admittedly, there are some people who arouse your hostility whom you must continue to see. Brothers- and sisters-in-law, fathers- and mothers-in-law, or brothers, sisters, and parents. There may be partners, bosses, or employees, too, who must be seen. Let us only say at this point that if you must see them, quit talking. Lend them your ears to trample upon, but swallow your tongue until they have bid you farewell. Don't be too surprised if, for the first time since you have known them, they seem genuinely reluctant to part company with you.

Far more serious is the situation in which *chronic* hostility arises between husband and wife. What then can be done? How efficacious is the marriage counselor, the family physician, the minister, or the psychiatrist in erasing this conflict? Let each of these professionals remember what seems to him to have been a victory on his part and let each take what comfort he can from their meager number.

It has been our experience that when hostilities arise between middle-aged husband and wife, the end of their battle comes not with the capitulation of either side, but with the arrival of a sort of indifference. At this point neither victory nor defeat appears any longer very important, so indistinct and blurred are the issues formerly in conflict, as well as the personalities of the opposing combatants. It may seem a gray and gloomy ending, but we believe that there are worse.

If you have confined your circle of friends almost exclusively to very hostile Type A persons, you might feel that we are condemning you to an anchorite's life. Actually, one's life *had* perhaps better be spent as an anchorite than as a companion of only very hostile Type A persons, but this isn't really necessary. Part of recovering from Type A sickness is to discover Type B persons, recognize that they, too, possess virtues and interesting failings. They will, if nothing else, listen to you without insisting that you listen to them, something your Type A acquaintances do not find easy to do at any time. And if they sometimes seem more interested in types of hummingbirds that visit California in the summer than the current price of IBM shares, attribute this penchant to their naïveté and also the fact that persons possessing lively disease-free coronary arteries oddly do seem to be partial to the more exotic and nonmercantile aspects of life in the world.

To find these new Type B friends of yours, scan the people you know and see which ones prefer to remain silent and to listen to the conversation of others—the ones whom you thought might be dull because they competed so little to be heard about anything. If you have friends who have libraries filled with books they *read*, take a new look at them; some just have to be free of hostility. If you have friends who can eat a luncheon or play a game of bridge without peering nervously at their wristwatches, take a long second glance at them, too. We have found that there are many Type B's among such people as presidents of giant corporations (particularly utility corporations), federal judges, patent attorneys, authors who specialize in writing up the histories of local county and state historical societies, and artists who have not yet been propagandized by the Madison Avenue art dealers. A few decades ago, we would have advised you to seek out the company of university professors, but it is our impression these days that too many of them have become Type A.

REENGINEERING FOR THE ATTAINMENT OF THE THINGS WORTH BEING

Unlike the things worth having, the things worth being, as we've already suggested, are primarily those concerned with the refinement of your character and the development and maturation of your spiritual and intellectual faculties. But our "everyday world" does not invariably reward those who strive to attain the things worth being. We have known few men of commerce whom the world has treated as its special favorites simply because they strove for a greater honesty in dealing with their customers or because they happened to know in what century Chaucer lived or what laws Newton discovered from watching sunlight after it had penetrated a prism.

All young college graduates within a week of their graduation become aware of the fact that the "everyday world" will not reward them for their acquisition of the things worth being. The majority of them thus go about learning how to force this same world to give them the things worth having. The demands of this process become so unrelenting that most of them begin to neglect the search for the things worth being. Finally, the search for the things worth having completely usurps their attention.

If you have made this mistake and hope to do something about it, you must begin right away. We are not urging that you do so because we are primarily interested in your soul or your mind, but because we are interested in protecting or saving your heart. Nothing can serve as a more cogent and powerful counterforce to the frenzy unleashed by the unbridled acquisition of numbers than a resumption of the quest for the things worth being. Why is this so? Because the things worth being have nothing to do with the sheer acquisition of numbers. A collector of things worth having gets his real satisfaction by counting his things. A possessor of things worth being receives his satisfaction by noting the maturation of his sensibility.

You must find the simple common sense to discover and realize once and for all that you cannot continue to avoid all that man in the past has considered lovely and humane without becoming the sort of person whose death saddens no one. Your common sense must serve to give you a preview of this sordid fate. It is your common sense that in the final analysis must reveal to you the life you will be forced to endure if you lose interest in the welfare of your friends and find less and less reason to visit a library, museum, art gallery, concert hall, theater, park, or even a sports arena.

But you will require a special variety of courage to allow your innate common sense to recover its sovereignty after so many years of subjugation to the false charm of quantification. It will require a considerable degree of bravery for you to face up to the probability that your death will sadden no one—and even gladden a few! Remember Scrooge?

So you must begin to search out distinguished "guests" who will aid you in your search for the things worth being. These "guests" are the greatest historians, philosophers, novelists, poets, social scientists, and statesmen of our Western society. And they are all to be found in the same place, in books.

Of course we are not suggesting that you turn yourself into a bookworm, or try to become knowledgeable in all the arts and sciences. To offset one extreme with another doesn't appear to us to make therapeutic good sense. If you've never liked poetry when you were in high school, it's likely that you won't really enjoy it now. And similarly, if physics was a mystery to you in college, it probably still will be. Yet the total neglect of the humanities is inexcusable and spirit-corroding. There must be some areas of human thought and creativity that should eventually appeal to you. A fair idea of what those areas may be can be gained by recalling what used to interest you prior to your total absorption in the acquisition of numbers.

Obviously, it will require a certain dogged persistence on your part to reacquire a taste for reading. Often your new "guests" will be difficult for you to follow and to understand because they will demand your *total* attention. You may find a poor sales record or some other familiar bit of mental debris attempting to seize your attention as you gamely try to follow the Wife of Bath's Tale in Chaucer's *Canterbury Tales*. And you may not always find it pleasant to search repeatedly in your dictionary for the meaning of various words employed by these new "guests" of yours.

And how your smoldering hostility may flame up when one of them firmly demolishes one of your favorite prejudices! Here again your doggedness will undergo its most grueling Gethsemane. For, if you are like many hardbitten Type A men who have been accustomed for years to substitute deep feeling for actual knowledge about various subjects, you may find that it requires a rare sort of courage to keep your bearings when one of your own long-held and equally long-loved opinions or beliefs is revealed as sheer nonsense.

Books, of course, are not the sole guides to the things worth being. The proper regard and appreciation of friends must also be nourished. You, however, must not confuse acquaintances with friends. You should not fool yourself into believing that exchanging a few more pleasantries each day with your usual acquaintances can substitute for the spiritual sustenance afforded by real friends. A friendship enhances your life in part because of what you must give of yourself in order to appreciate the friend.

We have mentioned the subtle charm and magic that myth, ritual, and tradition used to bestow upon communities treasuring these abstractions. You can still draw upon them, and they can enhance the quality of your life. Remember that the repetition of any pleasant event eventually gives far, far more pleasure than the initial event possibly could have done. In experiencing a pleasant event previously experienced, you not only enjoy it in the present, you also enjoy your recall of the pleasure you received previously. An adult enjoying a Christmas morning does so in part because of his having experienced so many other pleasant Christmas mornings.

Were this book being written a century ago, religious belief would be mentioned as the principal source of the things worth being in life. This may no longer be so widely true, but even now religious belief, when allowed to do so, can savor and sweeten a life. And there are other activities such as various hobbies and avocations, love of nature, and enjoyment of art and music, that can yield the things worth being.

But any thing worth being can only be attained if you manage to find the time to find yourself—and this can come only from that huge amount of time you now devote to the acquisition of those things you have considered worth having! It is therefore necessary for you to make some sort of decision about the allocation of your time. You must ask yourself, "What do I want to sell my time for?" If you are to achieve the things worth being, your answer must be: "I wish to sell as much of my time as possible for my own development as a human being." Such an answer surely furnishes you a path toward the things worth being in your lifetime.

Chapter 17

WHAT TO DO
IF YOU'RE TYPE A:
DRILLS

Type A Behavior Pattern, while originally growing out of a rather natural desire to acquire more and more things in less and less time, quickly reaches a stage in which the habits developed to achieve this goal break loose to take command over the person's whole life. They emerge to harass their possessor even when there is no longer any real need for him either to hurry or to fight.

We know a dentist who very early in his career took great pride in filling teeth expeditiously and rapidly. He would glance at his wristwatch every three to five minutes to be sure that his pacing or timing was exactly correct. Now, thirty-two years later, though he no longer practices dentistry, he still glances at his watch every three to five minutes whether he is listening to cocktail conversation or playing a game of bridge. He usually doesn't even really notice what time it is. One of us, seeing him a few months ago glance in this fashion at his watch, asked him for the time. Rather startled, he then deliberately and consciously looked at his watch again and informed us of the correct time.

We also know a physician who quit smoking his pipe over six months ago. Yet each day, on leaving his home or office, he still pats the right pocket of his trousers as he has done for decades, to be certain that he did not forget his pipe. Even now he confesses to feeling just a bit of disappointment that it isn't there.

Unless you establish new habits meant to supersede and replace your old ones, you will not free yourself from the Type A illness. Here are some suggested "drills" that may help you do this.

A DRILL AGAINST "HURRY SICKNESS"

1. Perhaps one of the most important new habits you can establish is to review at least once a week the original causes of your present "hurry sickness." Just as a doctor is far more likely to be able to cure a disease if he knows what causes it, you, too, will be better prepared to alter your degree of "hurry sickness" if you know why you have it.

2. A second new habit is to reread regularly the philosophical guidelines set down in Chapter 15 for combating your behavior pattern. Many persons, while drilling beautifully the first week, begin to forget what they're drilling about the second week, and as a consequence forget to drill entirely in the third and subsequent weeks.

3. Each morning, noon, and midafternoon, remind yourself—preferably while looking at yourself in a mirror—that life is always an unfinishedness. We suggest this because so often persons badly sick with a sense of time urgency doggedly persist in believing that they can "fin-

ish" all the events of their life at the end of every day. Actually, of course, they can do so only by bullet, poison, or a jump from a high building or bridge. You are only finished when you are dead.

4. Begin in your *avocational* hours to listen quietly to the conversation of other people. Quit trying to finish their sentences. Never interrupt with such hurrying phrases as "Yes, yes," "Uh, huh, uh huh," or "I see, I see." Just remain quiet and listen to them. An even better sort of drill for you if you have been in the habit of hastening the other person's speech rhythms is to seek out a person who stutters and then deliberately to remain tranquil. Always remember during these drill sessions that you are trying to overcome your own sense of time urgency by exposing yourself to "slow-down" maneuvers and tactics.

5. Quit trying to think of more than one thing at a time, an activity we've labeled *polyphasic thinking*. Remember that even Einstein, when tying his shoe laces, thought chiefly about the bow.

6. If you see someone doing a job slower than you know you can do it, don't interfere with him unless you are positive he can't do the job at all. But if he can do it, but will finish perhaps five minutes later than you would have, remember that he is not suffering from "hurry sickness"—you are. In other words, don't allow his "slowness" to make you take on something you shouldn't —and merely waste your own time.

7. Never forget, when confronted by any task, to ask yourself the following questions: (1) Will this matter have importance five years from now? and (2) must I do this right now, or do I have enough time to think about the best way to accomplish it? Asking and answering these questions allow you to determine, first, whether the task is a trivial one, suitable for delegation to someone else or to be executed "with your left hand" or not even done at all, and second, whether it has a deadline attached to it. Your established sense of time urgency, of course,

will tend to make you believe that everything has to be done by yesterday. Asking questions like these, over and over again, brings things back into perspective.

8. It will be difficult for you ever to be a leader of men if you never say anything. But it will be impossible for you to be such a leader if you habitually utter nonsense, and at inconvenient times. Make it part of your drill to ask yourself, before you begin to speak, these questions: (1) Do I really have anything important to say? (2) does anyone want to hear it? and (3) is this the time to say it? If the answer to any of these three questions is no, then remain quiet even if you find yourself biting your lips in frustration. Many Type A persons insist on taking over conversations, repeating subjects they've mentioned before, and talking far too long, thus leaving themselves terribly behind schedule. And of course, nothing aggravates the "hurry sickness" of a Type A person more than the feeling of being behind in his schedule.

9. *Tell yourself at least once a day that no enterprise ever failed because it was executed too slowly, too well.* If you find this difficult to believe, begin making a list of the men whom you know who have failed and then ask yourself which of these men failed because he did something too well, too slowly, and which failed because he erred in his judgment or in a crucial decision. Almost invariably, you will find that it was an error of judgment or decision. Then ask yourself, "Are good judgments and correct decisions best formulated under unhurried circumstances or under deadline pressures?"

10. Whenever possible, shy away from making appointments at definite times. Admittedly, almost all work-connected appointments must be made and kept at definite times. But your nightly arrival time at home should be elastic. Remember, the more unnecessary deadlines you make for yourself, the worse your "hurry sickness" becomes.

Carry reading matter with you whenever you go to the airport, barber shop, or anywhere else where there may be delay, so that being occupied, you won't fret. And since most of the classics are now in paperback, try to select a classic that you've always promised yourself you would sometime read if you could "find the time." The next time your plane is delayed, "the time" for the classic has come. Sitting luxuriously at the airport, a cup of coffee by your side and reading Thucydides' description of the Peloponnesian War, you might find that you wouldn't mind if your plane were delayed a second hour —an utterly unthinkable reaction prior to your conversion.

11. Try never to forget that if you fail to protect your allotment of time, no one else will. And the older you become, the more important this truth is. Whenever you can save some of your time by offering money in its place, do so. Strangely, from their earliest beginnings, men have always seemed quite happy to trade the very limited days of their lives for disks of copper, bronze, silver, and gold. They have always taken such pride and joy in stamping, trading, and hoarding. How many minutes or hours was an ounce of coin gold worth in Pompey's day? And while we are asking the question, how many seconds or minutes is an imitation silver coin worth in Nixon's day?

12. Desist from projecting your own sense of time urgency upon those with whom you come into contact. Most persons are not infuriated or even upset if they are kept waiting a bit for you, particularly after you have explained to them the reason for your delay. Most persons, when they are guests at your home, at a restaurant, or at your club, do not demand instant service. Nor are most persons so seriously afflicted with "hurry sickness" that they become impatient with the rate at which you talk or relate an anecdote. Only too often, Type A persons aggravate their own "hurry sickness" by believing that all their friends and acquaintances are as sickly impatient as they are.

13. Purposely, with a companion, frequent restaurants and theaters where you know there will be a period of wait-

ing. If your companion happens to be your wife, remember that you spend far longer periods of time alone with her in your own home without fidgeting. If you and your companion cannot find enough to say to each other as you wait in a restaurant or a theater, then you had both better seek different companions.

This is an important drill. If you cannot indulge in waiting—with someone or alone—without your sense of time urgency beginning to erupt, you are still far from free of Type A behavior.

14. Whenever you catch yourself speeding up your car in order to get through a yellow light at an intersection, penalize yourself by immediately turning to the right at the next corner. Circle the block and approach the same corner and signal light again. After such penalization, you may find yourself racing a yellow light a second, but probably not a third, time. When you are following a car whose speed seems too slow for you, again penalize yourself by not passing it even when you are able to do so. And never forget that while there may be a slight excuse for hurrying to the office in the morning, there is none at all for rushing home at night.

After all, your car is not some form of "rocket" designed to flash you from place to place at the speed of light. Why not practice seeing it rather as a sort of home in itself? Detroit has been trying to turn a car into a home for quite a while. Actually, the seats may be far more attractively styled and more comfortable to sit in than the chairs you have in your home. The radio is often just as good. And when you are stuck in traffic, there is nothing to stop you from enjoying the scenery.

15. You must regard every number and your possible fascination or intrigue with it as a telltale aspect of your Type A Behavior Pattern. Each time you glance at a clock, each time you peruse the prices of stocks and bonds, each time you translate the lira, franc, and pound prices you see attached to foreign articles of merchandise or

menu items into American dollars, each time you become intrigued with baseball batting and pitching statistics, you may unconsciously be aggravating your sense of time urgency. After all, your sense of time urgency would wither away if you could once tear yourself free from your bondage to numbers. A man without "hurry sickness" is a man who does not serve numbers.

16. For drill purposes, attempt to read books that demand not only your entire attention but also a certain amount of patience. We have repeatedly advised our own Type A patients to attempt reading Proust's seven-volume novel *The Remembrance of Things Past*, not because it is one of the great modern classics (which it is), but because the author needs several chapters to describe an event that most Type A subjects would have handled in a sentence or two. Proust cannot be hurried. When a Type A attempts to skim, he is likely to find himself totally lost in a pageful of Proustian prose. It is only by deliberate acquiescence to Proust's pace that the reader can understand and enjoy the novel, and it is this acquiescence that makes such reading a drill.

There are, of course, other books, too, that demand a slowdown in the Type A subject's usual pace of doing things. The Will Durant series of world histories and McNeil Dixon's *The Human Situation* are good examples.

We do not claim that this particular drill is pleasant. Sometimes it will appear to you to be almost a form of torture. But if you persevere long enough, you will have struck a mighty blow at the "hurry sickness" lying at the core of your Type A pattern.

17. Learn to interrupt long or even short sessions of any type of activity that you know or suspect may induce tension and stress before it is finished. Such stress is particularly apt to arise in the course of writing long memoranda, reports, or articles. It also can arise whenever you are constrained to execute a long series of delicate manual procedures, particularly if you have set a deadline for their successful execution. What should you do during these interruptions? Well, almost anything, just as

long as it allows you to relax. Caress a pet, stroll about the premises, peruse a magazine, stare out the window at trees, an airplane, or the adjacent building. But it doesn't make too much difference what you do, just as long as you manage to break the interior tension.

18. Find periods each day during which you purposely seek total body relaxation and peace of mind. Since hundreds of thousands of Americans enthusiastically insist that their adoption of various Yoga-inspired techniques manages to accomplish just these ends, you might be well advised to investigate one of these procedures.

A DRILL AGAINST HOSTILITY

1. If you are overly hostile, certainly the most important drill measure you should adopt is that one in which you remind yourself of the fact that you are hostile. Being forewarned, you are far less inclined to flare up at any stimulus short of one that would induce hostility in anybody.

Try throughout the day to enhance your awareness of the wants and needs of your friends as you simultaneously strive to diminish your own sensitivity to possible affronts. No one who is himself certain of security wishes to undermine the security of another. Remember that as you develop your *sensibility* and reduce your *sensitivity,* your hostility will gradually fall away.

2. Begin to speak your thanks or appreciation to others when they have performed services for you. And do not do so, like so many hostile Type A subjects, with merely a grunt of thanks. Take the time to look the man or woman who has served you well full in the face and then in *full* and gracious sentences let him or her know how grateful you are.

This may be a difficult drill for you to perform. You may not be grateful for a favor, or you may feel too "shy" to express your appreciation. It is under these latter circumstances that you should probe for the causes of such reluctance. You might begin to realize that part of the reason for your hostility springs from your own inability to believe in the innate goodness of your fellow men. We have seen hundreds of hostile persons during these past few decades and not a single one of them ever believed that most persons are generally altruistic. Conversely, of the hundreds of gentle, nonbelligerent folks we also have met, we cannot remember a single one of them who was truly convinced that some people are absolutely evil.

3. Quit talking about your ideals and your disappointments in finding so few ideals in other people. Most so-called "idealists" are frustrated and hostile little gods who have taken it upon themselves to draw up their own "rules" for life's living and get angry when other people pay no attention. Over and over again, we have listened to Type A's rationalize their hostility as stemming from their disappointment over the lack of ideals in their friends. We always have advised such sick people that they should cease trying to be "idealists" because they are in fact only looking for excuses to be disappointed and hence hostile toward others. So, if you pride yourself on your "idealism" and have condemned other persons for their lack of your brand of it, go back and reread drill item 1. After having done so, if you still find you do have some glorious rules to live by, call them principles and stop inflicting them on other people.

4. Begin to smile at as many persons as often as you can. Begin first to smile regularly and frequently at the persons you may meet in corridors and elevators of your building. Simultaneously begin to smile at persons whom you may encounter while walking in a city square or park or in your own neighborhood.

This drill may appear to you to be quite contrived and hypocritical, but that will be true only if you fail in trying to find the qualities in other people that might command your respect, admiration, or affection. Of course, the more often you succeed in this, the freer you become of the tyranny of your own hostility. We can't

explain precisely why sincere smiling so effectively ap-
peases the nascent wrath of so many Type A subjects;
we only know that it does.

A DRILL TOWARD THINGS
WORTH BEING

1. Perhaps no change in your life has taken place so in-
sidiously as the gradual ascendancy of your struggle to
achieve the things worth having over your attempts to attain the things worth being. Indeed, so treacherously is
this ascendancy usually accomplished that as wise and
percipient a man as Charles Darwin, having reached late
middle age and discovered to his horror that he no longer
could enjoy poetry, painting, or music, complained bitterly:

> My mind seems to have become a kind of *machine* for
> grinding general laws out of large collections of facts
> but why this should have caused the *atrophy* of that
> part of the brain alone on which the *higher tastes* de-
> pend, I cannot conceive. . . . The loss of these tastes is
> a loss of happiness and may possibly be injurious to
> the intellectual and more probably the *moral* character,
> by enfeebling the *emotional* part of our nature.

Now if this catastrophe took place unobserved in one
of the most astute minds that Western society has ever
produced, you need not be embarrassed if a similar tragedy has befallen you. On the contrary, it should make you
realize how important it is that your personality and in-
tellect be retrieved, improved and developed. It is precisely
such improvement and development that will provide you
with the steel to fight against your frenzied tendency to
acquire numbers.

Your first drill measure should thus consist of a daily
reminder to yourself that no matter how many things you
have acquired, if they have not improved your own spirit
or mind you have only become a more prestigious "care-

taker" of the creative works of others. Now it is time for you to concentrate on making your own character one of worth. This is the message you should relate to yourself as your most important drill measure. And don't forget to give yourself this message daily. Otherwise, a spanking new car, a motorboat, or a square of emerald surrounded by diamonds may pull you back into the exclusive quest for the things worth having.

2. Drill yourself in improving your speech. Remember that you employ far fewer different words than the dollars you earn annually. If you are like most Type A subjects, your vocabulary has shrunk, not expanded, since your high school or college days. This is because, harried by your hurry sickness, you probably have not attempted to expand but rather to abbreviate the reaches of your speech. Then, too, when reading, if you came upon a word whose meaning was unknown to you, too often you felt that you didn't "have the time" to look up the word's meaning in a dictionary. Most Type A subjects don't recognize the truth of old Seneca's aphorism: "Where the speech is corrupted, the mind is also." Learn new words, expand your mind and your thinking processes, perhaps even discover new ideas bubbling up again.

3. Drill yourself in the art of holding opinions loosely. Consider most of them as at best *provisionally* correct, particularly if such opinions are concerned with politics, race, and religion. And if you are apt to become angry when a particular opinion of yours is not considered valid by others, it may be a wise tactic to begin to doubt the validity of it yourself. Whenever you can, try to examine your opinions about various subjects critically, by learning what distinguished experts have to say on the subject.

Remember that no small part of true wisdom is the capacity to bid farewell *quickly and without fanfare* to any opinion you previously held when it is shown to be erroneous.

4. If you are ever guilty of saying or even intimating "I told you so," discontinue it. Besides its uselessness, it points out to the listener a pettiness in you that hardly

compliments your character, and needlessly arouses whatever latent hostility he may possess.

5. Continue to seek some "loneliness" for yourself. Since Type A subjects are rarely introverts, there is probably very little danger of your overdoing your quest to be alone. But you must lop off some of the time you have devoted heretofore to the scurryings connected with your Type A pattern, employing it instead to acquire things worth being.

6. You also must find the time to consolidate a few of your acquaintanceships or friendships into firm and spiritually rewarding intimacies. Only living things provide joy, and joy is a peculiarly necessary emotion. As Sophocles pointed out, when joy is killed, man no longer lives.

7. You must allocate time for your reading, for learning any new avocations you have chosen to pursue, and for visiting museums, galleries, and theaters. There must be time for you to recall your past. This need not be carried out on a fixed schedule, but certainly should be frequent; the true enrichment of your life is possible only by bringing back into it the things and thoughts of your earlier life.

8. Drill to improve your mind in such a way that when you have forgotten almost everything you have newly learned —as you will—the residue left will be of value to you, personally. Don't try to "cram" on intellectual fare as if you were going to be examined. Don't try to organize "culture" or "reading great books" clubs and certainly don't join one. Such organizations only too often degenerate into amateur exhibitions of pedantry.

9. Finally, begin drilling again after you have given up the attempt to drill. Remember that success has been described as largely the ability to survive failure. And it is precisely in the six to eight months after you have begun to drill that your old habits begin to strike back. Remember to review the progress of your drill at least every six months. When you detect the return of tyrannizing habits, rebel once again and take up the drill with even greater enthusiasm—and grit! And remember that if you can't succeed in altering your behavior pattern, you aren't

being protected against heart disease, no matter how little cholosterol you now eat, how little cigarette smoke you inhale, or how many miles you run each day.

Chapter 18

COPING WITH
CORONARY HEART
DISEASE

Up to this point, we have concerned ourselves almost exclusively with describing those measures which, we believe, if introduced early enough, can prevent the onset of coronary heart disease before one turns seventy. But, unfortunately, millions of Americans have eaten too much and too often, smoked excessively, exercised infrequently, and have followed Type A Behavior Pattern for many decades already. Then, too, hundreds of thousands of Americans have suffered from those diseases—hypertension, diabetes, hereditary hypercholesterolemia, and hypothyroidism—which, having been untreated or inadequately treated, hastened the onset of coronary heart disease.

Because of errors in life habits, or of the particular disorders described in Chapter 9, or of both, it is probable that at least 5 million Americans now suffer not just from coronary artery disease but also from coronary heart disease. That is, the narrowing of one or more of their coronary arteries has become severe enough to produce either symptoms of coronary distress—angina pectoris, shortness of breath, a serious irregularity in the rhythm of the heartbeat, or easily induced fatigue—or actual injury to the heart muscle. To repeat, coronary heart disease is coronary artery disease that has become severe enough to produce symptoms.

If you are one of these persons who has suffered such symptoms, then you must face the fact that at some time in the past your coronary artery disease became so serious that one or more of your coronary arteries failed to deliver sufficient blood to all parts of your heart. This critical interruption in a portion of your coronary circulation may have been relieved or compensated for by the efforts of some of the less diseased segments of your coronary arterial system. At present you may have no symptoms whatsoever. Nevertheless, you must consider yourself, now and forever after, a patient who has *serious* obstructive disease of at least one and possibly two of your three main coronary vessels. We do not stress this attitude to depress you, but rather to make you aware of the necessity of following a regimen designed to prevent a rapid return of the symptoms you once suffered.

Almost all of you have heard of—and perhaps been frightened by—various statistics on the length of survival of patients after they first become aware of their coronary heart disease. In general, these statistics suggest that approximately one-third of patients with coronary heart disease will succumb to the disease five years after its appearance. We bring up these statistics not to deny their past validity, but to emphasize their worthlessness for any future prognostic purposes.

These statistics are anachronistic because they were collected on coronary patients before two recent medical and surgical advances. The first advance was the detection of the major role of Type A Behavior Pattern in exacerbating the course of coronary artery disease and coronary heart disease. Most if not all statistics we now have concerning the prognosis of coronary heart disease pertain solely to patients whose Type A behavior, the probable major cause of their disease, was not even detected, must less treated, at any time during the course of their illness. Once therapeutic attempts are made to alter or eradicate the effects of Type A Behavior Pattern, future statistics relating the long-term survival rate of coronary patients may bear no more relation to the ones we now have than the present statistics relating the survival rate of tubercular, typhoid, or meningitic patients bear to their statistical counterparts half a century ago.

The second advance that has been made in the past six or seven years, and that may also render the value of our present survival statistics obsolescent is in surgical procedures. Surgeons are now able to extract a small segment of a superficial leg vein of coronary patients and use it to construct a bypass around the obstructed area of a coronary artery. In a second type of operation, one of the arteries originally supplying the breast can be brought down and sewn to a coronary artery immediately below its obstructed area. This deft maneuver, so brilliantly simple in concept, yet demanding technical excellence for its execution, serves to supply adequate quantities of bright, fresh blood to areas of the heart muscle previously bereft of it.

Because one or the other of these two operations are now being performed daily upon a hundred or more patients suffering from coronary heart disease, hundreds, perhaps thousands, of men and women who a year ago were unable to leave their bedrooms are now able not only to leave their houses but also to walk, run, and even perform jobs or play games requiring moderate to severe physical exertion.

To you patients who already have coronary heart

disease, the above facts mean, first, that most of you have no legitimate cause for either pessimism or gloom about your future. Second, these facts strongly intimate that if you have Type A Behavior Pattern and it is not *actively* ameliorated, or if you fail to obtain surgical relief for arteries already too severely obstructed, then your chances of survival will be no better than they were for coronary patients in 1900. If you really desire the best medical aid to prevent further deterioration in your coronary vasculature and heart muscle, part of the responsibility for finding such aid devolves directly upon you. We know of no other disease whose outcome depends so little upon what is done *for* the patient and so much upon what is done *by* the patient.

1. First, and most important of all, you must select the proper physician for yourself.
2. Under this physician's advice and counsel, you should be willing to submit to all necessary diagnostic procedures in order to learn the extent of your coronary artery disease and what may be done to improve the situation.
3. If coronary artery surgery is advised, you should accept and act upon such advice.
4. You must eliminate or control any disease or disorder that predisposes you to coronary artery disease (see Chapters 9 and 10).
5. You should introduce those changes in your dietary, smoking, and exercise habits which we've already recommended for the prevention of coronary artery and heart disease.
6. *It is absolutely essential that you eliminate all or almost all facets of Type A Behavior Pattern from your daily living.*

YOU MUST SELECT THE RIGHT DOCTOR

The best physician for those of you who already have coronary heart disease is one who, in addition to supervising your dietary, exercise, and smoking habits and administering various specific drugs to lower your blood cholesterol level (if it is elevated), will also do everything in his power to alter your behavior pattern.

Now at this writing, as we have pointed out, very few doctors in the United States are *systematically and continuously* concentrating their efforts to rid their coronary patients of their Type A Behavior Pattern. There are several reasons for this shortage. Even among the doctors who recognize the probable lethality of Type A behavior, many are still sincerely doubtful whether the pattern can be altered. Also, not many believe they have the time to spend in the attempt over a period of many weeks or months. But we are almost positive that this situation will change. Indeed, it is in this hope that we are writing this book. And when our professional colleagues read it, we won't mind at all if at first they are quite skeptical. We only hope that if they are skeptical, they will still begin to look at their patients with new eyes.

We know what will happen! Many of these doctors will begin to see their coronary patients in a fresh light, as we did. They will note their haste, their competitiveness, and even their hostility. We are positive that they will then be convinced of the relationship of the behavior pattern to coronary heart disease and will begin to treat their patients accordingly.

Thus, you must seek out a physician for yourself who will concern himself with a good deal more than with just the things you eat, inhale, or even think about. For example, if you are suffering from angina or bouts of irregular beating of your heart, your physician must make it his business to find as soon as possible a consultant somewhere in the United States who will be able safely to perform a coronary arteriogram on you, in order to find out exactly how diseased your three coronary arteries are. If it shows serious obstructions, which may be life threatening, he must see to it that a very competent cardiac surgeon is called in to determine whether one of the above-described operations should be performed.

Incidentally, neither coronary arteriography nor the coronary bypass surgery, when done by superbly trained doctors, need be painful or particularly distressing. We did not find it so, at least, nor have any of the patients whom we have followed. Here again, we had superbly skilled diagnostic cardiologists and an equally skilled cardiac surgeon.

So your physician should know how to advise you not only concerning your dietary, smoking, and exercise habits; he should be willing and eventually able to tackle the problem of your behavior pattern; he should discover and refer you (unless there are very strong medical reasons for not doing so) to a consultant who will *safely* visualize your coronary arteries by X-ray techniques and discover precisely where and how badly they are diseased.

Finally, it is the duty of your own physician to inform you fully concerning any procedure that he and his colleagues may recommend. He should inform you not only of its possible benefits but also its risks. He would be doing you a terrible disservice if he also did not inform you of the risks of *not* subjecting yourself to any particular procedure if he believed it was indicated.

Unquestionably, provided you can find him, the best physician for you is a doctor who will help you to alter your behavior pattern. He must be a man whose general philosophy of living you find yourself respecting. You won't be able to respect your doctor in this way unless you are convinced that your physician not only likes you as a patient but is also interested in you as a human being. You must know that when he looks at you, he really sees you; and when he listens to you, he really hears you.

And of course he should be a man you like and respect. Certainly, if you find yourself wishing to avoid him because you can't stand his manner, then you can be reasonably sure that he is not the physician for you.

COPING WITH CORONARY HEART DISEASE IF YOU HAVE UNDERGONE BYPASS GRAFT SURGERY

For those of you who have undergone a bypass graft operation, the greatest peril—and it is a very real one—will be overconfidence. Certainly, after being unable to walk even a block without chest-clutching pain or to climb even a half dozen steps, to find yourself suddenly able to walk for miles, even to run, play tennis, and swim without any distress of any kind is an almost miraculous experience indeed. And how natural it will be for you to feel that you have a "new" heart and that the dietary and smoking restrictions that plagued you prior to the operation can be done away with. And if you had also been struggling to alter your behavior pattern before the operation, it will be tempting to revert to your old ways. Yet there must be *utterly no change* from your preoperative medical regimen except for the possible elimination of some of the drugs for which you now have little need.

You should continue your preoperative medical regimen for a number of reasons. First, the new vein segments from your legs or the internal mammary artery employed to bypass the obstructions in your coronary arteries can also, in turn, close off. We have very good experimental evidence that suggests that in the first few weeks after the insertion of a vein in the arterial system, during which time the walls of the vein thicken to withstand the high pressure of arterial blood, the vein is extraordinarily susceptible to the deposition of cholesterol. This is particularly apt to be the case if the cholesterol traveling in the blood has been absorbed from the cholesterol present in food. And, unfortunately, such cholesterol deposited in the vein acts to narrow the lumen of the vein segment. *For this reason we advise any person who has undergone an aortocoronary saphenous vein bypass operation not to eat any food containing even a tiny amount of cholesterol for at least ten weeks after his surgery.* By that time, judging from our laboratory studies of vein transplants in rabbits, the walls of the veins become as impermeable to the dietary cholesterol present in the blood passing through the vein bypass as any healthy vein or artery. It is quite probable that the same sort of dietary regimen should also be followed by all patients who receive arterial instead of vein grafts.

After this period of ten weeks of a cholesterol-free diet, you should then continue to eat a low cholesterol diet for the rest of your life. No matter whether you have one or more new vein or artery bypasses, even they must finally empty into your original coronary arteries. And usually these latter arteries were at least 20 to 50 percent obstructed at the time of the operation. If they continue to narrow, then the time will come when once more your heart muscle will not get enough blood.

Another reason for continuing a low cholesterol diet is the possibility that other of your coronary vessels will continue to thicken, making a second operation necessary in order to bypass the new obstruction. Also, there are other important arteries besides the coronary arteries in your body, and their thickening should be retarded, too.

For essentially the same reasons, you should continue to abstain from smoking. Once again, it is altogether probable that heavy cigarette smoking (over ten a day) does increase the rate of narrowing that takes place in the coronary arteries, and it certainly cannot enhance the integrity of vein transplants. Besides, it would be a pity to resume smoking after you already suffered—and survived—giving up the habit.

It is not usual for persons who had accustomed themselves to exercising regularly to discontinue such exercise after having had the coronary bypass operation. Certainly if exercise does promote the development of new coronary vessels, then it should continue following surgery, but *properly*. The new blood being brought to the heart should be equally distributed to the more peripheral areas of the heart. Therefore, go on with your daily hour or more of *moderate* exercise.

But once again, no matter how fine you may feel, *never* indulge again in any form of violent exercise. Your operation, if it was even moderately successful, has given you a better blood supply than ten thousand hours of jogging could. Be content with this gain. Walk, swim, fish, garden, gently play *at* tennis, bowl, throw horseshoes, indeed take almost any kind of exercise except any one that makes your heart race violently and your breath come with difficulty.

If a coronary bypass operation is performed upon you before you have had a real opportunity to begin to combat and alter various facets of your Type A Behavior Pattern, you naturally will be most inclined to cease even thinking of your behavior, much less changing it. And the more successful the operation, the more you will be tempted to abandon your emotional rehabilitation.

Unfortunately, however, if you do not attempt to alter your behavior pattern, you may be facing a perilous future, more perilous than you faced if you had not had your coronary operation but *did* alter your behavior pattern. If we are correct in believing that Type A Behavior Pattern is the most lethal of all the factors causing coronary heart disease and death, then allowing it free reign to continue to damage your coronary arteries—and possibly your cerebral vessels, too—is totally foolhardy.

We remember the case of a man who had a bypass operation on his left anterior descending artery. He felt well after this operation, so he made no attempt whatsoever to abolish his Type A Behavior Pattern. Six months later he died suddenly from a thrombus that had obstructed another of his severely diseased coronary arteries. A vein or artery shunt, or even a series of such shunts, can't compensate forever for the continuous obstructions set up in many portions of your three coronary arteries by a complex of pathogenic agents of which Type A Behavior Pattern appears more and more to loom as of primary importance.

On the other hand, if a coronary patient has succeeded in altering significantly his Type A Behavior Pattern *before* he undergoes coronary bypass surgery, it has been our experience that he usually continues to work on his behavior pattern with even more gusto after surgery. He recognizes the role his original behavior pattern played in bringing on his disease and understands how it could continue to erode his remaining arteries.

But he also persists in altering his Type A pattern for another reason: having *partially* freed himself from the tyrannies of time urgency, free-floating hostility, and the craze of unbridled numeration, he recognizes the serfdom he had endured for so many years. "Better I die of a heart attack than return to that sort of senseless slavery," said a physician-patient to us recently, and he meant precisely what he said. We do not know of a single person who, having really managed to free himself of the major components of Type A Behavior Pattern, ever again allowed himself to be totally recaptured and degraded by it.

Finally, no matter how brilliantly successful your bypass operation appears to have been, don't ever fail to attend to any of those diseases—hypertension, diabetes, hereditary hypercholesterolemia, and hypothyroidism—that lead to coronary heart disease.

COPING WITH CORONARY HEART DISEASE IF YOU HAVE NOT HAD SURGERY

Relatively few of you who already suffer from coronary heart disease have been subjected to coronary bypass surgery. There are hundreds of cardiologists and even a number of very competent cardiac surgeons who aren't very enthusiastic about bypass operations. The operations, however, certainly give satisfactory results when done upon patients suffering from severe or disabling angina. But whether these operations will prevent the shocking deaths—usually coming instantaneously or suddenly—from coronary heart disease remains to be seen. In our opinion, as time passes these operations will be found to lower the coronary mortality rate. We would be almost positive of this if the patients *continued to alter their Type A Behavior Pattern and to refrain from smoking.*

KEEP OTHER DISEASES UNDER STRICT THERAPEUTIC CONTROL

There is an understandable tendency on the part of many persons to become terribly discouraged if, after having religiously followed their physician's instructions concerning the control of their hypertension, diabetes, familial hypercholesterolemia, or hypothyroidism, they nevertheless suffered a heart attack. "What good has it done to have taken these pills for over ten years to keep my blood pressure (or blood cholesterol or even blood sugar) within normal limits, if I end up with this heart attack?" they argue. And being totally dejected and discouraged, they may discontinue their efforts to keep these diseases in check.

If you first encountered your heart symptoms after years of trying to keep in control one of these "precursor" diseases of coronary heart disease, you, too, may have been tempted to stop. If you have, resist by all means. You must realize that two probabilities exist. First, if you hadn't taken pains to control those diseases, you probably would have suffered your heart attack years earlier than you did—and the attack might have been far more severe. Second, despite your efforts, no one had informed you of the heart-disease-inducing propensity of Type A Behavior Pattern. Accordingly, you did nothing to combat *it*. And this behavior pattern is potent enough in itself to bring on a heart attack in the complete absence of any "precursor" disease. It also is potent enough to bring on a heart attack even if your diet is low in cholesterol and animal fat, if you don't smoke, and if you exercise vigorously every day.

FOLLOW THESE DIETARY, SMOKING, AND DRINKING INSTRUCTIONS

Patients already suffering from coronary heart disease are usually expected to ingest the sort of low cholesterol, high polyunsaturated fat diet we have already described in Chapter 11. There is at best only suggestive evidence that adherence to such a diet can play a very great or effective role in retarding the progress of your disease once it evolves into coronary heart disease. Why, then, do we so strongly encourage coronary heart disease patients to adhere to it? Because we know it won't hurt you, and adhering to it gives both you, the patient, and us, the physicians, the feeling that at least we are trying to do something to stop the onslaughts of this disease.

But there is one dietary precaution that may be of life-and-death importance to you. At no time should you eat a meal rich in protein or fat—whether the fat is unsaturated or polyunsaturated—within two hours of bedtime. Osler was not wrong when he wrote, "Late suppers should be interdicted—there is 'death in the pot' for angina patients and a surfeit [of food] may be as fatal as poison." Over seventy-five years have passed since Osler wrote this, and we still don't know why it is true. But certainly one of the best ways to make sure that you will live to see the morning sun is to enter your bed with a reasonably empty belly. This, of course, means that the evening meal is eaten earlier and that it is no longer the main meal of the day.

The same advice should be followed in regard to eating before you indulge even in moderate physical exercise. When you plan to work, play, or sleep, do so with a stomach that is not distended with food. Allow at least three hours to lapse after a moderate or heavy meal before you indulge in physical activity. Earlier we suggested that normal persons might benefit from consuming their daily food in five or six settings instead of just three. Certainly such a regimen would not hurt those who have coronary heart disease.

Likewise, we recommended that those wishing to avoid coronary heart disease should eat only enough to maintain the body weight they had during their senior year in high school—assuming that this was normal. However, if you already have coronary heart disease, maintaining your high school weight is not just desirable, it is mandatory. Why is this so necessary? Just perform this simple experiment. First walk up twenty or more steps. Then repeat the action, except this time carry an object weighing twenty-five pounds. We believe that after you have tried this just once, our reasons for insisting upon your slimness will become obvious to you. Then, too, it is far easier to keep your serum cholesterol at lower levels if your weight is similarly maintained.

As a coronary patient, you no longer dare to smoke cigarettes. Admittedly, in an earlier chapter we pointed out that the evidence incriminating cigarette smoking in coronary artery disease was not absolutely conclusive. Nevertheless, once the symptoms of coronary heart disease make their appearance—particularly angina or shortness of breath—cigarette smoking has repeatedly been observed to aggravate the intensity of these symptoms. There are certain cardiologists—whom we respect very much—who refuse to continue to see a coronary patient if he persists in smoking. And while you are making these changes, you had better desist from smoking cigars and pipes, too. It has been our experience that when heavy cigarette smokers try to turn to cigar or pipe smoking, almost invariably they inhale the dreadfully rich, nicotine-filled cigar and pipe smoke. This, of course, is even worse than smoking cigarettes.

And what about whiskey? Well, hardly a month goes by that some article isn't published whose results have led its author to conclude that even a jigger of alcohol may be quite dangerous to the damaged—or even the normal—heart muscle or liver cell. From our own laboratory and clinical experiences, however, these articles lead us to suspect that their authors are more crank than physician or scientist. If a drink or two—but mind you, two is the limit—relaxes you at the end of the day and changes some of the day's previously black-colored events to light purple- or bright pink-colored ones, then take a chance. Two jiggers of liquor will not corrode your arteries nearly as much as they will help to jettison the particular wretchednesses that may have frustrated your day.

Finally, what about lecithin, vitamin E, vitamin C, and any other substance you've read about or seen displayed in a health food store? Might these have value? In our own practice, we always have used one principle to decide these matters. We only ask ourselves: "Will any of these substances harm the patient?" If the answer is no, then we say okay, go ahead. It would be salutary for all our medical colleagues to act similarly. We have so very little hard evidence that any medicine we advise our patients to take is any more efficacious than the substances some of our patients spontaneously ask to try. Then, too, these substances are often much less expensive than the dubiously effective drugs we may prescribe.

Finally, there are the specific drugs that can calm your nerves, lower your serum cholesterol, strengthen your heart's contractile power, regularize an irregularly beating heart, and prevent possibly fatal arrhythmias. A book is not the proper place to give advice about them. They are the concern of your physician. Remember, however, that if you are given a drug and notice any new phenomenon—whether it be a rash, a joint ache, a failure to get on with the sex act, or any other abnormality—notify your doctor immediately.

FOLLOW THESE EXERCISE INSTRUCTIONS

As a coronary patient, your danger does not lie in the inability of your heart muscle to contract well or to extract oxygen from the blood passing it. Your only danger lies in the tough, stone-containing scars that are obliterating the interior portions of your coronary arteries. And if you were to ascend and descend the Pyramid of Cheops at Giza a dozen times a day at jogging speed for a decade, you still would not widen or open any of your coronary vessels where they had been severely narrowed or entirely closed. You would succeed only in breaking your neck or dying instantaneously of a cardiac arrhythmia.

We are obdurately opposed to a patient with coronary heart disease indulging in any violent exercise. We have already declared we are opposed to a seemingly normal, middle-aged male person so indulging, having known far too many of these patients to die of abnormal heart rhythms (such as ventricular fibrillation) as they were jogging or playing handball or tennis. We now see groups of coronary patients cavorting in gymnasiums or on the track as if they were about to qualify for some Olympiad for Senior Citizens. We only feel sorry for them, but we experience a dull sort of rage against their medical or paramedical mentors.

Recently, one of these physician exercise-enthusiasts bitterly criticized us for saying that jogging could be a form of "mass murder." This doctor thought that we should have qualified our statement. He pointed out that whereas we were correct in stating that jogging can lead to cardiac arrest—and death—it was his belief that if the joggers are accompanied by an electric defibrillator and also by persons who know how to apply this complex, very expensive machine immediately to the chest of a person whose heart has stopped beating, then even though a jogger "drops dead" he can immediately be revived.

The doctor was very proud of the fact that six of his jogging coronary patients did "drop dead" and were revived. Moreover, he talked all of them into resuming their jogging in the next few weeks. Of course, the same doctor, like all other such enthusiasts, has never examined the coronary arteries of a group of patients he exposed to this sort of supervised Russian roulette, comparing them with the arteries of a group of patients not so exposed to determine whether his violent exercises actually change the coronary arteries in the slightest degree. Can we be blamed if we find the practices of this doctor rather terrifying?

We still do advise you to exercise at least an hour daily. If on walking you develop angina, do not continue walking, but stop and rest immediately, and if necessary, use your nitroglycerin. Exercise gently at anything that gives you pleasure, but never to the extent that you suffer angina, extreme shortness of breath, excessive pounding or irregular beating of your heart, or a sudden drenching sweat. And always remember that it is your mind and your entire body, not necessarily your heart, that are getting the benefit of the exercise.

One thing more! Never take a wristwatch or stopwatch with you when you do your exercises. Coronary patients, being Type A subjects, tend to want to time themselves. This miserable offshoot of numeration and/or "hurry sickness" is a particularly pathetic—and deadly—characteristic of some Type A joggers.

YOU MUST MONITOR YOUR SEX ACTIVITIES

Peculiarly, during the many years of treating hundreds of coronary patients, we can remember less than a dozen male and no female coronary patients who ever voluntarily asked us for advice about their sexual relations.

Perhaps some of our patients were too shy. Perhaps, too, some of our patients' sex drives and capabilities had dwindled even prior to the onset of heart disease.

But we suspect that the main reason our patients so rarely thought it necessary to ask us for sexual guidance is that they themselves consciously or unconsciously had decided that they could solve their own sex problems. By finding out how much general physical activity they can take without suffering angina or severe shortness of breath, and knowing how much expenditure of physical energy their sexual activity prior to their heart disease had required, they make their own decisions about sexual activity. We see no essential fault in this way of handling it.

If we are asked directly about these matters by a male patient, we attempt to determine whether he is himself interested in resuming sexual activities or believes his wife feels and needs his sexual attention. Now, it happens not too infrequently that when both husband and wife are well over fifty years of age, neither particularly cares about the sex act, but continues, each believing the other desires it. If one partner of such couples does get coronary heart disease, this pretense should be ended.

But if you had enjoyed the sex act prior to your heart attack, the odds are very good that a few months after the initial phases of your illness you will again be able to enjoy it. And it should be continued if you enjoy it, and if your angina or shortness of breath does not become too severe. You might remember, however, that the very worst and most dangerous time for the sexual relationship is one to three hours after a meal that was heavy with food and drink, particularly wines.

IF YOU DO NOT CHANGE YOUR BEHAVIOR PATTERN, YOU AREN'T COPING WITH YOUR DISEASE

Throughout this book, frequently at the risk of being considered medical cranks, we have tried to pound out the message that in bringing on coronary heart disease no single factor or combination of factors may be as important as the biochemical influences set loose in various ways by Type A Behavior Pattern. If this is so, no regimen designed to prevent the recurrence of a heart attack can be of much value if it omits measures to counteract this behavior pattern. Even if you never touch a cholesterol-containing food again in your life, or smoke another cigarette, and manage to exercise several hours a day, but leave your Type A Behavior Pattern unchanged, your chances of getting a second heart attack are about the same as a coronary patient who has not changed his dietary, smoking, or exercise habits.

Therefore it is mandatory that you return to Chapters 15, 16, and 17, which describe in detail how you are to go about ridding yourself of your "hurry sickness," your free-floating hostility, and your greed in numeration. The time to begin this battle, possibly the greatest of your life, is now.

If you do succeed in extricating yourself from the tyranny of this behavior pattern, your coronary arteries, perhaps for the first time in decades, will no longer be forced to bear the savage, unceasing biochemical attack caused by unbridled Type A behavior. Second, you may very well begin to experience far less frequently the irritating symptoms so often attendant upon coronary heart disease. Third, you may be able to stave off a second infarction or serious arrhythmia for an indefinite period of years. Most important of all, you can begin to lead a life whose depth vies with its variety. The world will offer you an existence that is not stereotyped but kaleidoscopic.

Chapter 19

AND BEFORE WE LEAVE

We are finishing this book in the middle of 1973. We can't help but wonder what sort of book we would have been able to write about coronary heart disease were we finishing it in 1983, a decade hence!

Of one thing we are certain. The surgical measures available to partially correct the ravages of obstructive coronary artery disease, which now seem exquisitely sophisticated and helpful, will appear rather crude by 1983. A decade hence, artificial hearts in various models and of various sizes may well be pumping away in hundreds of thousands of breasts. New divisions will have been created in some of our giant corporations to fabricate and service these hearts.

How the private insurance companies will face up to the astronomical costs that will accompany the purchase and insertion of these artificial hearts is a problem about which we don't feel qualified to hazard even a guess. Somehow or other, though, we are certain that they will discover a financially sound way of "getting into this act." The government will have to do so, too.

Probably long before 1983, we physicians also should have available for our patients new and very potent drugs to prevent the death-dealing onset of ventricular fibrillation which now is claiming so many hundreds of thousands of coronary victims. If our major pharmaceutical companies concentrate their marvelously keen research teams on the task of finding these antiarrhythmic drugs, they will be found in the next several years, or even months.

But will there be less coronary heart disease to treat in 1983? That is, will we have made progress in preventing the evolution of coronary artery disease into coronary heart disease? Perhaps we can be faulted for envisioning an unwarranted pleasant ending to the present disaster conditions, but we do believe that the incidence of coronary heart disease will wane during the next decade in this country.

First, we are absolutely certain that more and more pediatricians will recognize that coronary artery disease may be the most dangerous disorder to which their young patients are exposed. Such recognition will then be followed by detailed studies of their patients' cholesterol, fat, and sugar metabolism and therapeutic measures then will be taken to correct any defect. Most important of all, we believe that the pediatrician—and American parents—will recognize that as now constituted the average diet of American children, particularly when aligned with a later developing Type A Behavior Pattern and/or heavy cigarette smoking, can destroy the integrity of coronary arteries. When this is recognized, drastic changes will be instituted—by doctors and by parents, and possibly by the children themselves.

Second, we believe that the frequency of cigarette smoking will subside in the next decade, bringing down with it the incidence of coronary heart disease. Never before have so many thousands of middle-aged American men and women quit smoking. It is what the elders actually do—not what they sermonize about

—that the youngsters eventually emulate, no matter how much they seem at first to grumble and shy away.

But the young will stop smoking primarily because they, too, can read and think. Every advertisement and every package of cigarettes they purchase drives home this message to them: You are doing everything possible to cause your early death by lung cancer. Those youngsters who still smoke despite these well-understood warnings do so in part because they, like most young people, find it very difficult to imagine dying of anything! Time, however, has a way of correcting this erroneous belief.

The third and certainly the strongest reason we have for believing that the incidence of coronary heart disease will diminish is our conviction that the incidence of severe Type A Behavior Pattern will wane during the next few decades. The American man and woman are not stupid, nor have they inherited any great liking for tyranny. Even if this tyranny is being exerted over them by their own habits, drives, and greeds, they are quite capable of revolt.

Already many of our young people have been trying to tell us that they are no longer impressed with our acquisitive frenzies. It is obvious that many of them have sickened in a spiritual sense because they either had not been given, or were not able, to accept the components of any myth, ritual, or tradition once enjoyed by their elders. So bereft, is it any wonder that they have organized their own myths, rituals, and traditions? We should keep this in mind lest we sneer too readily at their sallies into astrology, psychedelia, and cults of Jesus freakiness. At worst, these are only phenomena blooming in a spiritual vacuum.

We don't believe for a second that it will be easy for any of you who are already severely afflicted with the Type A Behavior Pattern to escape from its subtle but tough meshes. But it can and has been accomplished repeatedly. Just as we were finishing this book, a middle-aged writer on the staff of one of America's most prestigious business journals sauntered into our office. It had been a full year since we last had seen him. At that time he was a typical Type A New Yorker, and more than slightly cynical about our work.

Now as he sat, relaxed, talking with us, it was difficult to believe that he was the tense, terse writer who had interviewed us a year earlier. He no longer chain smoked; he didn't smoke at all. He smiled and laughed easily, and the hostile glint in his eye had given way to a twinkle. His speech was no longer sharp and staccato but carried the smooth, rather soft quality it probably possessed when he was at college. Nor did he once try to hasten or interrupt our speech. In short, he had become a Type B person. How had he managed to execute this transformation in the space of just a single year? Let us listen to him.

"I had to have enough courage to look realistically at my life in New York and to realize, that with an apartment in the city, a home in Connecticut, and all of us strung out between these two places and sometimes other places, too, we didn't exist as a family. The article I wrote about your work helped because I received two national prizes for it. I knew that my article didn't win those prizes because I wrote the article rapidly or because while writing it in New York I managed to do a dozen other things at the same time. I realized that I had written a good article because there were some good new ideas in it, and so it won these prizes despite my other activities that you doctors here call Type A stuff.

"Even before I got the prizes, though, I kept mulling over in my mind what you had told me last year. I also kept thinking of those taped interviews with Type A persons you let me listen to. Finally, it began to dawn on me that I was so busy trying to avoid wasting time, just like those fellows in the tapes, that I was managing to waste my life instead. I didn't have time to read the books I really wanted to read, I didn't have time to spend with either my wife, my kids, or friends who talk my sort of language. What then in hell *did* I have the time for? I asked myself. And you were right, only some numbers and deadlines.

"Well, I discussed this with my wife and both of us agreed to change our way of living. We've sold that expensive apartment in New York City and we've also accomplished a lot of other economies. And what the Joneses think of us, or who the Joneses are—well, we discovered that actually it didn't even matter.

"The hardest job was to look at myself. I had to face up to the fact that I'd never be a Proust or a de Tocqueville." Our friend then looked at us for a few seconds, shrugged his shoulders, and continued. "But I know that I'm still a damned good writer, and that will have to do. And during the next six months I'm going to take a 'Sabbatical.' I don't know exactly what I'll do during this period, but I don't much care. It's enough for me to know that for the first time in a long, long while, I'll feel free."

We congratulated him and complimented him on his ability to rid himself of his wristwatch. A year previously he had looked at it constantly. He smiled, then pulled a silver watch out of his pocket, old-fashioned but slim. "I carry this one, but I rarely look at it. I carry it mostly because my mother gave it to me when I graduated from high school."

We rather suspect that during his Sabbatical this talented writer may find new and valuable ways to further diminish his old Type A Behavior Pattern. And we will be the most surprised physicians in the United States if he should suffer a heart attack during this Sabbatical of his, or for that matter, during the next several decades—assuming, of course, that he continues to possess a Type B Behavior Pattern.

It would be easy for us to give you other examples of Type A's who converted themselves into Type B's. Such conversions, of course, happen far more frequently to Type A persons already suffering from coronary heart disease than to Type A's who harbor coronary artery disease without obvious symptoms.

It would also be easy for us to give you many examples of Type A subjects who totally failed to alter their behavior patterns. The chief reason for their failure, of course, is not their personality but the tyrannous habits plastered on this personality by the ceaseless quest for numbers. These habits of hurry and hostility become so firmly established that the afflicted person thinks or feels that they are integral components of his personality.

Another cause of failure is the total inability of some Type A subjects to read books or to communicate with people who have a wide cultural background. Obviously, if part of ameliorating the Type A pattern consists in beginning to accomplish the things worth being, then Type A subjects will have to learn new things. If, however, they cannot find the patience to read books, and if they have no instructors to help them find these new cultural pathways, how can they even begin to obtain the things worth being?

Luckily, the behavior pattern of most Type A persons is not crippled beyond repair. Most still retain, to some degree, a sense of humor; this is a priceless aid to recovery. Another is sheer courage. It takes courage to look back at one's career and brand an error as an error. It takes courage to look critically at the person you are today. But the highest species of intellectual courage is required to see numbers for what they are. And this is the great stumbling block for so many Type A subjects who would become Type B subjects if only they could do so without giving up their dearly beloved "numbers."

Again, we should like to emphasize to those of you who have suffered one or more heart attacks that no matter what your diet, no matter how vigorously you exercise and how valiantly you shun cigarettes, if you have not altered your Type A behavior, then the probable chief cause of your first heart attack is still operating to produce another one.

There is extraordinarily good scientific evidence in hand to indicate that Type A Behavior Pattern is the major cause of premature coronary artery disease in this country. What we lack—but confidently expect to get eventually—is equally good evidence proving that removal of the pattern can prevent or forestall advent of the disease. A new set of experiments should be able to show us, for example, to what degree damage previously done can be reversed; the relationship between the duration of behavior pattern and vessel damage; and the effects of the removal of the behavior pattern on other probable causes—such as hypertension and hypercholesterolemia—of coronary heart disease.

We do not know exactly what such experiments will reveal in terms of detail. But in our own practice we have already observed enough patients to predict with some certainty what will happen when Type A behavior is altered. The advent of either the first or second heart attack is forestalled indefinitely. That's what happens! You might call it empirical evidence, but it's good enough for us. And for our patients!

Finally, we can hope that in changing your behavior pattern you will have received not only a truly powerful protection against the premature advent of coronary heart disease but something more—the joyous gift of a life lived in accord with what the ancient Greeks called "the golden mean," a life also good and useful enough to echo the poignant truth of Boris Pasternak's verse:

> *For life too is only a moment*
> *only the dissolution*
> *of our selves in all others*
> *as though a present to them.*

GLOSSARY

adventitia: the outermost of the three coats comprising the wall of all arteries. The fibers making up the adventitia are rather loosely interwoven and some of them are quite elastic. The adventitia serves not so much to give strength to an artery as to envelop and protect the other two coats.

angina pectoris: classically used to describe a pain in the front and middle of the chest that has a tendency to radiate down either arm (most frequently the left) or up the neck to the jaws. Angina pectoris is considered to be caused by a temporary scarcity of blood to one or more areas of heart muscle.

aorta: the main trunk of the arterial system. All the blood ejected from the left ventricle of the heart enters the aorta. The aorta then gives off all the arteries of the body. The first arteries it gives off are the right and left coronary arteries (see Figure 1, page 21), which bring blood back to, and hence nourish, the heart muscles.

aortocoronary saphenous vein bypass operation: This is a new operation (first performed in 1967), in which segments from veins in the thighs (saphenous veins) are used to make new connections between the aorta and coronary arteries, bypassing any obstructions. Doctors frequently call this simply a "coronary bypass operation."

arrhythmia: the term employed to describe any variation from the normal rhythm of the heart. There are many forms of arrhythmia, but the most common and important are extrasystoles, auricular fibrillation, ventricular tachycardia, and ventricular fibrillation.

asymptomatic: without symptoms.

atherosclerosis: the lesion or disorder directly responsible for coronary artery and coronary heart disease. Technically, atherosclerosis defines an arterial deposit that initially contains chiefly cholesterol and fat but later also contains calcium and is subject to internal ulceration. If the atherosclerotic process is well localized, it is frequently referred to as an atherosclerotic plaque.

Atromid-S: the commercial name for the cholesterol-lowering drug clofibrate.

auricle: a pumping chamber in the heart. The heart has both a right and left auricle (see Figure 1, page 21). The *right* auricle receives all the venous blood returning to the heart from all parts of the body and it gently ejects this blood into the right ventricle. The *left* auricle receives all the newly oxygenated blood coming to the heart from the lungs. The left auricle gently pumps this oxygen-rich blood into the left ventricle.

auricular fibrillation: an arrhythmia in which the auricles no longer submit to the master rhythm initiated by the sino-auricular node but contract wildly and ineffectively at rates well over four hundred beats per minute.

calcification: conversion of tissue elements into bone.

catecholamines: a group of chemicals with at least one property in common—the ability to stimulate those functions of the body not under conscious nervous control. Adrenalin (or epinephrine) is one of the catecholamines manufactured in the body.

cholestyramine: a commercial name for a cholesterol-lowering resin complex.

Choloxin: the commercial name for the cholesterol-lowering drug dextrothyroxine.

chylomicrons: very small particles composed of fat derived from the diet, but also containing some cholesterol and other chemicals. All fat absorbed by the body from the gut is taken up in the blood in the form of chylomicrons.

clofibrate: probably the most popular drug now in use for lowering of an elevated blood cholesterol. It is not equally efficacious in the treatment of all forms of hypercholesterolemia. It also produces far more side effects than most patients (or doctors) presently suspect, including a loss of male sexual potency and other effects, some of them long delayed. Clofibrate is by no means a totally satisfactory drug for the control of the serum cholesterol level.

collateral vessels (coronary): as a coronary artery becomes occluded and can no longer supply its share of blood to heart muscle, it is believed that the remaining coronary arteries develop new branches. These take over the function of supplying those segments of heart muscle whose nutrition otherwise would be endangered. Such new branches are called collateral vessels.

"a coronary": a frequently employed, abbreviated term to connote a myocardial infarction. Formerly even physicians used this term to designate a heart attack. Now, however, more physicians are apt to refer to a heart attack as an "M.I." (an abbreviation for myocardial infarction) when speaking to one another.

coronary arteriography: an X-ray visualization of a coronary artery. Radio-opaque material is injected separately into the right and left coronary arteries as a series of X rays are being very rapidly taken. This technique allows complete visualization of the coronary vasculature and must be done before any surgical approach to the coronary arteries can even be considered. If not performed by an expert, however, this procedure can be dangerous and even fatal.

coronary artery disease: a *symptomless* disorder in which one or more of the three coronary arteries is partially or totally obstructed by one or more atherosclerotic plaques. When and if these plaques give rise to symptoms (for example, angina pectoris or an acute myocardial infarction), coronary disease may be considered to have evolved into coronary heart disease.

coronary thrombosis: the formation of a clot in a coronary artery obstructing the flow of blood through the lumen of this same vessel. Although a myocardial infarction (often called a heart attack) can occur in the absence of a thrombosis, usually it is produced by the interference in blood flow effected by this clotting process.

dextrothyroxin: a form of thyroid hormone that is able to reduce the serum cholesterol of some individuals, and yet not cause the distressing symptoms usually observed when an excess of the usual form of thyroid hormone is given.

diastole: the period of the heart cycle when both ventricles of the heart receive blood from their respective auricles, hence do not themselves contract.

dyspnea: difficulty in breathing or getting one's breath.

edema: (see also *pulmonary edema*): an accumulation of excess fluid in various tissue spaces of the body. When such accumulation takes place in the lower half of the body, it is usually due to a partial pumping failure of the right ventricle.

electrocardiogram: a graphic record of the total electrical current produced by heart muscle just prior to its actual contraction. Unfortunately, an electrocardiogram taken at rest is almost always found to be normal in persons having coronary artery disease but not coronary heart disease. Moreover, it is abnormal in only half of those persons who do suffer from coronary heart disease.

endothelium: the tissue forming the internal lining coat of all arteries. The cells composing this tissue are flattened and allow the blood with its own formed cells to flow easily and with a minimum of friction over their surface.

epidemiologist: a scientist who studies the relationships of the various possible factors that determine the frequencies and distributions of various diseases in a human community.

epinephrine: one of the catecholamines. A hormone produced in the adrenal gland to circulate in the blood as an "emergency" hormone, in that it can speed up the heart, increase the blood pressure, and alert the brain. It also is known as adrenalin.

extrasystoles: extra beats of the heart, usually followed by a compensatory pause. This type of arrhythmia can be and usually is harmless. However, if it arises *de novo* in an adult, it deserves medical scrutiny.

fats: technically, esters of glycerol with various fatty acids. If these fatty acids contain carbon atoms that lack their usual quota of two hydrogen atoms, they are called polyunsaturated fatty acids and fats containing them are called polyunsaturated fats. Almost all vegetables and fruits (exception: coconut oil) contain only polyunsaturated fats, whereas the fats of most terrestrial animals (but not fish) are relatively saturated. Fats are also called triglycerides.

fibrillation: see *auricular fibrillation* and *ventricular fibrillation.*

heart block: inability of the electrical impulse preceding and responsible for each contraction of the heart to pass from the auricle to all parts of the ventricle. If the block is complete, the auricles beat at a different (usually faster) rate than the ventricles.

hypertension: high blood pressure. A blood pressure that is over 150 (systolic) at the time the heart contracts and that does not fall below 90 (diastolic) at the time the heart relaxes may be considered high.

hypercholesterolemia: elevated serum cholesterol. Although some epidemiologists and physicians consider a serum cholesterol elevated only if it exceeds 270 mg./100 ml., it seems far more likely that any serum cholesterol level consistently above 200 may be considered hypercholesterolemic.

hypothalamus: a portion of the brain between the basal surface and the pituitary gland that coordinates all our unconscious nervous functions. The hypothalamus is very intimately connected with the emotional phases of the total personality and of all parts of the brain it is the most neglected medically.

infarct: see *myocardial infarction.*

intima: the innermost of the three coats making up the wall of an artery. It is chiefly composed of endothelial cells; hence *endothelium* and *intima* are almost synonymous terms.

ischemia: inadequate blood to any part of the body, almost always due to constriction of the artery (or arteries) supplying that particular part. When any portion of cardiac musculature becomes temporarily ischemic, angina pectoris usually signals this ischemia. If the ischemia is not temporary but sustained, an acute myocardial infarction usually occurs.

ischemic heart disease: exactly the same as *coronary heart disease.* English and European doctors appear to prefer this term.

lesion: an area of tissue injured by trauma or disease; thus, a boil is a lesion just as a stab wound is.

lipids (blood): the fats and fatlike substances in blood. These include fats, free fatty acids, cholesterol, and phospholipids.

lipoproteins: the blood proteins (globulins) that carry all the cholesterol, fat, and phospholipids present in human blood. There are three general types of lipoproteins: (1) alpha, (2) beta, (3) pre-beta. In persons possessing too high a serum cholesterol, the excess cholesterol is usually carried in either the beta or pre-beta lipoproteins.

liquefaction: conversion of solid tissue into a fluidlike mass.

lumen: the central opening of a blood vessel through which blood flows.

media: the tough middle coat of an artery. It is composed of muscle cells and myriads of elastic fibers. Thus, it allows the artery to expand with each cardiac ejection of blood and to contract during cardiac diastole.

myocardial infarction: an area of necrosis in heart muscle resulting from obstruction of circulation to this area. Usually such obstruction does not occur until two of the three main coronary arteries have become totally obstructed. Synonyms are myocardial infarct, heart attack, "a coronary," coronary occlusion, and coronary thrombosis.

necrosis: death of tissue, usually in relatively small, localized areas.

norepinephrine: a catecholamine closely resembling epinephrine, but one that is secreted by the nerve endings of all sympathetic nerves, thus controlling over half of all body functions not under conscious guidance. These include intestinal contractions, heart contractions, and sweating. This substance is strongly suspected by some scientists (including ourselves) to be more than casually involved in both hypertension and coronary heart disease.

normotensive: having normal blood pressure.

pacemaker: the normal, or nature's own, heart pacemaker is a very small area called the sino-auricular node. It lies in the right auricle and consists of very specialized cells that initiate the cardiac electrical impulse.

An artificial, or manmade, pacemaker is an electronic device that regularly discharges a current of millivolt strength. This current when led to the heart can elicit a synchronized contraction of this organ's musculature, thus causing the heart to pump blood in a normal fashion.

pathogenesis: the development of a disease or disorder.

phospholipid: a lipid substance composed of fatty acids, glycerine, phosphorus, and a complex nitrogenous compound. Phospholipid circulates in blood usually as a constituent of various lipoproteins.

plaque, arterial or *atherosclerotic:* a scarlike mass in an artery, containing varying amounts of cholesterol fat and possibly also calcium, which projects into the lumen of the artery. A plaque is actually a localized area of atherosclerosis.

plasma: the liquid portion of blood. Thus, plasma is blood minus its red and white blood cells.

premature beats: the same as *extrasystoles.*

pulmonary edema: a leaking of the fluid of the blood into the tiny air sacs of the lungs. This condition is apt to develop when the left ventricle of the heart functions so poorly that it can't prevent blood "backing up" in the lung.

Questran: a commercial name for a cholesterol-lowering resin complex.

septum: the fibrous wall separating the right auricle and ventricle from their left counterparts.

serum: the liquid portion of the blood lacking not only red and white cells but also platelets and all elements of normal blood that cause it to clot. Thus, serum never clots.

sympathetic nervous system: the network of nerves governing the majority of body functions not under direct conscious regulation.

systole: the period during which the heart contracts.

tachycardia: rapid beating of the heart. There may be various forms of tachycardia, most of them not very serious, with the exception of ventricular tachycardia. This type of tachycardia stems from a new pacemaker arising in the ventricle that challenges and overcomes the basic rhythm initially instituted by the normal pacemaking cells of the sino-auricular node. The great danger of ventricular tachycardia is the possibility of its abrupt transformation into ventricular fibrillation.

thrombus, coronary: see *coronary thrombosis.*

ventricular fibrillation: an arrhythmia, that if not very quickly converted back into a normal rhythm by a special machine delivering an electrical current of specific character, always leads to death within a few minutes. Although it sometimes is heralded by extrasystoles or ventricular tachycardia, it also may develop abruptly. In this type of lethal arrhythmia, the basic heart beat is lost and the various muscle bundles of both ventricles quiver rather than contract so that blood is no longer pumped from the heart.

A Note about the Authors

MEYER FRIEDMAN was born in Kansas City, Kansas, in 1910 and was educated at Yale and Johns Hopkins. He has been a practicing physician and a leading researcher in the field of cardiology for nearly forty years, and since 1939 has served as director of the Harold Brunn Institute for Cardiovascular Research at San Francisco's Mt. Zion Hospital and Medical Center. He is the author of three monographs and more than four hundred articles dealing with coronary heart disease.

RAY H. ROSENMAN was born in Akron, Ohio in 1920. He received his training at the University of Michigan, and joined Friedman at the Harold Brunn Institute, where he is now associate director, in 1950. Dr. Rosenman has also published many articles, and divides his time between research and the practice of internal medicine and cardiology.